Basics of Private and Public Management

Basics of Private and Public Management

A Humanistic Approach to Change Management

Stahrl W. Edmunds
University of California,
Riverside

Lexington Books
D.C. Heath and Company
Lexington, Massachusetts
Toronto

Library of Congress Cataloging in Publication Data

Edmunds, Stahrl.
  Basics of private and public management.

  1. Management. 2. Public administration. I. Title.
HD31.E37   658.4'06   77-9147
ISBN 0-669-01679-9

Published simultaneously in Canada.

Printed in the United States of America.

International Standard Book Number: 0-669-01679-9

Library of Congress Catalog Card Number: 77-9147

To young people everywhere that they may learn to manage change and live lives of their own design, rather than have them molded by yesterday's institutions.

Contents

List of Figures

List of Tables

Introduction

The thesis of this book is that the basic elements of management are similar throughout the range of private and public institutions. If this thesis is correct, then the most skillful manager is one who has learned to apply his art across-the-board, generically, to all types of situations or institutions despite their differences. The differences among institutions are inherent in their mission (purpose) in the social process, because the mission alters the form of the decision criteria. The incipient manager will find it to his advantage, then, to learn management from a generic point of view—that is, from the view of the similarities in applying basic management techniques—because he will then be able to cope with more situations throughout his career.

The similarities and differences in management practices among institutions in society are, then, the major concern of this book; but this approach may cause some readers an initial problem of understanding (which is easily overcome), depending upon their normal thinking pattern. People reputedly think in two basic modes: (1) by noting similarities among parts in a whole, or (2) by noting differences among parts in detail. The second mode of thinking (noting differences) is by far the most prevalent, probably because education conditions people in the scientific method, which is basically differentiating, reductionist, and analytical.

This book asks the reader to think primarily in the first mode. The reader is asked to look at management as dealing with the social process as a whole, in which any institution is merely a part or subsystem. Parts differ in their detail, but they perform functions or work that contribute to a common output in the whole social purpose. The whole social purpose is to enable individuals to fulfill their needs for individuation and maturation—that is, fulfilling human ends and needs is the purpose of management. This approach forces us to examine human individuality and how management comes into being—it looks for similarities among human needs and similarities in management functions to fulfill them. The thinking mode is one of synthesis rather than analysis, looking for similarities rather than differences.

The book starts with an overview of human needs, the social process, how a management function originates, and how authority is delegated to make the management function operative. From this overview of the management function (chapter 1), the discussion then proceeds (in chapters 2 through 5) to break down the functions into more explicit detail.

Readers who have had some exposure to systems thinking, reasoning by similarity, or experience in general management, will best grasp the concepts by reading the chapters in the order in which they are presented. Other readers, more accustomed to thinking in differences or in terms of the detail of management, may find the order of chapters somewhat abstract or general. Such readers will find the book more understandable by starting with chapter 5 and then going back to chapter 1—or indeed, perhaps reading the first five chapters in reverse order (5, 4, 3, 2, 1), and then scanning the chapters again in the given order—because the level of detail with which most management books begin is found in chapter 5. This book begins at a broader overview of the whole social process so that the incipient manager will become better oriented to the situations and issues that he will encounter throughout a management career. After chapter 5 the book continues to cover topics similar to those in other writings on the principles of management, except that the decision structure is always kept in the framework of the whole social process. This leads to criteria concerning executive judgments which differ from traditional management texts, and which also lead, at the end of the book, to a difference in the method of evaluating the competence of management.

Thus the purpose of this book is to enable managers to think about their decisions in a broader context, one that will enable them to cope with more situations, more successfully, over the life of their management career, regardless of the kind of institution in which they work.

Part I
Environment and Structure
of Management

1 The Ends of Management

Management is usually studied from the viewpoint of specific organizations, such as business enterprise, government, universities, hospitals, or voluntary social institutions. This institutional approach has the advantage of imparting specialized knowledge and skills; but it has the disadvantage, being specialized and partitioned, of suboptimizing the decision process—that is, the decision process tends to achieve the ends of the special institution concerned, but not necessarily the ends of society. A decision process that seeks to achieve the ends of the whole society must ask first what those ends are.

Private and public management are jointly concerned with the whole social process, and the examination of their joint outputs is a way to examine the ends and mission of society. The basics of private and public management are the concepts that seek to optimize the whole social system. This chapter considers sixteen basic concepts of private and public management.

The Mission of the Social System

Society is an abstraction: it is in reality a collection of individuals. Institutions also are an abstraction—legal entities authorized to act on behalf of individuals. In the abstract, society and institutions have no ends of their own. They exist to fulfill human needs. Society becomes vitalized as a system only as people organize activity to meet individual needs. Institutions become organizational units only when managers are authorized to act on behalf of individuals to fulfill their needs.

The total social system functions to fulfill the individuality of its members, their economic needs, their intellectual development, their personality development, their cultural and artistic needs, their biological activity, their maturation, and their spiritual realization. These are not separate realms, each sufficient in itself, because an individual is not a bottle with many separate compartments, each to be filled at a different fountain. The individual does not simply fill his economic needs at work, his cultural needs at a symphony, his religious needs in church. At work the individual engages in economic activity; but he also develops his intellect, shapes his personality, sharpens his cultural apperceptions, matures, and, if work means anything at all, sees the relationship between his daily life and the greater scheme of things. Indeed, this latter fault—the individual's inability to see the grand design of his life in daily work—is the most shattering blow leading to alienation in an industrial society.

3

This alienation in an industrial society comes about because the enterprise is treated as a whole, with the individual as one of its interchangeable parts, whereas in reality it is the individual who is the organic whole to be served, and institutions are the subsystems with delegated functions to respond collectively to individual needs. Management should be approached as a system; and the whole system is the whole social process. Any other approach causes separate institutions to suboptimize on their own interests. For example, the critical environmental problems today are caused by businesses minimizing their direct, internal costs to suboptimize profit. The consequence is that health, biological, and ecological effects are ignored in the decision process, resulting in external costs to clean up emissions, effluents, and pollution.[1] A systematic approach to ecological problems would incorporate the biological and health effects into the decision process, with a result of optimizing both the environmental and business consequences. But even this would be suboptimization of only two elements of the whole social system, unless cultural, aesthetic, psychological, and spiritual values were incorporated into the decision process as well. Thus the only decision process that will serve the whole man is one that deals with the whole man's social environment.

A systemic approach to management for the whole man treats all the efforts to nurture individual maturation as costs and all achievements of maturation as outputs. The costs versus the benefits of these endeavors to develop the whole man become the crux of the managerial decision process, regardless of institutional setting. Until a managerial decision process is adopted that treats the whole man, the tendency toward alienation and disorder will recur.

Under a systemic view, the society is seen as a process rather than as a series of separate institutions. The processes are those actions, wherever they occur, which are undertaken in response to individual needs to achieve the individual's personal development. The institutional territory in which actions occur is of importance only to identify the cost center for accounting purposes. The validity of the action or the institution is dependent upon whether individuals do develop, mature, and are fulfilled. Institutions thus are the vistages of territorial imperatives that establish dominion over a certain class of actions; but since the institutions suboptimize on their own maintenance, the individual becomes a means used by the institution to achieve its own ends, being the human end which the institution should serve. As long as institutions qua institutions are the organic base for management studies, individuals will be frustrated in their maturation.

Assume, then, that individual development and fulfillment is the mission of a social system. Then the output of that system is a form of individual achievement and maturation. The inputs are a series of action or implementation steps leading to personal achievement. The action steps may have occurred partly in an educational institution, the family, a church, a small fraternal group, an individual adventure in nature, an artistic creation, and work. But, if the output is for the individual to realize his own identity, for example, then it does not matter where and in what pieces the realization occurred. The important fact is that the individual identity was realized. The costs were all the learning experiences that existed in the school, the family, church, fraternal group, adventure, or work. The management process is to see that all the implementation steps occur to realize the output. The decision process is to see that all the accumulated costs and efforts are equalized by results equivalently valuable to the individual.

Decision making in this sense is generic. It does not belong to any institution. It is the kind of decision making an individual would do for himself if he had all the knowledge and technique that has accumulated within the society. But no individual can have that range of knowledge and technique; hence it is society's role to organize a decision process that simulates his decision criteria and serves, in effect, as his collective and managerial alter ego. This kind of decision process is what is meant by *private* and *public management*, or business and social problem solving. Business and social problem solving is a decision process designed to serve the whole man—anything less is insufficient to serve the dignity of the individual or be dignified as the managerial function.

When a Management Function Must Be Performed

A management function originates when an individual, unable to meet his own needs, seeks the knowledge, resources, or technology of a larger group to satisfy them. Then the question arises as to who shall act, and who shall have the authority to initiate the action. In some cases, the individual himself may be the actor on his own behalf, as, for example, when he builds a house of logs for his own shelter. But he needs the authority to act from elsewhere, because he has to have access to land and materials—that is, he must have entitlement to a site and construction means granted to him by mutual consent; otherwise, someone else may claim his home. That grant of entitlement is authority bestowed by the social process with the agreement of others. Hence, authority has two major aspects, the grant of a right and consent.

Nature of Authority

Authority is a grant by individuals to a decision maker of the right to act on their behalf, and the use of authority requires the tacit or overt consent of the grantors. The grant may be of a right, such as the right to use land, or it may be the grant of a power, such as the right to direct other people in their labor. The consent may be overt, by acquiescence in a specific case, or it may be formalized into an institution. An example of overt consent would be the approval of an easement for one person to place a water line across another's property. An example of formalized consent is the delegation by a sovereign people in a constitution to Congress the authority to levy taxes on behalf of society. The constitutional consent allowing Congress to levy taxes is a generalized recognition that in all cases of revenue needs, Congress may act now and into the future. Formal consent, therefore, has the aspect of a timeless delegation of power to an institutional body.

Formal Consent to Authority

The timeless delegation of power to an institution to act on behalf of an individual is certainly one of the most powerful organizing principles in human history. Stated as a timeless delegation of power to an institution to act for and upon the individual, the concept becomes a potential for despotism; and so it has turned out to be in many epochs of history. The reason an individual must make this sweeping consent to authority is that there is not sufficient time in his own lifetime to decide everything that affects him; and even if there were time, he does not have all the knowledge. The delegation and consent to authority increases as the complexity of society, technology, and knowledge increases. If there is a crisis of authority today, it is due in no small part to the vast delegations and consent that an individual must confer on others (usually institutions) in a complex and changing society.

Protections against Formal Authority

Individuals seek protection from the potential misuses of formal delegations of authority by not delegating those things most vital to their being, and trying to place constraints and compartmentalization on authority. Individuals zealously protect their privacy, personal lives, thoughts, and expression—they avoid delegating authority over the most vital aspects of their being. They do not delegate to organizations the authority to make love or laughter, to witness beauty, nor to reason on their behalf. The personal side of life, which is the developmental side of personality, is carefully guarded from outside authorities or from authority delegations.

Authority is delegated by individuals on the more trivial aspects of their lives, such as what goods and services they shall have, how much goods, and how much taxes they shall pay. These matters are less vital to their being; and they frequently involve services which the individual cannot provide for himself as well or as cheaply as society, considering the time, resource, and expertise required in their production.

A management function is, therefore, in the interest of individuals to provide the knowledge, resources, technology, and time required to produce the optimal goods and services that augment the alternative ways by which humans may seek their individuality. A management function requires a delegation of authority for the manager to act on the individual's behalf. Delegations of authority are normally made as specifically as possible, and hedged with checks, balances, and regulations to prevent institutional managers from encroaching upon individuals. These checks, balances, and regulations are attempts to constrain and compartmentalize authority for the protection of individuals. The delegations, nondelegations, constraints, and compartmentalizations of authority form the structure of society, of institutions, and the decision process. These structures and decision processes must be understood by anyone who wishes to solve problems or to manage.

The Structure of Society

The structure of society, institutions, and the social process is formed by the delegations, nondelegations, constraints, and compartmentalization of authority. The basic form for delegations of authority is found in the charter, constitution, or incorporation of an institution. These are legislative grants by a sovereign people to a government, and by the government to business and voluntary institutions. The specific authorizations of business and voluntary institutions are found in legislation that delegates decision authority to them, usually in the form of contractual powers that are enforceable in the courts. The constructional powers include the authority to make contracts, hold title to property, issue negotiable instruments, buy, sell, exchange, and borrow.

Contractual authorities are also limited or constrained by regulations that further define responsibilities or prevent abuses. Regulations upon businesses limit their contractual power on mergers, acquisition, restraint of trade, discriminatory price competition, horizontal market power, food adulteration, advertising misrepresentation, labeling, securities issuance, accounting practices, labor negotiations, shipping practices, product standards, trading with the enemy, etc.

The total sum of all of these delegations, nondelegations, regulations, checks, balances, constraints and compartmentalizations of authority forms the social structure. The structure of the social system is illustrated briefly and schematically in figure 1-1. The schematic shows the social process initiated by individuals who have needs. The needs of individuals give rise to missions. Individuals assume the mission for themselves of their own individual development, to the extent they can realize it in their private lives unaided by others. To the extent they need the resources, time, knowledge, or technology of others (society) to meet their needs, individuals delegate authority to a management function to aid them.

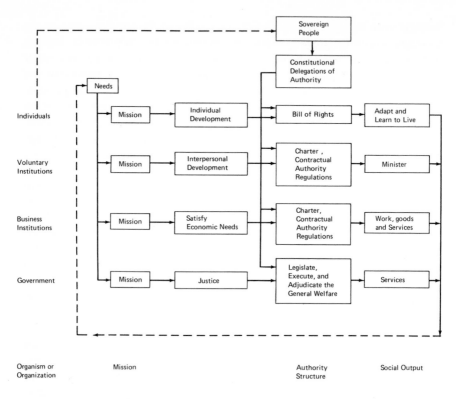

Figure 1-1. Structure of the Social System.

Voluntary social institutions, like schools, universities, churches, hospitals, health care associations, and community associations, have the mission (purpose) of aiding the individual in his personal or interpersonal development. These are the most personalized of institutions, and they are voluntary, by design, because they come closest to the individual's private life. By being voluntary, these organizations cannot mandate or encroach upon the individual's private life except by his overt consent on each act—the individual can always withdraw his delegation of authority by withdrawing his own person. Voluntary institutions generally operate under legislatively established charters, contractual authorities, and regulations.

Business institutions have the mission of satisfying the economic needs of individuals; and these include both employment and the provision of goods and services. Business institutions are also authorized by legislation to organize under incorporation charters and operate through contractual authority and under regulations.

Government is the institution of last resort to provide justice for individuals and equality of services to the extent that individuals as well as voluntary or business organizations do not provide the services in the social process. As the rectifying institution of last resort, the government can only provide minimal, mass services that are generally standardized to the point that they contribute little to individuation. Rather, government services contribute to survival and subsistence. The size of government is a measure of the failures of the social process, in the sense that government services are minimal remedies for injustices. If the injustices were not there—that is, if businesses, individuals, and voluntary institutions were able by themselves to fill the unmet human needs—there would be no need for governmental intercession.

Besides being the intercessor of last resort, the government, as agent of the sovereign people, is also the keeper of authority distributions—government legislation is the initiating act by which authority is dispersed and distributed to government agencies, businesses, voluntary institutions, and individuals. These enabling acts grant rights to organizations to act on behalf of the general welfare, and public consent is assumed to be inherent in the representativeness of the legislature. To the extent that legislatures are representative of special interest groups and lobbies, rather than the public at large, this consent is moot. For example, large portions of the public withheld consent for the Vietnam war, even though it had executive and congressional approval.

Return to figure 1-1. We have seen that individual needs give rise to missions for organizations. These missions are ensconced in law by delegations from a sovereign people to government through constitutional delegations of authority, and from government to business and voluntary organizations by enabling authorizations in charters, contractual powers, and limiting regulations (checks and balances in the economy). These delegations, nondelegations, constraints, and compartmentalizations form (1) the nature of organizational units in the social process, and (2) the distributions of authority under which the institutions can then exercise their decisions—that is, the authority distribution forms the design of the decision system.

The results of these decisions, as shown in figure 1-1, are a series of social outputs: adapting, learning, ministering, work, goods, and services. These social outputs are intended, if the social process is well articulated, to meet the sum of individual needs. To the extent the social outputs leave human needs unmet, the social process is deficient. The efficiencies and deficiencies of the social output are the feedback that tests the effectiveness of the social process to individuals. Individuals must be the final judges of effectiveness of the social process; and, to do this, they must have the ultimate ability to define and voice their own needs.

The Development of Individuality

The development of individuality requires that each human being retain the ultimate authority to define his own needs. The expression of needs is the activating purpose (mission) of the social system. If the individual cannot define his own needs, he loses the power to make decisions about his life and its fulfillment. Freedom exists when the individual retains the capability (authority) to search for his own identity (needs), and when the delegation of authority to others to help meet those needs remains decentralized, differentiated, and diverse—a free individual is one who can choose what his life style and life actions will be, and who has a variety of options as to the means by which he can achieve these actions. The variety of options open to him becomes larger as the variety of actions, procedures, programs, services or institutions increases. Therefore, individual freedom and creativity are fostered by decentralization, with differentiated and diverse institutions to serve him—none with overweening power to regulate him. The individual achieves this diversity and delimitation of power in societies where the authority has been constrained or dispersed among institutions.

The individual's first protection of his freedom, as we have seen, is not to delegate authority to anyone or any group to act on his behalf. The most central features of individuality have always been closely guarded and never delegated. Individuals delegate authority over mundane aspects of their lives—what they shall eat, how much, what clothing, recreations, mobility, fashions, entertainment, or public ceremonies they shall have. They are the authorities that institutions acquire and the services that they provide.

Unfortunately, institutions become vehicles for their own continuance and for the personal power of their officials. Then the services and ceremonies of the institution come to be propagated as the real experience, rather than individualized development. Thus, social institutions become ends in themselves.

Dispersal of Authority

For individuals to retain ultimate authority over their own needs, they must keep authority delegations to institutions differentiated, dispersed, decentralized, and diverse. The wide distribution of authority makes each authority holder (institution) anxious to serve the individual to survive, and this competition among authorities is both the guarantee of service and the insurance against domination of the individual. Those ages in history that have had diversity and decentralization of authority have been ages of human freedom. They have usually occurred, historically, when a society was opened to new ideas by trade, exploration or discovery, and new institutions were needed to exploit opportunity.[2]

Periods of human subjugation, alienation, and domination historically have followed crises and social disorders; and order was stabilized through social institutions that were large, established, centralized, few, and powerful. Institutions were given blanket authority to cope with a serious social threat, and individuals were not successful in maintaining their liberty against the institutions. In these past eras, individuals gave away too much authority to institutions to deal with the insecurities, threats, problems, or anxieties besetting the society. Such threats as war, ideologies, proselytization, insecurity, poverty, and depression have most frequently been the occasion for yielding too much authority to institutions. At the time, the anxiety of coping with threats to personal security have seemed to warrant such absolute delegations.

Institutions usually have been all too willing to accept these broad delegations of authority, serve the need of the time with masterful resolve, and retain power over the individual when the crisis has passed. Since these delegations of authority tend to be timeless, the power of the institutions builds and feeds upon itself until the individual is provided the security he sought by a beneficent and intricate set of controls limiting his freedom. Then it is the individual's turn to become constrained, serving the institution, frustrated in his own development, disaffected, and alienated until a new social movement and ideology enable individuals again to break the authoritarian hold of institutions and to start anew. But, again he will have to delegate some authority, because no individual has the time or competence to deal with all aspects of his needs himself. Hence, the cycle between freedom and authoritarianism, delegation and constraint, individualism and institutionalism begins again, historically running over the same circuit time and again. The question is whether there is sufficient human wisdom and managerial competence to avoid another round.

Where might we look for guidance in seeking to avoid another round of the cycle running from disorder to oppression? Among the curious places to find some guidance is in the twilight zone between conservatism and anarchism, so well described by Nisbet:

Even the great anarchists have insisted that there can be no freedom, no individuality, without authority. The essence of anarchism, and its link with such conservatives as Tocqueville and Acton, is that authorities must be many, dispersed, and closely united to objectives and functions which command the loyalty and talents of members. Freedom is to be found in the openings and crannies of authority; and it is nourished by competition among authorities.[3]

The Systematic Practice of Management

The systematic practice of management distributes missions, authority, functions, tasks, and allegiances within the social process in response to the individual needs of a whole man. The key priorities of management are, in order in which they must be decided, to determine (1) needs, (2) a mission, (3) alternative solutions to the needs, (4) functions, (5) tasks, (6) allegiances, and (7) the process of the social system.

Needs. Needs are individual in origin. They represent the aspirations and requirements of a human being to live in fulfillment of his own capacities within a larger social environment.

Mission. The needs of individuals may be viewed from many perspectives, and these provide the conceptual framework for the mission. One perspective is biological—the needs for food, shelter, mating, and familial protection. Psychological needs concentrate on basic drives, such as hunger, sex, identity, recognition, approval, achievement, self-assurance, individuation, and maturation. Sociological needs are described in terms of role, group relations, status, and hierarchy. Economic needs are viewed as material wants and satisfactions expressed in the purchases of goods and services, at exchange prices, for consumption. Political needs are expressed as social choices, leverage groups, bargaining, coalitions, lobbying, voting, and power. All of these views reflect a significant aspect of personality seeking to find a means of expression, and the list could be made much longer by citing artistic, cultural, intellectual, humanistic, and religious needs as well. The object here is not to catalog individual needs but to inquire how these needs become expressed in a way that requires a management function to be performed.

Alternatives and Authority. When a need is seen in the context of a technology, discipline, concept, or strategem that provides a solution to the need, then a management function: (1) is performed by the act of creation of a product or service, and (2) may be executed by allocating resources to perform functions and tasks needed to deliver the service. The act of creation—that is, seeing a mission and solution—gives rise to authority. Authority thus is the authorization to initiate actions (solutions) which fulfill human needs.

Functions. Functions are the allocation of performance requirements and the subdelegation of authority to organizational units capable of completing one element of the solution. In essence, they are broad divisions of labor toward a performance objective.

Tasks. Tasks are detailed divisions of labor made in the light of the technologies and human skills that are available. Tasks are essentially work orders that may be accompanied by appropriate levels of technical discretion or resources.

Allegiance. Allegiance is the loyalty that individuals yield toward those with delegated authority who serve their needs. Allegiance recognizes that authority is a two-way pact, in which loyalty is given to those who are responsive to individual needs. Alienation is the withholding of loyalty from those who do not serve individual needs.

Process. The process is the flow of inputs and outputs intended to complete the requirements of a mission. The inputs are materials, labor, land, capital, and management used in the transformation of productive process. The social outputs are the goods and services of all kinds—material, intellectual, cultural, or professional—that fulfill the totality of individual needs. The social system is the network of the missions, authorities, functions, tasks, allegiances, processes, and human interactions that link the initiating needs to the final social outputs.

The Accession to Authority

If the distribution of authority is the heart of the social management process, as argued here, then the most vital issue is how does anyone acquire authority in the first place? Certainly a contemporary individual will find the idea of his actively delegating authority to others somewhat unreal. Most of us have never been asked whether we agree that some authority figure shall levy taxes against us, conscript us for war, pollute our air, fire us from jobs, restrict us from trespassing on beaches or forests, determine who owns or runs giant corporations, decide what products we shall have and schools we go to, or control our actions in work and on the street. To any individual, at a moment in time, these regulations and restrictions on his life seem given to him. Some power, institution, or law-giver—some amorphous "boss"—has power over him.

Yet, in a more subtle sense, the individual can always make a choice, even if it is limited. He can choose not to do what seems required of him. He can walk away from that which he disapproves. Herein lies the power of Ghandi's nonviolent opposition, of the labor strike, of dissent. The East Germans who "voted with their feet" by walking out of Communist Germany required a totalitarian regime to put up the Iron Curtain to contain them. Student dissent caused two administrations to modify their stands on the unpopular war in Indochina.

Acquiescence to and participation in the existing social process is a tacit consent that perpetuates the accession of authority in on-going institutions. Acquiescence is a permit for continuance, and discontinuance is possible only when delegations of authority are withdrawn by acts of overt dissent. Society must be badly divided, and obstacles to individual development very critical, before individuals are willing to risk widespread, overt dissent, because dissent forceful enough to change institutions is also violent enough to create chaos in social processes. Social chaos is something the individual is reluctant to precipitate.

The social order is the sine qua non of individuality and individuation. Without it, life is an animal existence; with it, even when it is pretty bad, the individual has some chance to seek his own humanity. The social order is a habit that takes care of mundane affairs, relieving the individual for other pursuits. With the mundane affairs of his life placed in a fairly predictable set of social arrangements, the individual can turn his personal decision process to more intimate and vital choices, such as loving, raising a family, writing a poem, or worshiping—without worrying about the mundane. The social order takes care of the routine and trivial affairs of life, and enables the individual to develop himself to the farthest reaches of his being; and this is the basis of his acquiescence even in a faulty social process.

Means to Succession

The succession of authority takes place by acquiescence to legal continuance of current institutional practice. Succession among individuals is normally accomplished by property rights and inheritance. For example, a man may have acquired title to property by purchase, with the consent of the body politic through enabling legislation to buy or sell property in fee simple; and he may transfer title to the property to his son by a will upon his death. Hereditary accession and transfer of authority by property right has been institutionalized in law, and hence the succession and continuance of territorial rights comes about tacitly without question. The son may take all or approve all actions that occur on the locus of his acquired property.

The succession of authority in the modern corporation is quietly efficient compared to the conspiracy and assassination that sometimes surrounded succession in feudal times. The title to the property of the corporation is held by its stockholders, who delegate the operational management of the enterprise to an elected board of directors, including the naming of its president. When a corporation president dies or retires, the board of directors quietly evaluates potential candidates, usually experienced managers within the firm, and names a new president. The stockholders are not consulted unless a proxy fight is involved. The workers, the customers, the suppliers, the managerial hierarchy, the public are not consulted even though they are vitally affected, and all of them tacitly consent because the voting procedures of the corporation are established by law.

The succession to authority in an educational or voluntary institution is usually with the consultative consent of the governed—that is, most universities and public schools name a new president or superintendent only after the governing board has consulted with the faculty or teachers, students, parents, and sometimes public agencies. The constituencies do not have a direct vote, but they have an implied veto power by expressing reservation or disapproval upon consultation.

The succession to authority in political office is by overt consent—that is, by election or vote. The casting of ballots determines who shall succeed to office, and the authority passes peaceably to the candidate with the majority vote. The politeness and acquiescence with which defeated candidates accept their defeat and do not challenge the succession of authority demonstrate the human proclivity for order.

All of these modes of succession seem commonplace to us. In that sense, these rules of succession are our tradition. Yet traditions change; it was not always so. Business leadership was once conferred by royal decree, and the regal crown conferred by divine authority. There is no logic now which says that a corporate president is best selected by a board of directors, or a political leader by a vote. It is just as logical to select political presidents by boards of directors, as in the parliamentary system, or to elect corporate presidents by a vote of constituencies, as in cooperatives. The point is that the form of succession is largely a matter of happenstance and history. The only significant fact about the succession is that it is an institutional procedure that has common consent. Institutionalization and consent give succession a settled routine. Succession becomes a social habit.

Without this routine or social habit succession is potentially the most perilous and disruptive of social processes. The power and tragedy of Medea, Oedipus Rex, Hamlet, and Macbeth are due, in no small part, to the ambitions, hatred, trauma, and guilt that accompany contested successions. The replay of these tragedies is too painful and conspiratorial a process to repeat with each change of leadership in every institution. Without habitual succession, we would all be engaged in conspiracies or expressing ambition and hatred most of the time—claiming new positions of power or marshaling the allegiances to make the claim. Given the capacity of the human being for avarice and evil as well as good, unbridled succession would be chaos for and pose a peril to all. Recognizing this peril, we move to the other extreme of routinizing succession to the point where it may stultify the social processes by failing to revise constituted authorities upon changes in leadership.

Consent and Dissent to Succession

The tacit nature of consent to succession, and the revolutionary nature of dissent, give society a bias toward alienation and crisis, by letting mismatches of institutional authority and unmet human needs continue for long periods without remedy for the sake of order. Because social order is essential to individuality, the individual is reluctant to disturb orderly processes, even when they are mismanaged for long periods of time. A mismanaged social order presents the individual with annoyances, constraints, regulations, and petty grievances, but somewhere in the interstices of authority the individual usually can find a loophole to get around his annoyances. Only when the loopholes are systematically closed and his intimate life is threatened does the individual find it worthwhile, in his decision trade-off, to seek to change the social order. If the individual is threatened by death in senseless wars, by capricious imprisonment that preempts his intimate life, or denial of his freedom to love, think, speak, create, only then does the individual find it essential to rebel against the social order. By that time he has lost his intimate life anyway, so he has nothing more to lose or fear.

Institutional authoritarianism, which pushes individuals to the point where they have nothing to lose or fear, makes a fatal error, because it causes individuals to see order as oppression rather than a personal benefit. Since order is oppression, they seek to destroy order, by violence, by systematic disobedience, and by dropping out. All of these forms of dissent bring disorder and social change.

Essence of Leadership

Consent is the essence of leadership, and every leader in every institution continually seeks consent. Consent is what bestows leadership and authority upon him, because consent is the affirmation by individuals that he serves their interests and needs, that he has their allegiance, that he may continue in office, that his ends or programs are regarded as desirable, and that he will prevail. These allegiances are what bind the institution into a membership or community. The withholding of consent and allegiance is a vote of no confidence. The leader may remain in office for a period of time as a mere boss, who individuals tolerate for the sake of order. Or, if he is intolerable, dissent can cause his termination.

Every manager is also a leader, whether in business, education, or government. The manager needs consent even in a business corporation, where the authoritarian legal structure makes dissent and removal of managers by constituencies very difficult, because dissent can sap productivity, drain interest in the job, and diminish a manager's effectiveness.

The means by which leaders obtain and retain consent is by demonstrating the systematic practice of management. Most particularly, leaders visualize and communicate their need-mission-solution to prospective followers. Successful leaders are those who can convince others to accept their creative solution to the problem of satisfying individuals' needs.

Leadership Conflicts of Interest

Leaders face a conflict of interest between their institutional selves and their public constituencies that in the long run can only be resolved by repression, or balancing interests in favor of the public constituencies. A conflict of interest inevitably arises because institutions come into existence to perform defined missions or services; but as times and needs change, individuals (consumers) demand alternate services. However, the alternate service may be outside the capability of an existing organization. The leader thus is faced with a choice of either trying to change the demand, trying to change the organizational capability, or trying to repress the demand.

For example, the automobile industry came into being with the mission of providing personal transportation, but the internal combustion engine is a significant atmospheric polluter. Should the auto companies (1) try to stimulate demand for smaller cars, (2) design a pollution-free engine, or (3) repress the air quality standards that they are required to meet? Thus far they have concentrated on (1) and (3).

The Vietnam war had initial support as a means to contain communism, but as the costs became too high in lives and dollars, the demand for withdrawal mounted. In 1963-1976 the government consequently tried to alter public opinion and support regarding the war and repress opposition to the war, particularly by the students who were being drafted as soldiers, before being forced by dissent and violence to negotiate an early settlement and withdrawal.

Institutional leaders try first to change demand and then to repress demand before they try to change the institution's internal capability. The reason is twofold: (1) the cost of changing institutions is large, if indeed it can be done at all, and (2) the leader has a conflict of interest that impels him to maintain the institution as it is.

Leaders are influencers of their workers as well as captives of their workers. The technological staff of an executive is his most personal power base. These are people whose loyalty he needs to remain as leader and carry out operable goals and programs. The technostructure of an institution has a historic mission and capability which its members understand and were recruited to do. They know the process they are doing, but they know few other processes. In manufacturing, heavy capital investments are also commitments to existing processes. To try to change a technostructure staff is to ask them to do what they have never done and do not know how to do. The implication of such a request is that the technostructure should leave and a different one with different capabilities should replace it. Professional staffs resist being displaced, and the executive is required to try to change external demands before changing internal staff.

This reluctance of the internal organization to change presents the leader with conflicts, because the public constituency is simultaneously demanding that he change to meet new individual needs. The leader must now choose between two sets of loyalties and allegiances, both of which he needs. His public constituency must affirm he is responding to their changing individual needs for him to retain allegiance and loyalty from the public. He is also under pressure to maintain the existing bureaucracy, within the limits of its capability, to maintain internal loyalty.

The leader's conflict of interest is that, to exercise the power of the institution and his office (that is, himself) he must first retain the loyalty of the internal organization that is capable of doing the institution's work (functions and tasks). If he loses the capacity to do organizational work, the institution terminates, as does his leadership and power.

However, unless he also (in time) satisfies the external needs of his public constituency to meet their changing requirements, the authority (allegiance or alienation) of the institution will wither. The leader normally has a short-term time perspective—namely, to stay in office. This leads him to opt for the alternative favoring the internal staff (the status quo) and maintaining the institution in the hope that in the longer run he can change or repress demand.

The only way the leader can get out of this dilemma is to resign his institutional job as his first act of management and start afresh with a new organizational capability; but this is a bold decision that few managers care to make. Failing to resign his job and start afresh to meet individual needs, the manager can only respond, as keeper of his organization, to try to maintain the institution first, and to try to change or repress demand second.

Institutional maintenance is normally the first priority decision made by institutional leaders. The evidence of this is seen in the lists of the leading business corporations from one decade to the next. The survival rate of businesses among the top fifty corporations through successive decades since 1900 has been less than 50 percent; and few stay among the top corporations over several decades. They are displaced by new companies who meet new needs, because the change process overtakes the old institutions that are captives of their organizational capability.

Optimization of Leadership Decisions

Management leadership decisions will suboptimize on few interests, including those of the decision maker, unless the decision system interacts with the whole social process. The few business corporations that do survive from decade to decade generally have one of two characteristics : either they hold an oligopolistic position by reason of barriers to entry, which give them a firm hold on resources, markets, or technology; or they have a means of adaptation within their leadership that enables them to change products and services with changing demands.

The longest surviving companies among the top corporations are, for the most part, oligopolies that hold their position by repressing competition, demand, or both. These are mainly manufacturing companies heavily committed to existing products by reason of large capital investment. Recently, another category of business corporations have shown tendencies to survive over long periods of time. These are largely research- or service-oriented companies with relatively fewer heavy, job-shop-type investments. These newer research-service companies tend to have many products and short product cycles (perhaps five to ten years). Because product cycles are continually phasing in and out, there is more adaptability to new demands. Moreover, the technostructure staff is more varied, flexible, and team oriented, enabling interdisciplinary project teams to combine and recombine as required to solve new problems and to meet new human needs.

The executive of such an interdisciplinary, flexible organization faces fewer of the conflict-of-interest problems that beset leaders of heavily committed or capitalized manufactures. However, he has a problem of a different order—that is, how does he maintain an interaction with the whole social process so that his organization can sense and create solutions to new needs? This is both a significant marketing problem (because needs are many and sometimes obscure) and a costly technological problem (because inventions required for new solutions must be developed regularly). Unless this sensing-creation phenomenon is handled with skill, the advantages of the flexible organization are lost. Then the leader will be tempted to suboptimize on what the firm is already doing, or upon his own predilections, which may not stand reality testing in the market.

One successful format for dealing with this management dilemma among technical companies is to have small market-product design teams continually making trial applications in the marketplace, then augmenting the pilot project when it shows signs of market acceptance or meeting new needs.

The Effectiveness of Management Decision Making

The effectiveness of management decision making can be evaluated by the extent to which decisions correspond with those the individual would make for himself, if he had the knowledge and technique accumulated within the society. The pilot-test approach to decision making is one way of obtaining sufficient feedback to evaluate whether the decisions of the institution are similar to the decisions that would be made by individuals. If the user response is positive either by purchases, support, or vote, the manager has some assurance that his actions are similar to those that would have been made by individuals. However, this pilot test is only effective insofar as the market or polling place is open and free. To the extent that forced choices are placed upon individuals, the evaluation is invalid. For example, faced with a choice between having no transportation alternative or buying a smaller car, individuals may necessarily but reluctantly choose the car. Or, faced with two presidential candidates who both say they will stop an unpopular war but who do not say how they will stop it, the individual may vote along straight party lines or for the most charismatic. In short, an individual must be able to make a free and open choice among differing alternatives if the effectiveness of a managerial decision is to be evaluated in terms of serving the individual's needs. Or, put negatively, the ineffectiveness of management decisions can be evaluated by the extent to which individuals tacitly or overtly withhold their consent to authority and displace it with alienation, dissent, and disorder. Alienation is difficult to detect unless it shows up in declining sales or nay votes. By the time dissent becomes disorder, the ineffectiveness of management decisions is obvious; but frequently it is then too late for corrective action.

The positive mode of attempting to evaluate pilot acceptance of solutions to new needs is, therefore, essential to the evaluation of managerial effectiveness and the maintenance of leadership.

Notes

1. Stahrl Edmunds and John Letey, *Environmental Administration* (New York: McGraw-Hill, 1973).

2. Stahrl Edmunds, *Alternative U.S. Futures* (Santa Monica, Cal.: The Goodyear Publishing Co., 1978).

3. Robert A. Nisbet, *Community and Power* (New York: Oxford University Press, 1953 and 1967), p. xii, preface to 2nd ed.

2 The Means of Management

Once missions, purposes, or goals have been established, the main function of management is to organize the means to realize these ends. The organization of means is the most time-consuming and, hence, the most costly aspect of management. In the federal government, for example, the goal-setting activities, as represented by the budgets of Congress plus the presidential offices, comprise about 0.2 percent of the federal budget. The other 99.8 percent of the budget is devoted to the means or execution of federal programs. Similarly, in business or voluntary institutions, the budgets of the goal-setting units (board of directors and executive offices, including the president and the vice-presidents) would be very small relative to the expenditures on means or implementation.

Thus the means of carrying out policy ends are costly because they are complex, detailed and difficult. Some of these complexities are seen in Part II, which deals with decision-making processes. At present, however, our purpose is to see management as a whole; and for that we need to look at the basics or concepts by which managers organize the means into usable output. Our first concern, therefore, is what are the means? Where are they? How does the manager get his hands upon them?

Nature of Growth

Human and economic growth are (1) the means for social development, and (2) measurable by productivity, gross product, and work satisfaction in the society. The development of a society or business enterprise depends upon the augmentation of its means, just as a biological organism grows by cellular multiplication. Growth is an addition to capacity or capability. In general system theory, this augmentation of capacity is looked upon as the storage of energy—that is, the storing and organization of energy reserves counteract the tendency toward entropy, decline, energy dissipation, or death. Biological species place their energy reserves in cells by multiplication. Society and social institutions store energy reserves in human capacity or by technical augmentation of human manipulative skills. Thus we may look upon an industrial motor as augmenting human muscular capacity, radio transmission as augmenting human communication capacity, and digital computers as augmenting human arithmetic capacity.

In more ordinary terms, growth occurs by increasing human performance through education, training, and development of skills, or increasing human performance by capital investment in productive equipment which raises human efficiencies. Education and training, as a means of increasing human growth and performance, may take place in schools, on the job, or in the organizational context of work. Education in schools and on-the-job training are effective means of transmitting skills; but they are frequently done outside of organization context—that is, without regard for the interrelations of people in work situations. The attempt to teach people a capacity for dealing with each other in work situations is often done tutorially, between supervisor and worker. Management has consciously tried to improve upon these interpersonal capacities by a variety of approaches, which together are referred to as organizational development. Organizational development is the expansion of the interpersonal capacities of individuals, in an organizational context, and thus improving organizational effectiveness (see chapter 10 for a more detailed discussion of this subject).

The use of capital equipment to increase human performance results in economic growth. Economics is concerned with the allocation of resources to satisfy human wants. Resource allocation decisions seek to determine which combinations of capital equipment, human skills, land, and management will yield the highest return and output. The American economy has become highly capital intensive—large inputs or ratios of capital equipment relative to land and labor yields the highest outputs per man-hour of work. This is true, of course, because the high applications of energy, mechanization, and machine output greatly extend and augment human effort. (The capital allocation process will be treated more fully in Part II. At this point, our main concern is to understand that economic growth occurs by expanding productive capacity through investment in capital equipment.)

The two means of development, then, are human growth and economic growth. These are jointly measurable as productivity, which is the physical output per man-hour of work. When productivity is expressed as physical output per unit of labor input, the measure is really reflecting a variety of inputs: productivity of capital equipment, hours of labor input, the learning curve of labor, technical progress, and effectiveness of management's capital allocation decisions. The measure is, therefore, a significant summation of the major growth forces in the economy. Productivity can also be measured as output per unit of capital input, but this reflects more exactly the productivity of capital.

A second measure commonly used to indicate social development or progress is the gross product of goods and services delivered within the social economy. The gross national product (GNP) is the most commonly used statistical measure of this type; and it has sectors or breakdowns showing the contribution to total social output from manufacturing, trade, services, government, and international transactions.

A third measure of social development is the human satisfactions that are generated by the social process; and, indeed, these are the final ends of management and society, as we saw in chapter 1. Presumably, the material satisfactions in the economy and the society are reflected in the gross product of goods and services. However, people seek a meaningful life, as well as material comfort, and this is more likely to be expressed in satisfaction with one's work. A measure of work satisfaction within a society is difficult to ascertain directly and is, therefore, usually done inferentially. Attitudinal and job satisfaction surveys in specific organizations are frequently used by management as one indicator. Other indicators are absenteeism, turnover rates (ratio of people quitting to those who do not), labor strikes, illness. Even more inferential are general social indicators such as mental health, drop-outs, drug abuse, crime, disorder, and violence—all of which in a very general way suggest disaffection.

In summary, the principal means of growth in the economy are through human development and capital investment. Management can measure its effectiveness of performance in human and economic growth by productivity, the gross product, and indicators of work satisfaction.

Productivity of Capital

The productivity of capital is the most tangible, short-term means for achieving economic growth. Human development is a long-run achievement dependent upon the motivation of individuals, the application of learning resources by management, and the availability of educational means in the community. The several variables in this mix of factors make human productivity gains through learning somewhat unpredictable, especially when the degree of individual motivation is related to work interest. If work interest or opportunity lags, the individual may leave the organization that has invested in his development. In other words, management does not have proprietary claim upon an individual in whom investment is made for growth and development, nor should it. The individual has unequivocable rights to his own development and accomplishments.

Management, therefore, often finds a greater short-term advantage in capital development than in human development because the productivity gains from capital equipment are often more predictable in both timing and yield than in human development, and management has a proprietary claim on the gains from capital investment, since it owns the property. These incentives lead to high priority for capital expansion. Indeed, capital investment has been the main management vehicle for achieving growth in the American economy, so much so that capital expansion has become the means for survival of the economy. This preference for capital expansion is not only a business choice; it is also a long-standing public policy.

The public policy to expand capital as a means of economic development goes back to frontier days, when resources were ample and labor was cheap. By giving resources to individuals at little or no cost, through mining claims, land grants, and homesteading, cheap labor could be applied to convert the resources into capital (such as farms, mines, timber companies, and processing plants). The conversion of cheap labor and ample resources into capital became the developmental policy, the modus operandi, for expansion in the United States.

As resources became more scarce and labor more costly, the government has continued the developmental policy of capital expansion through incentives. Many of these incentives are tax advantages to those who invest in capital productivity—for example, rapid amortization, favorable treatment of capital gains, depreciation allowances, expensing of research, as well as government research grants to businesses and universities. The effect of these incentives is to motivate business executives to find new innovations, technological improvements, labor-saving devices, and capital equipment that will increase productivity. The justification for these public tax incentives, which in a sense are also public subsidies to the capital expansion process, is that such investments are the means for economic growth and rising living standards for the society and the general welfare.

The counterargument to this developmental policy is that, to the extent incentives and subsidies to capital expansion are powerful enough to cause underemployment and underdevelopment of human beings, the means (capital expansion) become counterproductive to the ends of society, which are the development of individuals. This trade-off between human (individual) development and capital expansion is one of the paradoxes and unsolved problems of the U.S. socioeconomy, as we see later in this chapter when we discuss the problems of social disorder and change.

In general, the problem is that the human costs of capital expansion are few as long as resources are ample and cheap. But as resources become scarce and high priced, a diminishing rate of productivity of capital is felt—that is, more and more capital has to be invested for diminishing social returns. Once the easy resources have been exploited—for example in minerals or petroleum—the extraction costs become higher, wells and shafts go deeper, the quality of minerals decrease, processing costs increase, and the pollution wastes become greater. All of these mounting costs mean that larger aggregations of capital are needed to keep the expansion going. New incentives, larger institutions to amass capital, and more authority delegations are needed to keep aggregating the capital for these intensifying investments. The capital intensive society becomes capital intensifying—the declining productivity of capital has to be offset by more intensive capitalization to maintain the same rate of economic growth.

In the process of capital intensification, the means may well become the ends. Institutional decision makers are necessarily so intent on trying to raise capital productivity that the human needs for individuality assume second priority. Human work must be fitted to machines and machines must displace labor to make capital productivity work and to maintain ecomomic growth. What Jacques Ellul calls the dehumanization of technique occurs. Unemployment, poverty, and underemployment of human skills become endemic. The ends of individual fulfillment are no longer being primarily served.

In summary, capital investment has been the main management vehicle for achieving economic growth because of the incentives, predictability, and proprietary claims related to capital productivity. However, capital productivity achieves diminishing returns as resources or technologies become finite, and this declining productivity of capital requires that capital investments be intensified to maintain the same rate of economic growth. Capital intensification may then become so difficult that managers shape employment to the needs of technology rather than to the needs of individuals. If this happens, then the means (technique of capital investment) become defeating to the social ends of individual fulfillment.

Capital Flows

Investments in capital productivity are dependent upon the organization of orderly flows of financial capital. The sources for financial capital to be invested in capital equipment are savings and credit. Individuals are sources of substantial personal savings, which are organized for investment use by their deposit or collection in savings institutions, such as banks, insurance companies, and savings and loan associations.

Corporations are substantial savers of funds through their internal earnings and cash flows. The cash flow of a corporation is made up of its profits, depreciation allowances, increases in debt, or liquidation (sale or reduction) of assets. This flow of funds in a corporation can normally be found in an accounting statement called the sources and uses of funds, or the fund statement.

The federal government is also a source of capital flows through its own use of funds and its management of credit. The government's management of its own funds (that is, tax revenues and expenditures) is called fiscal policy; and the management of its borrowing or credit is called monetary policy. The federal government uses fiscal and monetary policy as two gross means to manage the economy in an attempt to foster economic growth, stability, and equity. Monetary and fiscal policy may be used separately or together. Monetary policy is a determination of the amount of money supply that should be allowed to flow into the economy relative to goods. The principal means for increasing money supply is to increase borrowing, particularly government borrowing. The government must borrow when its expenditures exceed its tax revenues; and this is the link between monetary and fiscal policy. Government borrowing from banks or Federal Reserve System increases the amount of credit outstanding.

The government has four main options in monetary and fiscal policy: (1) An expansionist monetary-fiscal policy increases borrowing and money supply through a fiscal deficit (overspending), which tends to increase capital flows, employment, and inflation. (2) A restrained expansion policy seeks to tighten the money supply by high interest rates in the private sector, while simultaneously increasing public spending and the fiscal deficit for welfare purposes. (3) A tight fiscal policy (balanced budget) with an expansionist monetary policy tends to increase credit and capital investment in private business. (4) A neutral policy, or balancing the fiscal budget and constraining the money supply to the rate of change in goods, tends to leave the economy in equilibrium and let economic change take place by internal reallocation of resources in the private sector.

The first two policy options create expansion in the public sector (government), which leads subsequently to increased consumer purchasing power and, it is hoped, to capital investment. Unfortunately, these two policies also lead to inflation. The first two policy options have been used heavily by government since 1930 as a means of trying to reduce unemployment. The second two policy options favor expansion and adjustment within private business. Option (3) was the principal policy prior to 1930 and was accompanied by wide cyclical fluctuations in business. Option 4 has the advantage of being noninflationary, but it has seldom been tried because it relies upon internal market adjustments to renew expansion, and meantime capital investment may lag and unemployment may increase. In summary, there are three major sources of financial capital: individual savings, corporation cash-flows, and government deficits. Note that all of these channels for funds are highly institutionalized—that is, the capital flows are controlled by decisions in savings institutions, large business corporations, and the federal government.

The institutionalization of capital flows means that the capital allocation decisions are largely made by institutional managers rather than by individuals on their own behalf. The question then becomes: do institutions make the same type of capital investment decisions that individuals would make for themselves? This is a vital question because, if not, the ends of society may not be met. The logic is: (1) individual development is the end of society; (2) economic growth is the means for social and individual development; (3) economic growth is achieved by capital expansion; (4) capital investment depends upon an institutionally channeled flow of funds; therefore, (5) the capital allocation decisions of institutional managers must be similar to those which would be made by individuals—otherwise the ends of individual development will not be served.

We have already observed several ways in which institutional investment decisions do not serve the needs of individuals: (1) business prefers investment in capital development rather than in human development due to more certain, short-term payoffs, (2) private managers, faced with declining productivity of capital, make capital-intensifying decisions that increase underemployment of people and their skills; and (3) government managers are so intent on expansionism to prevent unemployment that they create inflation, which erodes individual savings and purchasing power.

Property Rights

If the correlation between individual and institutional capital-allocation decisions is questionable, or at least moot, we are impelled to ask the question: why is this so? Why is capital decision making in the hands of institutional managers? For the answer we must go back to chapter 1 and the distribution of authorities. One form of authority distribution enacted in legislation is the right to purchase, own, hold, and transfer property, including productive property like plant and equipment. The ownership of property confers the right of decision on the property manager; and much of the productive (manufacturing) property in the United States (about two-thirds) is owned by large business corporations. *Property rights are a means for maintaining orderly capital flows and of distributing income.* The result has been a growing concentration of economic power and increasing centralization of corporate decision making.[1]

Property-owning practices are a legislative grant, or an authority grant from the sovereign people. Property rights granted by a sovereign people could also be altered by the people. Historically, there have been many forms of property ownership: common ownership of land as among American Indians; common field ownership as in the English town government or village; private ownership subject to a prior public claim, as in Scandinavia; or private ownerships in fee simple, as in the United States. The United States has one of the most extreme forms of private property rights, in which the owner's use rights are almost inviolate from public influence (except eminent domain and minor regulations). The origin of this extremely private view of property rights goes back to frontier days, when resources were ample, cheap, and land was treated as a commodity. Land and property as a commodity meant that people could do with them as they wished without constraint of public purpose. These customs still prevail. Meanwhile, times have changed. Land and resources are scarce and dear. Land is more than a commodity; it is living space, an ecology, a food chain—the source of sustenance. Productive property is more than commodity; it is the means for social and individual development.

Changes in property rights would be extremely difficult in the United States, because they are so imbedded in custom as well as in law. Still, we must recognize that property rights are an extremely complex and multifaceted grant of authority from a sovereign people to property holders. They grant the right to own a store of wealth over time; a right to income from the property in the form of rents or profits; a right to make decisions regarding the use of property; the right to aggregate and channel investment funds through institutions holding property; the right to make capital allocation decisions regarding the use of those capital flows; and the right to determine human employment in the use of capital equipment.

Are all these authority delegations inherent in property rights equally cogent and essential to the owner, to the public interest, to individual development? Could these authority delegations be separated? These are questions to be explored. The point is that if capital allocation decisions do not necessarily correspond to the ends of social and individual development, there are two obvious places to make the adjustment; one is the usage authorizations of property rights, and the other is in the decision process.

Income Distribution

Economic growth has been treated so far as an augmentation of the capacity or means of the society, through capital intensification. Capital productivity also increases income (as the output is sold). This income from economic growth is distributed first on the basis of property rights to owners in the form of rents and profit. Management also distributes productivity gains within the rest of society in the form of wages and salaries, as a result of collective bargaining, or their intent to retain the allegiance of employees. At times, competition also causes some productivity gains to be distributed to consumers in the form of price reductions.

Competitive Position

Competitive position is a means for influencing prices, incomes, and capital flows. Competitive position is determined by control over output, supply, or channels of distribution through the market. An enterprise that controls all the output and supply is a monopoly. An oligopoly occurs when a few enterprises control supply. Competition can also be dominated by controlling marketing channels and outlets. This is referred to as horizontal market power.

Enterprises use various strategems to reduce competition. When competition is limited to a few companies (oligopoly), prices can be administered or artificially kept high to increase profits and internal capital flows. The means for limiting competition are by merger and acquisition, price leadership practices, patents and technical superiority, brand advertising, and large capital requirements to enter the industry.

Government, too, influences competition. Antitrust laws are intended to keep businesses competitive. However, price maintenance laws by government, on the other hand, reduce competition. The government itself maintains a monopoly on taxation, conscription, and the military (presumably for the public interest). Government condones oligopolistic competition (among the few) in the provision of postal services, money and credit, research grants, military procurement, medical services, and public utilities.

The government's ambiguous policies on competition stem, in part, from its development policies to stimulate economic growth. Since capital intensification is the means to growth, business enterprises are usually not precluded from reducing competition to a few companies, if it occurs through product or technical superiority, economies of scale, large investments, or brand identification. In effect, only price competition in restraint of trade and horizontal market power is proscribed by regulations.

The importance of improving profits and capital flows through administered pricing is so great an advantage that most business executives are deeply concerned about market share and competitive position. Competitive position is, in a sense, a self-acquired authorization to charge more than an equilibrium rate of prices, profits, and capital flows. As such, competitive position is an authority distribution from society writ by one's own hand, making it an anamoly since authority distributions are normally legislative acts made on behalf of the public.

Determinants of Income Distribution

The pattern of income distribution is directly related to authority distributions in society. The distribution of income is determined by property rights, tax structure, capital flows, competitive position, and the productivity of capital—that is, income distribution is determined by those who have the first claim upon it. Profits are sometimes said to be a residual after paying all costs including wages, but this is true only in an ex post accounting sense.

Decision making is anticipatory, looking to future income streams. Decisions are made to invest where profits and income streams are highest, which builds in a claim to future income. Anticipatory decision making establishes for profits and rents a prior claim on income, while employee compensation is residual—that is, the decision maker has a manipulative choice on what his future income shall be. This choice (decision) can be based upon capital flows, property rights, tax avoidance advantages, competitive position, and the productivity of capital. Having these authorizations and knowing their yields, the decision maker seeks to maximize future income; and this establishes the pattern of income distribution along with his own share.

The second-ranking claim on income is that of the government through taxation. We have already seen that the tax structure is designed to provide incentives and subsidies to capital investment and expansion. These incentives become tax advantages or loopholes that private decision makers use to avoid taxes and maximize capital returns. The government then has an opportunity cost or tax loss, which spreads more of the tax burden to others (other than the capital decision makers). This tax burden upon others is presumably the cost or sacrifice they must pay for the capital expansion process (economic growth). However, aside from the opportunity cost of tax incentives, the government's claim on the taxable portion of income is preemptory and manipulative— institutional decision makers in government can manipulate the definitions of taxable income; and once the tax is defined, it is preemptive over other claims.

The individual as employee (which encompasses more than half the population) has neither a manipulative choice over income, nor a preemptive claim upon it. The employee has some choice over his education and skill, whether to work, and whether to join a union. These choices will influence his income in a narrow, low range. But since the individual employee lacks authorizations to make decisions over the use of property, capital, or taxation, he has neither preemptive or manipulative choices over future income—that is, income distribution is directly related to the authority distributions in society that are determined largely by property rights, tax structure, capital flows, competitive position, and the productivity of capital. The effect of these authority distributions and incentives is to skew income distribution in favor of high incomes. High incomes are presumed to facilitate savings and thus induce the capital intensification process.

The skewing of incomes to the high side also has the effect of creating rich-poor extremes in the society. The government then attempts to ameliorate the poverty extreme by transfers of income, such as welfare payments, to supplement low incomes. The income distribution policy may be viewed as counterproductive in the sense that government incentives and subsidies create high incomes—rich-poor extremes make government subsidies necessary to supplement low incomes. This paradoxical policy would be avoided by more equal distributions of income, together with savings incentives for the general population, which is already producing a substantial portion of the savings needed for capital expansionism.

Technological Progress

Technological progress is a means for capital investment and economic growth by providing the flow of innovations necessary for productivity gains. Capital investment places improved technical means into use as equipment for the purpose of increasing efficiency and productivity. Such capital expansion is possible only when improved technical means or technological progress are available. Technological progress depends upon the advancement of new scientific theory, usually called basic research, plus the application of that theory to usable equipment, which is called applied research or engineering development.

Basic research is carried on in private research laboratories, research institutes, and universities; and most of the findings enter the public domain as published scientific articles. However, research must be applied to become useful to decision makers in government and business. Applied research creates new products, services, and more efficient productive equipment. Hence, applied research and development are the key to new innovations for the capital intensification process and to economic growth.

The funds for applied research are largely in the hands of the federal government and large corporations—that is, research funds are institutionally channeled in the same manner as capital investment funds. This provides for efficiency of decisions coupling research and investment; but it also has the effect of creating ownership or proprietary rights out of applied research ideas. These proprietary invention rights create market advantages to their owners, enhance their prices and their future income claims. In this way, innovations also create a competitive advantage, which is desirable from the viewpoint of the private decision maker. From a social viewpoint, however, the concentration of applied research funds and technical innovations reinforces the pattern of oligopoly already inherent in capital and income distribution practices.

Educational Attainment

Educational attainment is a means for achieving technological progress, and educational distribution affects technological accessibility. Education is the principal means by which individuals, without capital, can develop their knowledge and skills to participate in technological and economic progress. Human beings, without capital, enter the economic development process by using their knowledge of science, engineering, economics, and management. These combined skills are sometimes referred to as the technostructure of business and government. Individuals trained thusly are the thinkers and decision makers equipped to choose among alternative technoeconomic means for achieving expansion and growth.

The distribution of education opportunities in technoeconomic skills is generally wide in the United States. However, the staffing of technostructures is costly and can generally be undertaken only by large institutions, government, and businesses, which have intensive capital-technical decisions to make. These institutions are generally oligopolies by reason of their high income-technical-capital flows. While educational opportunities are fairly wide, technostructure employment is narrowed mainly to oligopolistic institutions. This means that the distribution of educated people is affected by employment possibilities. Those educated people most capable of making technoeconomic or managerial decisions are concentrated in the larger institutions. Consequently, the intellectual resources of society are collected into relatively few institutions, and this further restricts competition and the accessibility of technology. The width or openness of educational opportunity may be looked upon in terms of the numbers of persons educated, or the applicability of education to living and to individual fulfillment. Educational accessibility in the United States has generally been extensive in terms of numbers of people attending public schools, although women and minorities have until recently had limited educational opportunity.

The applicability of education to human living has been less wide. Education traditionally has been narrowly defined by the research methods that various disciplines use for the advancement of knowledge. Research and the advancement of knowledge are crucial to technological progress, as we have already seen. Research tends to produce specialized individuals, interested in and capable of disciplinary research. But research is not living; and living is not research. Living is action and interaction with the social and ecological environment. Education has been less relevant to these interactions of living and self-development. Since most of the population is interested in the interactions of living and self-development, rather than in research, education is currently going through a crisis of credibility: falling enrollments, declining financial support, skepticism regarding research, and a general ennui regarding the importance of education to individual realization. Therefore, education can be said to be wide in a numerical sense but narrow in academic range of applicability. A narrow range of applicability tends to produce specialized people; and wide range of human applicability in education would produce adaptable people.

Employment and Living Standards

Employment and living standards are a product of capital and educational distributions. From the managers' view, employment is the means of staffing the capital-intensive productive process. From the employees' view, employment is a means of sharing in economic growth and fulfilling their own work satisfactions. These are two quite different objectives, which can lead to diametrically opposed results. Management seeks by capital investment to minimize the amount of labor and the amount of skill on the job, as a means of reducing costs. The employee seeks the maximum number of employment opportunities (jobs) with the widest range of skills to employ all his talents. The matching of these opposing objectives is done in a very imperfect employment market, where neither the employer nor the employee knows the range of jobs or skills available. The result is that employers specify minimum skills (to lower costs), and employees accommodate their talents and interests to the jobs they learn about. Thus employment becomes determined more by technique (skills and technology) inherent in the capital investment process, than by the state of human talents and development available. Employment is, therefore, shaped by the same forces that determine economic development, namely the state of income-technological-capital flows, which are basically institutional.

Within the definition of the job or employment offered by the capital-intensive process, the income of the employee is determined by his level of performance, which depends in turn upon his educational attainment and learning on the job. Therefore, employment is shaped by capital distributions, and income of living standards of employees by educational attainment. Employment and living standards together are, thus, the product of capital and educational distributions.

Living standards are also affected by the manner in which capital costs are charged in accounting systems to arrive at prices. The clearest illustration of alternate accounting methods is found in environmental pollution cases. Chemical and paper companies, for example, require large amounts of water for processing their products. This water is drawn from stream flows that are part of the total hydrologic cycle upon which all life depends, and stream flows move in interstate commerce across state lines. If the water is drawn fresh from the stream by industry, but discharged polluted by effluent, the downstream quality of life has been diminished by fish kills, unsightly streams, or human ingestion of chemicals. To maintain the quality or amenities of life downstream, costs must be incurred to clean up the water.

There are two ways to charge these water quality costs: one is to let municipal government clean up the water by water purification plants, which places the cost of water quality upon the public through taxation or water charges. The second way is to require industry to discharge the water of the same purity or quality that it took in from the stream, which would mean a capital cost and charge for the industry to install effluent control equipment. The first method, of throwing the social cost on the public, is called an external cost, because it is external to the business accounting system—that is, water costs are regarded as free to the industry, and the accounting system only recognizes direct labor, material, and capital equipment costs. The second method (requiring the industry to purify its effluent) is called internalizing costs, because the capital charges for the effluent control equipment are internal to the business accounting system and are part of its normal costing and pricing.

This same fine line of cost accounting applies to all the business costs. Should unemployment be an internal cost of businesses who use labor, or an external cost of government? Should the education and training of employees be an internal cost of businesses who use their skills, or an external cost of government? Should welfare be an internal cost of business to maintain its market of consumers, or should it be an external cost of government? Should air pollution be an internal cost of automobile manufacturers who make air polluting engines, or should it be an external cost of government?

The more business externalizes its costs and throws them upon society, the larger government must become to remedy the deficiencies and assume the social (external) costs. Also, since government remedies are minimal by reason of mass, the amenities of life are less under external costing. The highest quality of life, and the least government, would occur if all social costs were internalized into the accounting systems of business producers who assemble goods and services for society.

Barriers to Entry

Barriers to entry are inaccessibilities to the social process arising from capital, income, competitive, technological, and educational distributions. The means to maintain incomes (personal, corporate, or government) skewed to the high side is by exclusion—that is, by excluding some people from participating in high income from economic growth. Barriers to entry are a systematic means of exclusion. Barriers to entry place obstacles in the way of some individuals—the less trained and less aggressive—from participating in the social process.

These barriers to entry and exclusions from the social process are not necessarily done consciously, or by Machiavellian design; they come about more by separate institutions suboptimizing on their own goals and interests. Nevertheless, they are there. That barriers to entry are there is attested by the exclusion of nearly one-fourth of the population of the United States from the social process—the welfare poor, aged, unskilled youth, minorities, women, handicapped, and the overeducated.

The barriers to entry are building blocks put in place, often for public purpose. The government, for example, creates property rights and tax incentives to induce economic growth through capital expansion. The property rights and tax incentives are used to channel capital flows through institutions and skew income distributions to the high side. The concentration of capital flows and incomes restricts competition to the few; and the few create proprietary interests—such as product, patent, market, competitive, price, technological, and intellectual advantages—which become barriers to entry. The barriers to entry then exclude those who cannot amass the capital flows, high incomes, product, market, price, competitive, technical, and intellectual superiorities needed to participate in economic growth. In the process, the less well-prepared individuals are excluded from the social system.

Welfare and Transfer Payments

Welfare and transfer payments are a means of retaining as consumers those who have been left out of the productive process. While unskilled portions of the population are not needed as producers in a capital-intensifying economy, they are needed as consumers to buy the output. Moreover, the underemployed constitute a large enough voting bloc to influence legislators to provide at least for their subsistence. The provision of subsistence to the underemployed is accomplished through the means of transfer payments; that is, tax revenues from the well-off segments of society (corporations and higher income individuals) are collected and then paid out (transferred) to those with deficient incomes for subsistence. The form of these transfer payments are many, including unemployment insurance, social security, public assistance to the poor, child and foster care, school lunches, food stamp plan, public housing allowances, old age and survivors' assistance, Medicare, etc. Taken together, these transfer payments, commonly called welfare, make up 55 percent of the federal budget.

While welfare and transfer payments are a means of providing subsistence and some minimal participation in economic output, they do little to satisfy the requirement that human beings need more than bread alone. Welfare and transfer payments keep the underemployed in the economy as consumers only, but not as producers. To the extent that individuals need useful work for their own development and self-realization, welfare fails to provide for human development; and, thus, it is deficient as a management tool that seeks individual fulfillment as the primary end of society.

Systematic Nature of Order

Social order is systematically related to authority distributions in society, and disorder is systematically related to barriers to entry. Social order is a necessary means of decision making, because order establishes predictability of decision results. Disorder vitiates predictability. The orderly segments of society are those which have some delegation of authority to make decisions affecting their own lives. The most notable segments having such authority are property owners, corporation executives, government officials, professionals, and the middle-management technostructure. These are the people astride the capital flows, who have both the funds and the authority to implement their ideas and thus satisfy their needs. Generally, this group, along with skilled employees, also has a favorable income distribution, enabling them to fulfill many of their needs in their personal lives. We have already seen that authority, income, and capital distributions are interdependent. Not only are they interdependent, they are systematically related to order—that is, the orderly segment of society is made up of those who have the means to share in decisions over their own lives by reason of authority-capital-income distributions.

The less satisfied segment of society are those without favorable authority-capital-income distributions; and they, in the absence of such authorities, have relatively little decision-making capacity over their own lives. Without property, position, power, income, capital, or employment, they do not have the means to choose activities that would fill their interests. These less satisfied individuals in the population in some cases accept their disadvantaged lot unhappily but peaceably. Others are more alienated and resentful of their deprivation, to the point of dissent, disaffection, demonstration, and confrontation. Still others are violently dissident, resorting to crime, riot, conspiracy, or revolt.

The rapid rise in crime, violence, and revolt in recent years is an indication that dissidence is a mounting phenomenon in the United States. Whatever the degree of alienation, dissenters have in common a feeling of nonparticipation in the social process. They do not have the incomes, rewarding work, or the ability to make decisions about their own lives that other individuals have. They feel excluded. The means of exclusion are barriers to entry in the social process; and these are many, including the inaccessibility of relevant educations, jobs, incomes, technological knowledge, skills, property, or capital. Their exclusion is systematic—that is, made up of the barriers that make economic growth and capital intensification available to some but not all. Again, perhaps the barriers to entry were not designed consciously to give advantages to some and not to others; undoubtedly, these systematic barriers, making possible the capital-intensifying design, came into being historically as a means of social survival. Still, the results can be viewed as invidious by those persons left out.

Occurrence of Social Disorder

Social disorder is a countermanagement means to displace power for the purpose of realigning authority distributions that have become mismatched with human needs. If alienation and disaffection reaches a stage of conflict, the conflict can frequently be resolved between the management and countermanagement by some compromise realignment of authority. Conflict resolution is a principal function of management. Conflict occurs over disaffections, which may take many forms: grievances, protests, petitions, strikes, confrontations, demonstrations, conspiracies, violence, riots, crime, or revolt. These are internal threats and may be likened to internal warfare. The leaders of the dissidents are challengers, presenting demands for change with a threat of unknown proportions if the demands are not resolved. Dissident leaders are a countermanagement, offering themselves and their ideas to a constituency to win their allegiance away from existing management.

In this situation, existing management should not be deluded either by the myth that all management is teamwork and consensus or by the presumption that authority bestows powers of repression. Dissenters frequently do not want consensus; they want a compromise that would increase their authority in the decision process. Managers have authority to fulfill human needs, but not necessarily to repress them. The coercive powers of management are directly proportionate to the allegiance it holds. By definition, a manager facing a confrontation with dissenters does not hold complete allegiances; he holds limited allegiances, and this confers only limited repressive or coercive powers. In this situation of tenuous support, managerial prudence dictates that he use compromise rather than strong coercive actions. This means, first, treating countermanagement as if it were indeed an alternate form of management by seriously considering the grievances of the alienated and disadvantaged. Management will then seek to co-opt the allegiance of the disaffected to show how their needs can be realized within the existing system; while countermanagement will seek to enhance its claim on the allegiance of its constituency by proving how it is wresting authority from the system and redistributing it to the disaffected.

These conflicts can be treated as games, politics, bargaining, or conspiracies, but whatever the frame of reference of the actors, they are serious contests to realign authority. Their purpose is to voice displeasure with the working of the social process, to cry for satisfaction of unmet human needs, and to demand that authority be realigned to fulfill these needs. Understood and treated in this context, conflict resolution is a constructive process of correcting mismatches that always come about over time between authority distributions and human development. Conflict is a constructive feedback for correcting the social process.

Viewed differently, as insidious conspiracy against an inviolate existing system, conflict can lead, not to resolution, but to challenge, coercion, further alienation, and further suppression, until real revolt moves underground. Dissent and disorder are troublesome, no doubt, but they are also challenges and opportunities to correct the mismatches in the social process to keep it vital, alive, and responsive to the people. It is also a means for building allegiances and keeping the social process strong.

Conflict Resolution by Voting

Conflict resolution which fails on the managerial level may be compromised at the societal level by voting, if voting is broadly accessible to individuals on specific issues. Too frequently, dissent is viewed by managers as insidious to their existing institutions, and they seek to repress or coerce the opposition. The labor-management disputes from 1890 to 1960 were frequently of this character. When coercion fails, as did management repression of strikes in the 1930s, conflict resolution may be taken to the public domain—that is, to Congress for resolution. In the labor case, Congress enacted the National Labor Relations Act, which gave labor spokesmen a countermanagement role on wages and working conditions, provided for collective bargaining, and provided for union-wide voting on the specific issues of contract negotiations. Whatever one may think of actual labor organizations the principle of specific-issue voting is a social invention of wide significance, because it is a means to give voice to and allow participation in specific issues that affect individual lives. As such, it is a form of individual decision making on vital issues. It is also a redistribution of authority from centralized decision makers to dispersed and decentralized decision making.

Perhaps the National Labor Relations Act was not a social invention, so much as a social reinvention of the Cleistenes reforms that made direct democracy on specific issues possible in ancient Greece. Having rediscovered the merits of direct Grecian democracy in the labor case, however, we have been reluctant to apply the principle of participative decision making to other areas of social strife and conflict.

The areas of strife and conflict in society are over the barriers to entry: employment, underemployment, living standards, living quality, income distribution, capital flows, prices, inflation, competition among the few, educational relevance, technological accessibility, violence in the streets, international violence and war. These are the means of social development and change. These are vital issues to individual lives. Yet, on none of them does an individual have the right to vote to influence how they affect him. True, the individual can vote for a candidate (usually from one of two parties) who has some amorphous posture on all issues; but there is no assurance how that representative will vote once the lobbying starts.

On the specific issues that have been crucial to our time—such as high prices, inflation, unemployment, violence, and war—the individual does not have a specific-issue vote, and hence cannot make decisions over his own life. Decision making is issue specific, as in the labor negotiation case. A decentralization and dispersal of authority for individuals to run their own lives would be characterized by a political process providing a wide spectrum of specific issues on which to vote, as in ancient Greece, early American local government, or labor negotiations. The centralization of decision making would be characterized by a political process providing a narrow spectrum of voting choices among a few elected representatives with vague stands on general issues, as in the present U.S. federal government. Vagueness of stance on issues inhibits conflict resolution, while participative choices on specific issues induce conflict resolution.

Sets of Policy Choices Regarding Means

The set of policy choices that a society makes on the means of seeking its mission configure the pattern of social change and evolution. The principal means of economic and social development have now been reviewed. Each institution has additional specific means of implementation that apply to itself, such as profit maximization in business, or forms of taxation in government. These will be dealt with in subsequent chapters on the character and problems of specific institutions. The general means covered in this chapter are used by all institutions and are, therefore, societal in scope. This is the way we wish to analyze them to see if they are indeed fulfilling the ends of society.

The principal means of private and public management of society are many; more than a dozen are apparent in this chapter. Each means may be applied in different ways over a spectrum; for example, more or less competition, more or less money supply, etc. Therefore the combinations of means may be arranged in many permutations; and these permutations of means will have varying consequences. Table 2-1 summarizes the spectrum of choices regarding each means, together with their consequences. The permutations of these thirteen sets of issues would make possible about sixteen thousand sets of policy choices as to means, if all possible combinations were explored. In fact, the practical sets of policy combinations are fewer because the means are systematically related to economic development. Hence, a pattern or set of choices conducive to economic development tends to be selected at the spectrum extremes as to incomes, capital flows, competition, price policy, employment, education, technical accessibility, barriers to entry, and narrow-issue voting. This policy set of choices as to means (that is, concentration of the means into the hands of fewer decision makers) is consistent with maximizing economic growth; and the United States has chosen to concentrate the means to achieve economic growth. What happened to human growth, which is the final end of society? Unfortunately, the concentration of the means altered the ends.

Systematic Practice of Management

The systematic practice of management coordinates and delineates functional means to perform the mission (ends) of the system. The missions of a system determine the functional means needed to perform the mission. The functional means selected determine the mission which is performed—that is, the ends affect the means, and the means affect the ends. The decision process is intercorrelated and interactive.

What went wrong with our systematic practice of management, when we started out with an end to maximize human growth, but ended up with a process that maximized economic growth at some human deprivation? The problem was that we had multiple objectives (missions) of human growth and economic growth, and it proved more feasible to maximize economic growth. Hence, the social system evolved to perform the feasible rather than to nuture human development. Besides, few people think about the social process systematically. Hence, the articulation of ends with means slips into the managerial process, and decisions suboptimize on what appears feasible and desirable to a subsystem decision maker.

Let us return again, then, to private and public management as a decision process for the total social system. The systematic practice of management suggests that decisions be made in the following order:

Individual needs: The ultimate need of the individual is to realize his intellectual, social, cultural, physical, and environmental potential. Such individual

Table 2-1
Spectrum Analysis of Major Means

Means of Management	Choice Spectrum	Consequences
Monetary-fiscal policy	Balanced	Equilibrium
	Unbalanced (expansive)	Inflation
Income distribution	Normal	Equitable
	Skewed to high side	Rich-poor extremes
Capital flows	Open markets	Less concentrated
	Institutionally channeled	More concentrated
Competitive distribution	Open	Less concentrated
	Competition among the few (oligopolistic)	More concentrated
Price policy	Free	Competitive, variable
	Administered	Profit maximized, fixed
	Rationing	Welfare maximized, fixed
Employment	Labor intensive	Service economy
	Labor extensive	Capital intensive economy
Living standards	Internalize cost	More amenities, less government
	Externalize cost	Fewer amenities, more government
Educational accessibility	Wide	Adaptable individuals
	Narrow	Specialized individuals
Technical accessibility	Wide	Less concentration
	Narrow	More concentration
Barriers to entry	Lowered	Equitable incomes
	Raised	Skewed income to high side
Voting	Wide issue	Direct democracy
	Narrow issue	Oligarchy
Internal order	Participative	Restless conflict resolution
	Coercive	Police order
International order	Participative	Political bargaining flux
	Coercive	Military conquest

development requires the individual to have capacity to make decisions over his own life relative to the substance of his work, reasoning, physical actions, social interactions, cultural pursuits, and environmental interactions.

Mission. The mission of society is to perform management functions when the individual cannot meet his own needs in such a way that management decisions are similar to an individual's decision in achieving that individual's development.

Authority. Authority over decisions must be distributed to private and public institutions so that the accumulated resources and expertise of society act on behalf of all individuals, as individuals define their needs. Such a distribution of authority must be dispersed, decentralized, and made diverse to respond to the variety of individual needs.

Functions. Functions are the broad work assignments to be performed by institutions or individuals. Managers make decisions on how these functions will be performed. How a function is performed is the means of execution. Therefore, functional means are arranged by management to perform the missions (ends) of society. The main functional means of social development are:

1. Human and economic growth
2. Investment in the productivity of capital
3. Organizing capital flows
4. Using property rights as a means of capital flows
5. Distributing income to contributors to growth
6. Competing for capital and income
7. Technological progress
8. Educational attainment
9. Employment
10. Barriers to entry
11. Transfer payments
12. Conflict resolution (that is, voting) to realign authority.

If these functional means concentrate on economic growth at the expense of human growth, the means can subvert the social ends.

Tasks. Tasks are the detailed work assignments and decisions that have to be made on the division of labor and the allocation of capital. (These detailed activities of management are dealt with in chapters 4-15 of the book.)

Allegiance. Allegiance is the consent that every manager at every level obtains to continue authority. Allegiance is a two-way pact, in which management responds to the desire for fulfillment of human needs, and individuals yield authority and loyalty to management for the continuance of that responsiveness.

Process. The process of private and public management is the network of missions-functions-tasks-loyalties that form an institution or society. This network of relationships can be explained, rationalized, and idealized into a socialization or learning process for new members in society as a means of transmitting skills and loyalties.

Alienation. Alienation is the mismatch of authority with human needs, so that some members of a community feel deprived of participation. Private and public management seek to bring such alienated members back into the community by enabling them to participate in decisions over their own lives; or, failing that, the social process enters a state of change and decline.

Note

1. Federal Trade Commission, *Economic Papers* (1969), p. 267.

3 Management Decisions

Change presents problems, problems require decisions, and decisions cause change. Where does management start in this circuitous flux?

Management starts with problems, because problems are a peculiarly human perspective. Without the human perspective, there are no problems. Nature changes constantly, but nature has no problems. Species come and go, grow and develop, mutate and change, evolve and decline, eat and are eaten, explode in population and outgraze themselves. These are not problems, merely change. Changes are problems only when they differ from human expectations. Management deals, therefore, in expectations, both its own and those whom it serves.

Problems are very difficult to define because of their expectative nature—but whose expectations, and about what? That is what is difficult to define. First, expectations are difficult to measure because they are subjective evaluations of need by an individual in relation to some norm or value that he has assumed, learned, or been socialized to believe is realizable. What is the norm? How was it assumed or learned? Is it realistic or realizable?

Even if these attitudinal questions about expectations are determinable for one individual, other difficulties occur in defining problems. What system are we talking about? What cluster of expectations, by what people, about what things? Are only the decision maker's expectations to be included? No, that would erode allegiance and authority. Are all the expectations of those in an institution, a business, or a government to be included? Yes, but they are only the producers. The consumers' expectations are even more crucial, because the institution exists to fulfill their needs. Who are the users or consumers? The direct buyers are consumers whose expectations should be included; for example, the buyers of the automobile. But the automobile affects many others as well: the highway patrol, insurance companies, service station operators, oil companies, auto repair, accident victims, hospitals, road construction workers, street maintenance men, highway tax collectors, state highway departments, and emphysema victims who die from air pollution. Are they all part of the system? If so, all their expectations should be included.

Problems are exercises in definition that try to delineate values, norms, realization of norms, attitudes toward departures from norms, and who in the complex of interactions is to be included in the system: decision makers, institutional workers, direct users, indirect users, victims of use, tertiary supporters of use, or logistic supporters of use. Or more simply, how peripheral may the expectation be and still be part of the problem?

The care with which all these expectations are defined constitutes the problem definition; and a problem well defined is partially solved for two reasons. First, the defined expectations give a performance requirement that management can treat as an objective to solve. Second, the exclusions by definition simplify the problem enough to make it soluable. The exclusions by definition may turn out to be a mistake, as we saw in the last chapter, by excluding many external costs from business accounting systems, or by excluding large segments of the population from participation in the social process by barriers to entry. Still, this indicates that the problem was not seen and defined whole before. Of course, problems can never be entirely seen and defined, because that would be omniscience, which, unfortunately, is not a quality of the human mind. Therefore problems are never fully defined, nor are they ever really solved. Management can only try to solve them more, to a greater degree than has previously been done by including more expectations, and then try again when the problem comes around once more. Management decision making is, therefore, partial, iterative, perpetual, and asymptotic—that is, management decisions may become increasingly holistic with each iteration, but at a receding rate as expectations in the system approach infinity. Assume that we can learn to define problems sufficiently to make decisions possible at some asymptotic rate; then we next would wish to inquire how decisions are made.

Decision Structures

Decisions are structured into three basic models: value choices of social ends, technical choices of effective means, and attitudinal choices toward human relationships. Value choices of social or economic ends are decided by a political or policy process, in government, business, or voluntary institution—that is, policy questions are basically a consensus of the value judgments of those participating in the decision. These value judgments are the perception of the needs and expectations of those in and served by the decision-making group. In government, a legislative-executive group seeks to perceive the needs and expectations of the voters or interest groups. In business, an executive group perceives the needs and expectations of stockholders, employees, and customers. In voluntary agencies, an executive-community group seeks to perceive the needs and expectations of the community for intellectual, health, or cultural services.

Policy is, therefore, perception, expectations, and consensus. These are all elusive qualities; and there is no exact way of arriving at policy by a precise, rational method. Consequently, policy is arrived at by a political method, which is an interpersonal assessment—that is, the political model calls for assessing the interest parties to a decision, their leverage, coalitions, bargaining position, compromise alternatives, protocols of negotiation, and the authority (cumulative allegiances) of the actors. Or more simply, policy is decided by bargaining and negotiation among coalitions of interest parties. These policy negotiations can be very complex in government and voluntary institutions, because the problem definition of these expectations are included in the decision is very elastic. In business, policy appears to be more straightforward because the interest parties have, in effect, a hierarchical representation—that is, the marketing department represents consumer expectations, the production department the employee-producer expectations, and the finance department the stockholder—lender expectations.

In business policymaking, then, bargaining is more highly formalized, and the executive is more authoritarian than in other institutions. While authoritarian formalization of policymaking expedites decisions, it does not necessarily enhance the accuracy of assessing expectations. Consumer and investor expectations, in particular, are likely to be underestimated in business; this perhaps accounts for the declining survival rates of business with age.

The second basic model of decision making is technical choice of effective means. These decisions involve two basic parameters: the level of performance expected of the products or services delivered to users, and the cost of delivering the services. Both of these parameters can often be quantified, at least partially. Performance level can be measured in terms of human requirements such as man-hours of effort or level of expertise, or else in engineering performance terms such as speed, accuracy, capacity, or output. Costs can be measured in accounting terms of the labor, materials, equipment, and fixed and overhead costs incurred to produce the service. The comparative evaluation of these two parameters is then an economic optimization formulation. If the cost-performance measures are highly quantitative and deterministic, elaborate mathematical or operations research models can be applied to the decision. If the measures are more probablistic (that is, subject to chance), econometric models can be used. If the comparative measures are rough, then simple benefit-cost or rate-of-return decision methods are used. These decision techniques are discussed more thoroughly in Part II. For now, note that all institutions (government, business, and voluntary agencies) use much the same optimization methods for making decisions among technical means. In business, the mass production industries are able to quantify the productive process to a degree greater than can be done in service industries, government, or voluntary agencies. The result is that such quantifying industries tend to use more elaborate operations research models. However, all institutional decision makers seek the best combination of resource means by some form of benefit-cost or rate-of-return estimation, even if the estimation is partially subjective or intuitive.

Attitudinal choices toward human relationships are the application of sociological or psychological models to personal interactions, such as those which occur between supervisor-employee, employee-employee, or employee-customer. These decision methods are subjective because they involve human emotions. Their purpose is to satisfy the aspiration level, to the extent possible based upon empirical evidence, of the stimulus-response interaction between individuals. The empirical evidence suggests that these are event-matching decisions, in which the series of satisfactions experienced in recent events tend to establish the aspiration level. The object of the decision, then, is to maintain or improve the response to personal interactions compared with recently similar experiences. (The behavioral aspects of decisions are discussed in more detail in chapter 10.) The human relationship decisions tend to be similar in all institutions, varying more by size and complexity of institutions rather than differing significantly by field, such as government, business, or voluntary agencies.

Mission of Decisions

The mission of decisions is to answer questions of identity, purposes, and relationships. Decisions may be thought of as having two parts, or perhaps three. The first part of a decision is defining the problem. Is there a problem, what is the problem, why is there a problem, what are the parts of the problem? The second part of a decision is the proposed solution, or alternative solutions. A third part of a decision is its proposed evaluation, effects, or feedback—that is, knowing whether the solution worked.

The first part of the decision—problem definition—is purposive and tied up with human expectations. For that reason, it may be said to have a mission. The mission of the decision is to identify the human purposes and expectations involved. The decision structure for identifying human expectations is to use the value and attitudinal choice models, which are the political and psychological methods, respectively. The solution portion of a decision, once the problem is defined, is heavily concerned with the optimum selection of effective means, or the economic optimization model.

Decisions become garbled when these two separable parts of decision making become mixed—that is, when solutions are used to define problems, or when problems are shaped to solutions (sets of data), then the ends and the means become reversed. The ends become means, and the means become ends. We observed (in chapter 2) that this reversal of means had occurred in the United States—that is, the end of society is the development of individuals. The means for social and individual development are human and economic growth. But economic growth is more short term, tangible, manipulative, manageable, and data prone than is human growth. Hence, management has defined the problem to fit the solution of economic growth by capital intensification. Then the means of capital intensification become so demanding, under the declining productivity of capital, that jobs and human growth are shaped to fit the economic process. Thus, the means become the ends. And the end, of human growth and development, becomes the means. The means-reversal occurred because of lack of clarity and structure to the decision process. It is important that decisions proceed in a strict order from their mission to careful problem definition to alternate solutions. The mission of the decision must first be determined—that is, what is the identity, human purposes, and relations of a situation which is alleged to be a problem?

Systematic Form of Decisions

The systematic form of decision structure inquires successively into the why, what, who, how, when, and where of a management problem. The intent of a decision is to create a series of actions responding to a problem. A series of actions constitutes a network of events that may be looked upon as a system (or subsystem, or process). If a decision is going to create a system (or network of actions and activities), the questions of management must be framed in a format which satisfies a system structure. For example:

System Elements	Decision Structure
Human needs	Why is a decision needed?
Mission	What is the system?
Authority	Who are the decision makers?
Functions	How is the work performed?
Tasks	When must specific work be done?
Allegiance	Where are the needs met?
Process	How is the institution maintained?
Alienation	How does the institution survive?

These relationships make it clear that unless management asks the questions of why, what, and who first, they will not know what the needs, mission, and authority of the system are. The why, what, and who questions establish the following:

1. Definition of the problem in terms of human needs, expectations, value judgments, attitudinal choices, and human relationships (this definition becomes the performance requirement)
2. Definitions of the bounds of the system, who and what parts of the world are included, and what parts remain in the environment
3. Definition of the decision makers—that is, who in the system influences and participates in the decision choices or alternatives

4. Definition of authority—that is, who benefits and participates in the output sufficiently to yield allegiance and authority to act on his behalf.

Once the problem, authority, system bounds, and decision makers have been defined by the why, what, and who questions, all the rest is solution and implementation. The how, when, and where questions are the organization and optimization of the technical means. They provide the solution once the problem is clearly known. Or another, perhaps simpler, way of saying the same thing:

1. The why, what, who questions yield the performance requirement of the system.
2. The how, when, and where questions yield the costs of the system.
3. The decision is to optimize the performance (why, what, who) at an acceptable cost (how, when, where).

But what does one do if the questions are not asked in the systematic form of a decision structure, but, rather, are asked in reverse order?

Truncated Decisions

The truncated, institutional form of decision making inquires into the how, when, and where of decisions, which yields a reversal of means with ends. Institutional decision makers seldom feel the necessity of asking searching questions about identity, needs, purposes, and relationships, the way an individual does. The individual continually asks these questions as he seeks the meaning of his own life and death. Institutions do not die, nor do they live. They are mere legal entities. Where does a business corporation, or a government agency, go when all its workers have gone home for the night? Does the corporation still exist? If so, where? In the buildings and records? Not in individuals, they have gone to some other more intimate, more vital preoccupation.

An institution is a legal fiction—in law, an "artifical person." The "artificial person" has an artificial identity and purpose as well as artificial relationships contained in its legal charter, authorizations, services, and organizational structure. This artificial person does not need to ask searching questions about its identity and the meaning of its life, because it is not going to die, its life has no meaning, and its identity is artificially given. That is to say, an institution's needs, mission, and authority are given to it, artificially, and it need not inquire further. Therefore the primary institutional question is: how is the institution doing? Are its functions and tasks being done? Is it surviving? Is it maintaining itself? Is it working? The decision structure of an institution, then, is truncated:

System Elements	*Institutional Decision Structure*
Human needs	None
Mission	What is the system? The institution. Look it up in the charter and bylaws.
Authority	Who are the decision makers? The institution. Look it up in the law and chart of approvals.
Functions	How is the institution performing? Good first question.
Tasks	When must specific work be done? Good second, cost-control question.
Allegiance	Where are the needs to be met? Good third question about institution's constituency.
Process	How is the institution maintained? Good fourth (maybe first) question.
Alienation	How does the institution survive? Really, the first question.

From this framework, the truncated institutional form of decision structure may be reconstructed as follows:

How does the institution survive?

How is the institution maintained?

How is the institution performing?

When must specific work be done?

Where are the needs to be met?

In business, the answer to the first three hows is whether the company is making a profit. In government, the answer to the first three hows is whether the citizens are supporting government by voting and paying taxes, especially reelecting officials. In voluntary agencies, the answer is whether the community is participating (enrolling in schools and using health or community services).

All of the truncated questions are addressed to means, and they become answerable or solvable as problems by an optimizing technique of effective means—that is, institutions can survive and maintain themselves by increasing their profits, sales, services, taxes, voting, and participation. The mode is to improve the service performance, reduce costs, or both. These are all means. By concentrating on the means, by asking means-oriented questions and solving them, a reversal occurs in which the institutional means become the ends of society.

However, the survival and maintenance of institutions does little to guarantee that human needs are met. Some are, of course, by the improvement in service performance and the reduction in cost; but these improvements in service performance apply only to the offerings of the institutions as they are constituted. Present U.S. institutions are constituted to produce capital intensification and economic growth. What they are not delivering (unmet human needs) are price stability, equitable incomes, access to capital, open competition, competitive prices, full employment, amenities, adaptable educations, access to technology, wide-issue voting, conflict resolution of internal violence, international peace, human growth, or individual development (see chapter 2). What institutions are not delivering represents a very long list of deficiencies in society. The institutions are working well, but society is not. The ends have become means. The truncated, institutional decision structure is asking the wrong questions and solving the wrong problems. Institutional society has developed a beautiful solution (economic growth) for which there is no longer a problem.

Decision Trajectories

Decisions have a mission, movement, and destiny along a trajectory of social evolution, which takes its form from the order in which decision inquiries are asked. Despite its grave human deficiencies, the truncated decision structure is working to maintain institutions, is ensconced in law, is the subject of social drill (socialization), is likely to continue, and will give us more of the same. The continuance of institutions and their decision structure, which overlays the social process, guarantees that the social evolution will continue on its present course or trajectory. The social evolution of the United States may be expected to continue to produce more and more capital intensification at declining productivity of capital, with a continuance of economic growth. The means (capital expansion) will have to be intensified to continue economic growth; and this economic intensification will continue to be at the expense of human growth. The future holds more inflation, concentrations of income-capital flows-technology, fewer amenities and more government, closed competition, administered prices, narrow educations, narrow-issue voting, internal crime and violence, and war, because that is what the truncated decision-structure is capable of deciding, and because that is the current set of policy choices of the United States (table 3-1).

This policy set constitutes the current U.S. choice and is a logically

Table 3-1
U.S. Set of Policies

Means of Management	Truncated Choice	Consequences
Monetary-fiscal policy	Unbalanced (expansive)	Inflation
Income distribution	Skewed to high side	Rich-poor extremes
Capital flows	Institutionally channeled	More concentration
Competitive distribution	Competition among the few	More concentration (oligopoly)
Price policy	Administered	Profit maximized, fixed
Employment	Labor extensive	Underemployment, capital intensive economy
Living standards	Externalize cost	Fewer amenities, more government
Educational range and accessibility	Moderately narrow	Specialized individuals
Technical accessibility	Narrow	More concentration
Barriers to entry	Raised	Skewed incomes to high side
Voting	Narrow issue	Oligarchic republic
Internal order	Semiparticipative	Partial conflict resolution
International order	Coercive	Balance of economic and military power (with periodic wars)

consistent means of achieving economic growth. The institutional decision structure overlaying society is geared to continue these choices; and, thus, the trajectory of U.S. social evolution is fixed, unless some heroic reforms change the decision structure from the truncated to the systematic form. If U.S. society continues on its present trajectory, the scenario of its outcome will be much like that of ancient Roman society.[1] Alternative scenarios are possible, but they would all require altering the decision structure and present set of policies.

Who Are the Decision Makers?

The present set of U.S. policies clearly arrive at a suboptimum solution—that of optimizing economic growth at the expense of human growth and individual development. The reason is twofold: the decision structure is truncated, as we have seen, and does not inquire into individuals' needs; and the reason individuals' needs are slighted is that all of the decision makers in the system are not included in the choices—that is, decision authority is not coterminous with the system.

The U.S. social system includes all those who have some activity in the network of interactions between the inputs and the outputs. As a system at its broadest, U.S. society includes the farmers who produce food, the ecology that makes food production possible, the workers in the productive process, the managers, the foreign producers in inputs—the Venezuelans who supply iron, the Arabs who supply oil, the Brazilians who supply coffee, the Eurodollar market which supplies money—the U.S. consumers, the minorities, unemployed, women, welfare recipients, corporate executives, and elected government officials.

The U.S. sociopolitical economy is an enormous system with millions of participants at home and abroad, and millions of interactions and transactions. But only the last two groups, corporate executives and elected government officials, exercise substantial authority in the institutional decision structure over economic growth—that is, authority is not coterminous with the system. Authority is narrowly and institutionally based, while the system parts (participants) are myriad with little voice to express needs and even less authority to effectuate them. Since individuals in the system have little authority to effectuate their own human growth, the institutional decision structure suboptimizes on economic growth. Decision authority must be coterminous with the system or solutions will be partial and suboptimum.

Decisions in Complex Systems

To avoid suboptimizing on means, all of the decision makers (that is, participant groups) of the system must be included in the decision process; otherwise, the choices to be made at the detailed levels of network interactions will not be made. Consider a complex organism such as the human body, for example, where myriad nerve endings connect cell groups throughout the body to the spinal cord and cerebellum. This vast cortical nervous system is diverse, decentralized, and dispersed, and is capable of functioning automatically and independently of conscious choice from the forebrain or cerebrum. A blow upon the finger will cause the arm to contract. An infection in the lungs will release white corpuscles into the blood stream. In the human body, the authority to act automatically is decentralized to the lowest network of interactions (nerves and cells) capable of responding—that is, the response mechanism (authority) is coterminous with the bodily system.

The social system is a more complex organism than the human body, made up as it is of four billion human bodies and all their interactions among themselves and their ecology. The response mechanism cannot occur at the detailed level of network interactions if there is no authority, means, or mechanism of response dispersed to that level.

In the United States, authority has become increasingly centralized in the federal government over the past fifty years, and in businesses through mergers and acquisitions over the past one hundred years. These centralizations of authority have preempted decision making at the human level, where the network of interactions are among individuals. The preemption has occurred by concentrating monetary, income, capital, competition, price, employment, education, technology, and participation into the hands of the few instead of the many. The result has been that the response capability in the individual activity networks has diminished, human needs have gone unmet through inaction, and alienation (violence, crime, and disaffection) has increased. The system is not working effectively at the individual level—decision authority must be diverse, dispersed, and decentralized for a complex system to function effectively at the individual level; and the more complex the system in question, the more diverse the authority distribution needs to be.

Function of the Decision Maker

The function of the decision maker is not primarily to exercise authority, but to disperse it to the lowest level at which action can be taken. The big man concept of leadership, that has been much in vogue assumes that the function of a leader is to be decisive and to make decisions for his institution that reach throughout the organization. This concept is ego satisfying and works quite well in mass production industries where the main decision is to optimize the mix of insentient parts—that is, when decisions are means oriented and have few interactions at the lower network levels, an executive can understand them well enough to be decisive.

A wise man, it is said, knows what he does not know. A wise leader knows that, when dealing with a complex system of sentient beings, he cannot know all the feelings and needs of the interacting individuals at the interpersonal network level. If he cannot know them, he must delegate and disperse authority to the level of interpersonal interaction networks so that a response can occur—that is, the function of a leader in a complex system is to disperse the power to act to the lowest level capable of acting. The wise leader of such a complex system will still have decisions to make, but of a different order. He will need to focus on adaptive change decisions rather than on decisions of the operational process, in the same way that the conscious mind in the human body focuses on adaptation rather than upon the reflex neuromuscular system. A leader who focused his attention on adaptation would establish a widely participative decision process to include all of the decision makers in a systematic-decision structure, and delegate authority to the lowest operational level of interactive networks to facilitate individual responses to human needs, development, and growth.

Function-allocation Decisions

Function-allocation decisions are made in direct relation to human capability, performance, and need. Function-allocation decisions are one step in delegating or dispersing authority. Functions are broad work assignments on how work is to be performed (see chapter 2). As such, they are decisions of means. A means decision is concerned with a performance requirement and cost.

The achievement of a performance requirement—for example, the successful performance of open-heart surgery—requires human capability and skill (for example, a cardiovascular surgeon) and a technology (such as a hospital surgical facility with all its medical equipment and supporting staff). The delegation of the function (work) of open-heart surgery would be to a medical unit that had both the human and technical capability to perform the work. The other basis for allocation of a function would be the presence of a need, or clientele. There is no point in allocating the function of open-heart surgery to a very competent surgeon and medical facility in the Antarctic if there are no heart patients there.

A function (work) allocation decision requires the decision maker to undertake an assessment both of performance capability and need. Need can be established by existing demand, sales or service trends, and marketing research techniques. Assessment of performance capability is somewhat more subjective but is customarily based upon credentials, track record, expert opinion (cross-assessment), and the executive's personal appraisal upon observation and interview.

Accurate assessment procedures for both need and performance capability are the key to good function-allocation decisions, and to executive success. The epithet, "he succeeded because he knew how to pick good men" is a tribute to an executive's assessment skill and function-allocation decisions.

Task-allocation Decisions

Task-allocation decisions are made on the basis of capability, economy, and time. Tasks are subdivisions of functions, or the delegation of the division of labor into detailed work requirements. Tasks are, therefore, subsystems or components of the major work function to be done. As such, they must meet the same performance requirement as the functional assignment. Therefore, tasks are assigned also primarily on the basis of capability to perform—that is, the task of an anesthetist in open-heart surgery is assigned upon the basis of his capability to administer anesthetics successfully to assist the surgical team in performing a successful operation.

As part of a detailed subdivision of labor, tasks have another characteristic beside capable performance. They must also be done on time and at a cost consistent with the total cost of the delivered service. It does not help the performance of open-heart surgery if the anesthetist is available on Wednesday but the operation is on Tuesday. Similarly, the anesthetic is not feasible if it is beyond the patient's ability to pay for it.

Tasks are part of a detailed network of activity that must proceed on time and meet cost objectives to make the total service feasible. This is the essence of the division of labor. Division of labor provides high skills and specialization, but it must be accompanied by a whole network of complementary supporting skills, which, taken together, must be done in a time sequence and at an aggregate cost to be able to deliver a feasible service to satisfy a human need.

The importance of time and cost in task-allocation decisions often require managers to make trade-offs. A trade-off occurs when one technique works nearly as well as another in meeting a performance requirement, but is available in shorter time period or at a lower cost. Suppose the builder of a warehouse, for example, is considering the use of either wooden or steel studs and joists in construction. Both meet the load-bearing requirement sufficiently to meet building performance specifications, but the steel has the added performance advantage of fire resistance. Assume, however, that the steel beams are available three weeks later than the lumber and at a cost of 75¢ more per square foot for the total construction cost. The trade-off is whether the fire-resistance of steel is worth the extra time and cost in construction. In such a case, management must make a value judgment about fire resistance versus time and cost. Such trade-offs are the essence of task allocation decisions. Good task-allocation decisions are based upon careful attention by management to accurate time and cost estimating, accurate capability assessment, and sound value judgments as to the essential performance requirements of the system (that is, neither overengineer, nor underengineer the final output).

Allegiance Decisions

Allegiance decisions are maximized in direct proportion to the use of persuasive rather than coercive authority to respond to human needs. Allegiance decisions are those which affect and respond to individuals' interests, such as giving people the kind of work they want to do, or the kinds of goods and services they want to use. These decisions may be viewed as marketing or employee-relations issues, whether in business or government; but they are more than that. They are management-design problems, anticipatory, looking ahead beyond what engineering or machines might require to what human beings may require in their work or usage.

Task-allocation decisions may be made with some preconceived idea of a technology or product requirement as one option; or task allocation decisions may be made with the possibility of a trade-off in mind between technical requirements and human requirements. For example, automobiles can be designed from the viewpoint of the simplest manufacturing technology, such as the internal combustion engine, or of the user who would prefer good air quality. Also, trash pick-up jobs by local government may be designed for the easiest means of collection or from the viewpoint of protecting the worker from hazardous materials, such as broken glass, sharp metals, and harmful chemicals.

Task assignments have a design aspect that anticipates work performance and usage. If the workers and users are consulted in advance by marketing research, hearings, or participative decision making, their needs and opposition to straight technical decisions would become apparent. Then management can discuss and evaluate the decision with the goal of making trade-offs with those affected in such a way as to persuade them that the final solution (decision) took all views into account. In the absence of such persuasive decision making, management is forced into a coercive posture, where its unilateral decisions place the worker and user with a take-it-or-leave-it option. The worker has no choice but to do the job as it is, hazardous, unpleasant, or monotonous. The user has no option but to buy or not to buy (for example, whether to use polluting, health-damaging automobiles) because there are no other automobiles or public transit options available. The coercive form of decision making induces alienation rather than allegiance; and, hence, persuasive decision making is to be preferred by managers who wish to build allegiance, consent, and authority.

Interpersonal Decisions

Decisions concerning human relationships relate the use of persuasive or coercive means to an informal or formal organization structure. Decisions that affect people will be effective only if management recognizes that organizational setting affects enforceability. In other words, the exercise of power needs to recognize as at least a two-parameter scale of variables. One variable is a spectrum from persuasion-to-coercion. The other axis is an informal-to-formal organizational setting. The interaction of these variables is depicted in figure 3-1.

Beginning in the lower left corner, we see that lovers represent the most personal and most persuasive relationship. Friends, single or in small groups, represent the next most informal relationship, but slightly more coercive because friends have socialized norms. Friends expect each other to behave somewhat as they themselves and their associates behave—not very demandingly, tolerantly, but still one cannot be completely strange and alien to their ways. However, among small, interpersonal relationships, social groups represent a higher order of socialization. They come together for a purpose, and the purpose must be

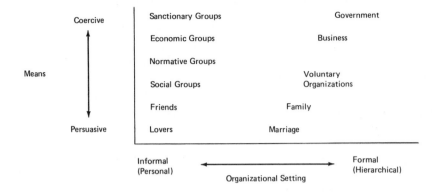

Figure 3-1. Structure of Human Relationship Decisions.

shared for commonality. Normative groups, like professional societies, come together to establish standards or norms of conduct for their professional field; and these are still more coercive or required for participation. Economic groups require socialization to accept economic standards and norms. Sanctioning groups consist of those who have penalty power, such as the American Bar Association with its penalty power of disbarment, or the parish priest with penalty powers of excommunication.

On the horizontal scale, marriage represents a more formal organizational setting than lovers, but remains similarly persuasive. Family, as an organized relationship of marriage, exercises mainly persuasive, but also some coercive powers, among its members. The main coercive power of the family is exclusion from family activities. Voluntary social agencies are rather formally organized and rely substantially on persuasion for cooperation. But voluntary social institutions do have rules, regulations, and norms by which they function to achieve a common purpose; and unless the individual accepts those norms of purpose, a voluntary institution will use coercive penalties, such as excluding the individual from service. Businesses are highly formal in their organization by law, mores, and hierarchy. They are also potentially coercive, such as by excluding individuals from compensation increases, employment, or service. Government is the most highly formalized and coercive of all institutions. Its organization is formalized in law, administered by rules and hierarchy, and enforced by courts. The potential penalties of government are the severest in society—taxation, conscription, deprivation of civil rights, imprisonment, and death.

Persuasive Authority

Persuasive authority's effectiveness is directly proportional to its personal application. Persuasive authority depends upon human contact to transmit by voice, eye, or manner a sense of authenticity and trust. Persuasive authority is a petition to be trusted, in return for which the petitioner promises to act in consideration and on behalf of the other. True lovers trust each other because they believe that each, by promise and authenticity, will act out of consideration for the other and not hurt the other in any way. This promise, authenticity, and trust is nurtured by the most personal and intimate of confidences, contact, and behavior. Sometimes this trust is ill placed, and the apparent authenticity was a dissemblance. Then the individual is deeply and traumatically hurt. The emotional hurt, which is potential in personal persuasive contacts, makes individuals reluctant to affirm love or trust blindly without extensive personal interaction and assessment.

Friends, family, and social groups may also exercise considerable persuasive authority with individuals by reason of their frequent personal contact, interaction, and establishment of authenticity. Business and government have very weak persuasive authority with individuals because their personal interaction is low or nonexistent. The larger and more remote business and government become, the less their persuasive authority exists. The main exception to this tendency is the personal supervisor-employee relationship in on-the-job situations. The supervisory relation can be very personal, confidential, and authentic—within limits. The limits of the supervisor's authenticity hinge on his speaking for the corporation as well as himself, in which case the employee may trust the supervisor as a person but still not believe that the corporation is acting in his interest.

The trend in past decades toward reliance on media rather than personal contact has increased the remoteness and decreased the persuasive authority of both business and government. For example, the reliance on advertising rather than warm, personal selling (whether in department stores or door-to-door sales of automobiles or spices) has decreased the feeling that business has any interest in what the consumer thinks or feels; and, if businesses do not care what their customers think and feel about their service, the allegiance to and persuasive authority of businesses are exhausted. Similarly, in politics candidates used to campaign by train, car, horse, and foot to reach their constituency, or else have an alter ego make personal contacts on their behalf. The tendency for campaigning to rely on television media has had the same effect as in business—it reduces the personal contact, authenticity, and apparent interest of the candidate in the citizenry. And, if candidates are not interested enough in what citizens think and feel to make some personal or surrogate contact with them, then the citizens feel that little trust, allegiance, or persuasive authority apply to the candidate. The crisis of confidence in America lies in this lack of trust because the avenues for personal contact and persuasive authority with business and government have been abandoned—not by citizens, but by media-prone institutional leaders.

Coercive Authority

Coercive authority is effective in direct relation to its reinforcement of the norms of sanctioning groups, and in inverse relation to the frequency of its use. Those formal institutions, such as business and government, that abandon the avenues of persuasive authority for their own convenience must increasingly rely on coercive authority for compliance. Coercive authority is a delicate weapon. Its use requires great expertise, because its effectiveness depends upon surrounding social and environmental factors. Coercion depends first on wide and near-unanimous consensus that a behavioral norm is inviolate. Second, coercion depends upon supporting confirmation from informal sanctioning groups who have personal and persuasive authority. Third, coercion depends upon the infrequency of its use.

Coercion used frequently becomes oppression, appears arbitrary, and invites further alienation. Coercion by definition is the enforcement of normal behavior upon a deviant. If coercion is frequent, the deviance of the behavior is questionable. When force and coercion are used on borderline or deviant behavior, individualism may be denied, because individuation is a deviation from a social norm. Thus, coercion used frequently becomes tyranny of an authoritarian decision maker over individuals.

Moreover, coercion does not stand alone. Institutional decision makers do not have absolute power, but, rather, they have power relative to the accepted norms and mores of the sanctioning groups. Take the rising rates of crime and violence in the streets, for example. The coercive authority of the police is used to fight violations of law that are crimes, but law enforcement does not work unless the violator can be first found and then convicted by evidence. Both finding the violator and punishing him for his crime depend upon the mores and norms of the community in which the criminal act was committed. If the crime was robbery by a disadvantaged person from a ghetto (where there is little employment and robbery is a means of survival), the community may not turn the criminal in nor testify against him, because the family, friends, and the social and sanctioning groups in the community do not confirm that larceny is deviant, nor do they admonish or condemn the perpetrator morally. Moreover, these sanctioning groups may not be willing to use their persuasive personal authority to stop the criminal acts, because they know of no alternatives that could provide for his survival. What should he do—look for a job, education, capital, or technical idea? Compete? Vote? Suppose the perpetrator has tried all these things, but the barriers to entry systematically exclude him. What should such an individual do then, condemn himself to starvation, and death? The community will not support such a judgment by informing upon him nor convicting him.

This argument is not intended to condone crime but merely to demonstrate that coercion does not stand alone. Coercion cannot work unless the local morality, where interpersonal contact occurs, confirms and supports coercion. Where the community mores do not support it, it is an ineffectual means for a decision maker to compel compliance with his wishes. That is why coercion is a delicate weapon. The decision maker must know in advance whether or not it will work. If coercion does not work, the leader increasingly edges toward tyranny, as occurred in the government's attempt to enforce the Vietnam War on an increasingly reluctant public—that is, coercive authority is effective in direct relation to its reinforcement of norms of sanctioning groups, and in inverse relation to its frequency of use.

Maintaining Decision Authority

A necessary condition for maintaining authority through consent is the minimization of coercive authority in favor of persuasive authority. Since coercive authority requires wide consensus on deviant behavior and infrequent use to be effective, a leader must use persuasive authority to the maximum extent possible to retain consent. When coercive authority is to be used as a last resort, and there is moral consensus for its use down to the communities affected, coercive authority should be used quickly, effectively, and dramatically. The quickness demonstrates infrequency. Effectiveness shows that the decision maker does not bungle a bad job. The drama demonstrates that the leader stands for the morality of the overwhelming community and acts on their behalf. Having used coercion in the only way it really can be used, the leader returns to persuasive authority as his main means of cooperation and compliance.

Social Design Decisions

By way of summary, the decision elements have now been described in order of organizational implementation. These decisions are very important for the effective use of the means; but they are not the end of the decision process. The systematic practice of management requires that all of the aspects of the decision named in this chapter be integrated into an output, a social utility, or a social design—that is, social design decisions are the integration of time-phased, task networks into technological, budgetary, control, organizational, and institutional packages.

All of these detailed tasks, activities, and events are capable of being classified into manageable units for subsequent feedback and follow-up. These packages are as follows.

Technological. Some of the activities and events require particular technologies or technical means, and the collection of these technical events specifies the engineering development work to be delivered.

Budgetary. Time is a cost in terms of payroll and material processing. Therefore, the collection of the time schedules of all the activity work to be done may be priced to yield a total cost for the delivery of final products or services.

Control. Budget and time estimates are means of control over actual performance, by comparing estimated time and cost with the actual experience as work is performed. A management information system may be created so that it is capable of making such comparisons and reporting exceptions.

Organizational. The functional assignment of task networks to organizational departments gives management control over the delivery of work expected of organizational units, and thus the organization is made accountable and responsible.

Institutional. The final delivery of outputs to a user group justifies the institution and determines its income, earnings, allegiances, authority maintenance, and survival.

Conflicts of Interest

The trade-off between human ends and minimizing the means in the social design of task networks presents every executive with a conflict of interest between individual versus institutional maintenance. The social design of an institution's final outputs to fulfill its missions has an ends-means trade-off built into its task networks—the tasks (technological, human, budgetary, control, and organizational) may be shaped to maximize the performance of the final service delivered to the user, or to minimize the cost to the institution. The user naturally seeks the best service (performance); and the user's allegiance in the long run is conditioned by that same satisfactory level of performance. The institutional interest is to minimize cost, make ends meet (if government), and maximize profit (if business).

The decision maker has, then, a final trade-off in his social design as to how far he should go in satisfying performance versus minimizing cost. This is not only a social design decision, but also a personal decision because the decision maker is institutionally appointed, or institutionally bound. He is an executive and a decision maker only as long as there is an institution to appoint him. Hence, he must maintain the institution to maintain himself. The motive to maintain the institution and the executive role biases the decision maker's decision toward minimizing cost, or maximizing profit, in the short run. Yet the long-run allegiance and claim to authority, which the decision maker has, depends upon the service performance of final outputs to users, as well as upon the persuasive authority that he exercises via personal contact with his constituency. The maximization of performance and personal contact with users maximizes cost, within the constraint of the institution's survival. The executive must at least go far enough in satisfying human needs in the long run to be able to retain authority through consent.

The decision maker might wish to avoid this dilemma by trying both to maximize performance and to minimize cost, but this is a logical impossibility; one or the other must be held constant. The decision maker must then choose some balance between institutional maintenance and satisfactory performance from a human (user or worker) viewpoint. This trade-off is the final achievement of management and should be made knowing that a conflict of interest is involved. This trade-off at least requires careful thought to the human ends of the system.

Perhaps this conclusion is obvious—that the final decision is a trade-off between minimizing cost and maximizing human ends. But if it is obvious, the socialization of managers makes them speak of their role in simplistic terms. Business executives assert that their job is to maximize profits. Politicians assert, in their campaign for votes, that their job is to maximize welfare. Some executives even come to believe what they are socialized to say, and then act accordingly. But these simplistic goals cannot be so, because a trade-off is involved. A business that simply maximizes profit has no social purposes from which to draw its authority, allegiance, and continuance. A government that merely maximizes welfare has no social accountability for the cost and worth to taxpaying citizens.

It is within the self-interest of the business executive to maximize profit for his own enrichment; and it is within the self-interest of the politician to maximize welfare for his own reelection. However, these realistic statements of self-interest only highlight the conflict of interest in the final decision. The interests of the decision maker, the institution, and the human ends are separable; and they must be kept separable to make an equitable trade-off in the final decision.

Note

1. Stahrl W. Edmunds, *Alternative U.S. Futures* (Santa Monica, Cal.: The Goodyear Publishing Co., 1978).

4 The Functions of Business

The distinctive characteristic of business, compared with other institutions, is that business has separable costs and discrete prices for its goods and services. Business derives its mission from the market; and the market place deals in the exchange of goods and services at discrete prices. Government and voluntary institutions, by contrast, deal mainly in joint services—goods whose benefit have such commonality that their costs are not allocable. For example, the police car that patrols the streets at night protects equally the homeowner in his living room who is not robbed as well as the one who is. Similarly, the educational services of a voluntary institution benefits equally those who learn and those employers who use the learning.

Business goods and services generally have a discrete demand, a single seller, a single buyer, a single price. The discreteness of buyers, sellers, and prices provides admirable advantages in equating the interests of parties, balancing supply and demand, and arriving at a fair equilibrium price by clearing a large number of similar transactions in the market. Business may have joint costs of production if it has multiple products produced by the same equipment; but these costs are frequently allocable on a reasonable basis, related to quantity, value, or usage. The existence of joint costs does not preclude discrete prices, if costs are allocable. In the case of government and voluntary institutions, truly joint services have costs that are not allocable except on an arbitrary basis. If the allocation is arbitrary, then the presumption of relating cost to benefit is lost, which is a principal advantage of market exchange.

That business goods and services are exchanged in the market at discrete prices provides for other corollary distinctions between business and other institutions. One is that the calculus of decision making is different, because resource allocation can be calculated in relation to costs and price, and supply quantities can be calculated from demand. Another is that rates of return can be calculated on earnings, after all costs, in relation to investment. These calculable characteristics of business decisions give them an air of precision, which is somewhat illusory. It may be illusory because of cost definitions—that is, the exclusion or externalizing of costs that properly belong to business but are relegated to government as social costs (see chapter 2). The precision may also be illusory because the sum of business services may not serve the ultimate end of human growth and development (see chapter 1).

Nevertheless, business is and remains the dominant institution in society by reason of its vital role in providing for human sustenance, in the ages-old fight against poverty. About two-thirds of the labor force is engaged in private economic activity, making business the largest employer in society. For these reasons alone, the role and contributions of business to society deserves attention and understanding. If it has shortcomings, so do other institutions; and, in any case, the purpose of understanding business is to strengthen it where it succeeds and improve it where it may be deficient.

Business Mission and Authority

Business receives its mission and authority by legislation and custom, which form its social contract. The social contract of business has three elements: (1) the chartering or organization legislation that brings an enterprise into being as a legal person; (2) the state legislation and federal regulations specifying authority and powers of a business that are enforceable by law; and (3) custom, which gives business a general role and mores.

Business licensing or chartering legislation provides for the initial organization of business into an identifiable legal entity for tax and litigation purposes, and a specified financial structure with known liability—that is, the initial organization of a business provides it with a tax, legal, and financial identity.

The uniform commercial code of the several states provides business with authority to make agreements, contracts, and decisions that are not only binding by common consent (to the authority of the decision maker), but are also enforceable in the courts in case of dispute. The authority granted to business in the commercial code covers the right to contract; nature of contracts; when contracts are formed and consummated; the liabilities of contracts; redress for breach of contracts; definition of damages; special forms of contracts, such as negotiable instruments; special recognition for the appearance of authority, such as in agency; and the liabilities of decision makers under various forms of business. Business and its authority is, then, substantially a creature of the law, for without the law, business would have no form, identity, or authority.

The law is relatively silent and permissive about what business can do, other than engage in production, commerce, trade, finance, and services. The mission and purpose of business is more a matter of custom and the market than a legal construct. Custom indicates that business exists to provide for human wants through the provision and exchange of goods and services. Custom assumes that goods and services exchanged in a market have a price and are brought into equilibrium, supply with demand, by bargaining over price. The demand for goods and services, at variable prices, is then the determinant of the purpose and mission of business. Custom also presumes that the self-interest of the seller is such that, caveat emptor, let the buyer beware.

The custom of caveat emptor is both an augmentation of authority and an embarrassment to business. Caveat emptor presumes that a business will act mainly in its own self-interest rather than in the interest of the buyer. Hence, let the buyer beware for himself and protect, if he can, his own self-interest. This concept of caveat emptor is at least partially recognized in common law, in such cases as—unless there is a specified warranty on a product—the buyer takes his own chances as to its quality and reliability when he purchases it; and the seller is not legally responsible for a poor or unusable product (unless he agreed in advance to be responsible by the warranty).

Caveat emptor, then, separates business from responsibility to the buyer in product performance and pricing. This has the effect of granting the business decision maker added authority to act solely, if he chooses, on the basis of internal considerations in the business. Thus, caveat emptor is permissive authority to maximize the interests of the business, profits, stockholders' interests, executive compensation, employees' interests, organizational mainten- ance, and the personal enrichment of the decision maker—all the while taking the view, if the decision maker chooses, adverse to the buyer. Seen in this light, caveat emptor is a substantial augmentation of authority, because it allows the business by custom to internalize its costs, interests, and maximize its profits.

Most businesses do not, in fact, behave with indifference to the buyers, if only for the good business practice that they want the buyers to buy again in the future. Hence, caveat emptor is mitigated by the interest of the business in its own survival. Most businesses do stand behind the performance of their products beyond the requirements of the warranty; and some, to mitigate the embarrass- ment of caveat emptor, go so far as to say and act upon the assumption that the customer is always right (which is also obviously untrue).

Caveat emptor is an embarrassment to business because (1) it reverses the ethics of normal community, (2) it destroys the foundation for trust, and (3) it undermines the ability of business to acquire authority through consent. The normal ethic is family, community, and nation is that a man's word is his bond, and a person stands behind the full truth and performance of his actions. This is expected in the family, among friends, and in community affairs. The principle of government is that it acts in the public interest, in the interest of others, not itself—just the opposite of caveat emptor.

The reversal of ethics means that all business executives and representatives have to be treated by buyers and public as schizophrenics who may be trusted for their personal words as individuals, but who are suspect as spokesmen and actors for their business. They are suspect because they have the moral and ethical option, under caveat emptor, to speak the full truth or part of the truth, to stand behind their acts or not, to assure reliability of their products or not, to price their products fairly based upon cost or not, and to act on behalf of buyers and employees or not. That most businessmen act honorably most of the time does not vitiate suspicion, because they have the option under custom to act otherwise, and a few sometimes do.

An institution that has the option, as its own choice, of acting against the interest of buyers or employees is difficult for the public to trust. The buyers and employees can never be sure whether they are being treated justly or being had; and their suspicion may cause them to overreact negatively to business when it is not warranted. The rise of both consumerism and the environmental movements are antibusiness phenomenon based upon this distrust. Consumers do not believe in the fairness of business pricing or product performance and seek legislation to force frankness and responsibility in these areas. Environmentalists do not trust business evaluations of alternative remedies and costs to improve air, water, and environmental quality. Indeed, business has a very difficult time getting a fair hearing before the public in environmental and consumerism cases, even when it is sincerely acting in the public interest.

The unfortunate part of caveat emptor as a custom is that it conceals information from the consumer-buyer, information he needs for his own protection and self-interest. The business seller has complete information on cost and performance of its services, and the consumer has little or no information (mainly what the seller tells him in advertising or sales messages). Caveat emptor implies: take a seller with full information, and take a buyer with little information, and let them protect their own self-interests equally. The inequality of information destroys trust. The information gap is so apparent and persistent between seller and buyer that, in the environmental and consumer cases, even when the seller discloses full information, buyers will not believe it.

Without trust, there is no consent to authority. Consumers and employees are not likely to yield their allegiance, consent, and authority to an institution that they cannot trust. This is the dilemma and crisis of business, which has been with society since 1930. During the Depression, a great groundswell of antibusiness sentiment and distrust brought into being myriad regulations and a social responsibility concept of government as more trustworthy than business and more likely to act in the public interest. The apparent trust in government to act in the public interest has, for nearly fifty years, brought wave after wave of new welfare regulation of both business and the individual. Business has stood by, in its postwar prosperity and self-affluence, content to see the erosion of its role and authority relative to government as long as it made good profits, and apparently content also not to ask how it might recover authority through consent. By not asking the embarrassing questions about ethics, trust, consent, and authority, business has become a suspect institution, beset by increasing regulation over price control, consumer issues, the environment, and political influence.

Perhaps business' critics are its best friends, asking questions that it subconsciously hides from itself—Why is there so much regulation? Why is government so big? Why is business not trusted more than it is? Whence comes authority to business? How can business build authority by its own acts and by consent? These are the most vital questions for business today. They are mission-oriented questions about purpose and values. They ultimately address the long-term strength of business as an independent institution, trusted by the populace, rather than as a regulated henchman of government.

Business is potentially a most equitable institution, because it has in the market (a free market) the potential for equating benefit with cost, and the interest of buyers with the interest of sellers. Government is potentially a more despotic institution, because it has in its hands the ultimate penalties of repression and death. Government has been centralizing power for fifty years; and without a reversal in sight, the potential for government repression must at least be viewed as an alternative possibility, particularly after the events in the 1960s and early 1970s. There is little evidence that either the wisdom or self-interest of government leaders will cause them to give authority back to the sovereign people from whence it came.

Business has a mission that is very confused. Law gives business an identity and authority, but custom gives business a schizophrenic role, that of a benefactor, that of a sharper (caveat emptor), or both. Business is so dominant an institution in society that the schizophrenia affects everyone. Ever since the 1950s, literature has held to critical light the organization man, the man in the grey flannel suit, the games people play, the antenna-oriented society, unobtrusive gestures, body language, duplicity of business role playing, and the lack of authenticity in society until young people have become so repulsed by the absurdity of modern social behavior that they retreat from society to a more authentic world of their own making. Business needs authenticity to recover its consent, allegiance, and authority. The business community needs to decide who it really is, Dr. Jekyl or Mr. Hyde. Then the rest of the society can decide how to react to either.

Objectives of Business

Legislative authorizations establish business, leaving it to business itself (with the market reflecting human needs) to define its specific mission in terms of products or services. These are policy objectives of business that are established initially by inventor-entrepreneurs, and subsequently by boards of directors and executive officers of the enterprise.

The selection of the field of endeavor usually is a combination of a product concept, a market demand perception, and financial feasibility. These ingredients are the continuous concern, not only of the originating inventor-entrepreneur, but also of all subsequent policymaking executives. The design, and continual redesign, of product-market-financial concepts that are deliverable as a service output to consumers are creative processes, perhaps the most creative in business decision making. These delivery concepts constitute the selection of the field of enterprise, the self-defined choice of mission, and the objectives of business. The objectives of business policy are its own chosen outputs.

Functions of Business

The major functions of business are policy and planning, research and development, marketing, production, finance, and control. Functions have their origin in the work to be done; they are literally work functions. The assignment of broad work functions by management makes possible the delegation of authority, the division of work based upon capability, and accountability for performance.

There are two main interfaces among the work functions: the outgoing interactions with the environment, and the internal focus on producing an output (table 2-1). All of the six functions are part of the internal core producing a deliverable output. Four of the functions—policy, marketing, finance, and product development—have an outward interactive layer as well. These interactions may be visualized as shown in figure 4-1, in which the market constitutes the environment and the enterprise is the system.

In this schematic, the policy and planning function is the search for concept, which are identifiable as the field of interests, product concepts, demand possibilities, and financial objectives. The marketing function assesses demand and need through market research, selling, and interacting with the public. The research and development function offers alternative technical

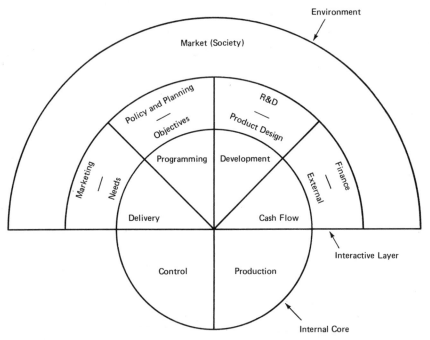

Figure 4-1. Major Functions of Business.

design concepts. The finance function examines the funds requirements, including external sources in the capital market, for the several market-product concepts. These assessments yield an evaluative decision by the policy and planning function about which specific products or services to pursue as implementable objectives.

Implementation then entails management of the internal core. Decision makers program the network of assignments, authorize product development tasks, organize the cash flows needed to finance the operations, place the developed products or services into operational production, assign the delivery tasks to marketing, and control the entire programmed network by a management control and feedback information system—that is, the business as a system conceives, programs, develops, produces, controls, and delivers interactively within a market environment.

Policy and Planning

The policy and planning function assesses the alternative combinations of client needs, technical feasibility, deliverability, company capability, and financial resources. The policy and planning function is sometimes performed by a department within a company, sometimes by an executive committee, and occasionally by the finance committee of the board of directors. Whatever its organizational form, the function is made up of the top policymakers of the company, and is an iterative evaluation process working with operating departments. Realistic assessments of needs, invention, and funding cannot be made without the marketing, research, and finance functions.

The top policymakers have the best grasp of alternatives, finances, and value judgments needed to pick a product concept and implement it as a business goal. Policymakers' value judgments may favor institutional maintenance or the executives own interests, but even so they also weigh consumer, government, stockholder, employee, and public interests in some manner. The final decision is essentially the priority interests among these groups (that is, is political), and thus cannot be delegated by the policymakers.

Research and Development

The research and development function creates alternative product or service innovations to fulfill client needs. The research and development function is sometimes performed by a department, especially in high-technology companies that have large research laboratories and sizable staffs of developmental engineers. The chemical, electronics, computer, pharmaceutical, optical, instrumentation, and defense companies are particularly likely to have such departments. In creative design businesses, such as advertising, printing, fashions, and greeting cards, an art department is likely to perform the equivalent of a research and development function. In mass production manufacturing, such as steel and automobile production, the function is likely to be split among a small basic research laboratory (concerned with metallurgy and engines), a styling studio creating new models or forms, and the production engineering department that has the greatest expertise on how to design products for mass production.

While the placement of the function varies according to industry technology, the research and development function entails assessment of technologies that may be applied; alternative performance specifications (with marketing); a creative invention or design; development engineering, or detailing the design; and production engineering, or designing productability into the product.

The research and development function is exceedingly difficult to staff, manage, and evaluate by higher level executives, because the work is at once highly creative and highly detailed. These two traits are not commonly found in the same person. Hence, the research and development function can waste a lot of money with applications people trying to be creative, or creative people trying to perform applications functions. From the outside, it is difficult to tell the difference until the money is all spent; and from the inside, research and development people will seldom tell which is which, or what is happening, either out of ignorance or to save their own skins. This is neither a flippant nor a snide observation, because creativity is difficult to detect anywhere. Think of the millions of dollars spent on Broadway plays or Hollywood films that were initially thought to be masterpieces but which turned out to be flops. Realistically, this difficulty of discerning creativity anywhere tells us that management's control of research and development (or creativity) is not possible by the normal means; and, hence, the best alternative is to make evaluations on technological assessments by bringing in independent evaluators, evaluating the track record of the designer, and scaling up from small designs to larger ones, or from conceptual designs to breadboard tests.

Research and development can be the heart of a growth business or the largest sinkhole in the organization. Even successful companies make colossal mistakes in research and development. For example, nearly every major electronics company invested millions in the computer business, and all but a few have failed and withdrawn, with similar experience in semiconductors and microcircuitry.

Marketing

The marketing function assesses demand, attitudes, distribution, and service requirements of proposed outputs, and then implements their delivery. Marketing has three basic functions: to sense consumer attitudes and needs, to deliver usable, desired services, and to measure demand as a control parameter. The sensing of consumer attitude and need is carried out by market research into consumer satisfactions and dissatisfactions with existing services as well as consumer loyalties, attitudes, unmet needs, buying power, price sensitivity, and quantity requirements. The delivery of usable, desired services is an operational activity of considerable magnitude involving the identification of market segments, territories, distribution channels, outlets, stocking inventories, and shelf lives, and the management of direct sales, service, and credit. Of these, the establishment of distribution channels and the act of personal contact in selling are likely to require the most manpower. The measurement of demand as a control parameter involves management of a sales statistics data base that shows quantities sold by type of customer, territory, product, model, price, sales rates, inventory, inventory turnover, and estimated new production quantities to maintain sales and inventory levels.

The marketing function is normally a department in most companies. In businesses where the value of product is very high, or when fashion and change are prevalent, the marketing function may be the dominant department in the business. In other types of businesses, where competition, change, or value are low, marketing may be quite perfunctory. The marketing function suffers more than any other department in business from confused identity caused by the caveat emptor syndrome. A company's internal organization, as well as those dealing with it from the outside, frequently expect marketing people to be either high-pressure hustlers or order takers, and marketing people are likely to respond to these expectations. As high-pressure hustlers, they confirm the image, internally and externally, of caveat emptor. As order takers, they dispel the caveat emptor image, but do the company relatively little good.

Marketing people suffer from a severe inferiority complex, caused by caveat emptor and their high-pressure ancestors. The marketing literature is filled with their hopes and guilt—for example, the marketing concept, the marketing concept revisited, the social-marketing resonsibility of business—but these concepts are aspirations and have no real effect unless adopted by management. Marketing has yet to come up with an implementable method for its own identity and mission.

Marketing is potentially the public interest arm of business. The surest method for becoming that, and giving marketing a mission, identity, and profession of its own, would be to close the information gap between the state of a company's knowledge and that of its customers' knowledge. Caveat emptor may have been a workable practice when technology was low and widely known, when people sold cloth and bread from camelback. But in a highly technological society the cost and availability of information is beyond the reach of any consumer, unless the seller shares the information with him. Marketing could be the public interest agency for sharing information on technical performance, price, costs, and profit. Instead of unbelievable advertising claims and cunning price concessions, marketing might simply try telling the whole truth, at least to those who inquire. This would require a degree of exposure of information uncommon in management, and might be viewed as the equivalent of going to confessional or the psychiatry couch. Still, several companies may be confident enough both of their product quality and the fairness of pricing to be truthful and fully disclose information that would make the buyer as equal in knowledge to protect his own interest as is the seller. An experiment in straightforwardness might even prove that the real interest of business is the public interest. When marketing men convey the full truth to customers, and represent customer interests fully to management, marketing will develop authenticity and business will cease to be suspect.

Persuasive authority is effective in direct relation to its personal application (chapter 3). Marketing lost the art of persuasive authority when it went almost wholly to media, departing from personal service and contact. Business lost much of its capacity for leadership from the demise of persuasive authority in marketing, and its lack of authenticity. Leadership and authority are grants by individuals to a decision maker to act on their behalf, and customers do not make this grant of allegiance and leadership in the absence of trust, disclosure, and personal contact.

Finance

The finance function organizes the capital flows needed to match resource and expenditure requirements in the enterprise. The major subfunctions in finance are those of treasury, cash flows, and capital acquisition. Frequently, the accounting and controller functions are part of finance as well because of the close relationship of accounting and budgeting to cash flows. However, we will treat control as a separate function because control has a quantitative feedback aspect as well as a financial aspect.

The treasury functions are to receive and pay all cash and check transactions, to be a repository for cash, to manage bank deposits, and to be transfer agent for stocks and bonds (or appoint one). The management of cash flows requires forward estimates of cash receipts and expenditures, so that the enterprise can meet its future bills and commitments. Cash flow management is the anticipatory extension of the treasury function. To be able to anticipate the rate of future receipts and expenditures, finance management needs to have good budget estimates of sales, sales receipts, payments on accounts payable, payroll expenditures, purchasing commitments, and the payment schedule on all contracts. These are, in fact, the major decisions that affect the accounts of the enterprise, and that is why finance and accounting are frequently combined.

The forward-looking budget estimates of all receipts and expenditures are reflected in three primary financial statements: the balance sheet, which shows everything that the enterprise owns and owes at the end of a time period (month or year); the income statement, which shows all the receipts, expenditures, and earnings during a time period; and the flow of funds statement, which shows the sources and uses of all money during a time period. These statements are prepared for the present and projected into the future based on budget estimates of sales and expenditures. Future statements are often called pro forma. The object of the pro forma statements is to draw up a schedule over time when cash will be received and paid out (cash flow). Unless an enterprise manages its internal cash flow to make ends meet, it must go out into the market to borrow money or go bankrupt.

The ability to acquire capital in money markets (banks, securities under-writers, stockholders, and lenders) is a finance function of utmost importance to keep an enterprise viable. The ability to acquire capital depends upon a business's earnings and ability to repay a loan—that is, on its profitability and the sum of its debts. Most firms do find themselves short of cash or capital part of the time and borrow to make up the deficiency, but the amount of borrowing must be marginal or small in relation to total earnings or other debts for a company to be able to borrow with ease. Thus, credit is most readily available to a business when it does not need it, and is difficult or impossible to obtain when a firm is desperate. The object of finance management is never to get into a desperate situation. A desperate financial situation is called a liquidity crisis and usually occurs when the cash receipts from sales drop so low that current bills cannot be met, or when a firm has contracted large capital equipment commitments that cannot be paid. Lenders and investors do not like to make money available during a desperate liquidity crisis because of the risk that the business may not succeed in recovering its earnings or ability to repay.

The strategy of finance management to deal with this reluctance to lend during liquidity crisis is twofold: to maintain a margin of safety in cash flow management to avoid a serious liquidity crunch in the first place, and to borrow money all the time to get the lender involved in the business's problems so that he has to put more money into the business to save what has already been lent. This latter strategy is called maintaining a line of credit, which provides lower and upper debt bounds within the business. Thus it is always able to borrow without serious question (although filing reasonable pro forma financial state-ments periodically is necessary). A line of credit costs money to maintain, because the business is always borrowing a small portion of its cash require-ments, and the bank lender requires a business to maintain a deposit or reciprocating balance in the bank up to about 20 percent of any loans. This reciprocating balance requirement raises the effective rate of interest for borrowing money by about 25 percent.

If financial management can keep a business out of periodic credit trouble by maintaining cash flow margins and lines of credit, there are at least two other crises in the financial career of most businesses to be avoided: acquiring the capital to get the business started, and getting capital for what might be called a midcareer changeover. Financing a new business is difficult because it is difficult to tell a good idea from a bad one (as in research and development or picking Broadway plays). Moreover, investors feel that they are taking a high risk, not only on the idea, but also on the manager's ability and a host of fortuitous events that cannot be anticipated. Since ideas are more plentiful than investment capital, the cost of money is very high to a new business—50-90 percent of the ownership frequently goes to the investors. This leaves the entrepreneur with the idea, his own life efforts, his life savings, and with minority ownership in his own idea. For this reason, new businesses are best started small and, when possible, with only the money of the owner and his associates in the business.

The second financial crisis of business is when it reaches a midcareer stage and must either expand significantly or lose its market and technical advantages. By this time, the business usually has a good earnings record, and may even have a high line of credit; but large capital expansion may be even beyond these means. The midcareer business will find the money markets quite anxious to lend or invest at this stage, based upon earnings and track record, but again at exhorbitant participation rates. This is caveat emptor at work again. The investor is a seller of money and wants to take over a good thing; let the buyer beware. Even wary and skilled buyers of money are often harvested by financiers at this stage. Howard Hughes lost control of TWA to a banker-management group when the airline needed to finance conversion of its fleet to jet airliners, even though he owned about 70 percent of its stock. Henry Ford, in a similar dilemma in the 1920s, was so incensed by the exhorbitant participation required to acquire capital that he decided to go it alone, which cost him so many years in retooling for the Model A that he lost 50 percent of the market to General Motors in the process (that is, Ford's market share dropped from 75 percent to below 30 percent). If Ford and Hughes could not beat the money market, it is difficult for any writer to suggest how to do it. The only precautions an individual can take are to build a cash reserve and to keep a keen eye out for early signs of market or technical changes which require large new capital investments.

The finance function is so crucial to the survival of the firm that frequently, particularly in a troubled company, it becomes the dominant department, absorbing even the policy and planning function. Still, the finance function can only preserve the firm; it cannot make the company grow. Growth depends upon product quality and marketing. This brings into play an uneasy balance and conflict in a business, depending upon what stage it is in, between finance and the product-marketing functions over policy and objectives. Finance tends too much to conserve the business, thereby possibly stultifying it, and product-marketing tends to overexpand the business, which gets it into financial trouble.

The skill of top policymakers is to resolve the finance-marketing conflict and establish a balance between them. Carnegie had a novel idea for solving this balance: expand the business (capital expansion) during depression and conserve it during prosperity. This is just the reverse of normal business practice and follows the dictum of Baron Rothschild to buy when blood is running in the streets. The technique worked for Carnegie well enough for him to take over the steel industry.

Production

Production assembles the resources to transform inputs into deliverable goods and services on time and on cost. The transformation of inputs into final outputs is the most costly single function in most businesses. In manufacturing firms, capital equipment, material, and detailed labor for transformation are costly. In services, the essence of service is personal contact, which is costly. Production departments are, therefore, very cost and time conscious, which is reflected in their organization: (1) production planning and programming, (2) material assembly, (3) work layout, (4) facilities planning, (5) processing (cutting, forming, shaping, mixing, retorting, refining, and blending), (6) assembly, (7) inspection, (8) service (repair and rework), and (9) control.

Programming and control are common to all production activities, in that they deal with planning the throughput of work into the transformation process, and seeing that the work is done as planned. The rest of the functions are technology specific—that is, the tasks vary according to the technology of the industry. In the production of integrated circuits, for example, the process is largely vapor deposition onto etched surfaces, an automated chemical process by which temperature-controlled gas mixtures precipitate conductive metals on a nonconductive surface. In automobile production, the process is mainly metal cutting and stamping, the cutting (as in boring engine blocks) to very fine tolerances and the forming by heavy presses capable of both great force and speed to handle the quantities needed.

Most production departments are very proficient at their technology and skillful at programming and control. Still, production departments have a chronic dilemma that goes back ultimately to a customer problem—that is, what is the trade-off in the user's mind between cost and quality? Production departments do not ask this question very much of themselves, but it is strongly imposed upon them by policymakers and marketing executives who set up production as a series of cost centers, set cost and time limits on final output production, and set quality standards on product performance. These goals and standards are highly quantitative in production functions, making production executives the most highly accountable in business. They respond to accountability (because their executive compensation depends upon it) by very tight control over time and cost.

The dilemma lies in the need to minimize time and cost results in maximizing profit, when increased time on human learning curves for production tasks is needed to improve product quality and meet consumer needs. This dilemma puts production executives squarely in the middle of the whole problem of human growth and satisfaction in industry, both among consumers and among employees. Consumers want a reliable product of maximum quality at a minimum price, but they cannot have both, because one cannot logically both maximize performance and minimize cost. One or the other has to be held constant. But production executives have no consumer contact or insight to tell them which one, so they have to listen to top management, which tells them to maximize profit, minimize cost, or hold performance at some constant satisfactory quality. What is that trade-off? What is a satisfactory performance quality? Production executives can only guess and then wait for complaints from the customer or marketing department. Or, they can overdesign redundancy and reliability into the product, often at very small incremental costs, but that takes more time and more learning.

The learning curve on production tasks is the time it takes a worker to reach proficiency in producing a satisfactory yield. Yield is the quantity (or ratio) of outputs that meet performance specifications. Some products are so difficult to make satisfactorily (meeting specification) that the yield may be as low as 50-60 percent (for example, in semiconductors and some glass-blown tube products). These low yield processes are known as "black arts." They typify the production dilemma. In black art production, given more time on the learning curve, the worker will frequently increase his proficiency sufficiently to meet or exceed specifications. Exceeding specifications, even by a slight margin, may significantly improve product quality and reliability. For instance, in precision machining, the improvement of tolerances by a thousandth of an inch can significantly improve the fit, wear, and durability of moving parts. But learning that degree of precision takes the worker some time. How much learning time versus how many thousandth inches of tolerance should the production executive trade off? The trade-off affects both customer satisfaction with product quality and management satisfaction with cost. It also affects worker satisfaction with his job, because learning has to be reasonably timed, supervised, tutored, inspected, trained, rewarded, appreciated, and recognized—all leading to pride in craftsmanship and work.

The production dilemma is not easily solved, because it takes top management time to understand the trade-offs. These trade-offs are best understood and decided when the chief executive is an ex-production executive, who knows the technology and the learning curve functions. But that is a trade-off, too, because such a chief executive may not know the marketing functions for growth or the finance functions for survival. The other alternative is for the policy level of management to organize itself to study the learning-quality-cost trade-offs, because this is at the heart of much of consumer and worker dissatisfaction.

Control

Control is the means by which managers ascertain that operations are accomplished as planned to meet objectives. Control is accomplished by some form of management information system that feeds back to management information on whether operating organizations have met their goals, objectives, budgets, cost targets, and quantity targets. The inputs for such a management information system flow from the following functions: (1) the marketing and production departments' report on physical quantities made and sold; (2) the accounting or controller's department compare budgeted versus actual expenditures; (3) the finance department estimates capital requirements and money costs; (4) the policy and planning function sets the performance standards for the organization, and (5) a statistical processing department integrates the data into an exception report.

The control data, then, come from most of the operating functions of the business; and the location of the control activity itself varies by type of business. In most corporations, the control function is performed by the controller's (or accounting) department within the finance organization. The controller usually has a computer information facility (with operations research staff to model problems) as the processing unit. Information processing, done by computer, is assembled from within the accounting-budgeting-finance complex. The management information facility has to go outside this organizational complex only for two sets of data: standards data from policy and planning, and physical quantity data from marketing and production.

Alternative forms of organization for management information systems are a separate, computerized information unit under a top management performing its own policy-planning function; a policy, planning, and programming unit; or the production department when the operations are highly quantitative and costly, and can easily be made into a model. The specialized information systems related to policy and planning usually is established when a company has had to utilize a specialized computer competence, and the chief executive demands that management meet objectives with a high degree of precision. The production-oriented information system occurs when an operations research group is put into the production function to model operations because they are difficult to manage by reason of cost, complexity, or quantity.

Control by management information systems present the common dilemma of having more information than management wants to see but seldom the right information for decisions. Management frequently sees itself buying stacks of paper that it cannot assimilate and is thus inclined to cut the cost of information gathering and processing. Yet, that the right information is not available to make decisions means there is not enough information. Again, management has a dilemma and trade-off, this time between the cost and the quality or pertinence of information.

The kind of information that management receives, and by which it feels inundated, is retrospective data that is cheap to assemble in large quantities from internal records. It is cheap because it is available, and the main cost is programming the computer to receive the data and make multitudinous cross-tabulations. The pertinent information that management wants for decisions is anticipatory—about the future. The data do not exist yet; and expectations data are hard to get and costly, if indeed they can be obtained at all. Expectations concern consumers and their future purchases, product developers and their future technology, bankers and their future money rates, government and its future monetary-fiscal policy, competitors and their future competitive advantages, labor and its future wage rates, and suppliers and their future materials prices. This is the information from which decisions are made; and the retrospective data in the internal data base sheds light upon these expectations only very little, by the extent to which extrapolation is valid. Extrapolation is valid only when rates of change are uniform, which is rare.

How does management move from retrospective to prospective data? One starting point is to build the information system around the physical quantity data from marketing and production, because these data are closest in time to the sales transactions, which are the ultimate indicator of current supply-demand situations, and because these data anticipate and precede in time, by several weeks, all the other data in the company. The second step is to spend less money collecting and processing retrospective data in the company, and to spend more money collecting at least a few pieces of anticipatory data. One vital piece of data, which is collectible at least in subjective terms, is consumers' expectations about their purchases and financial condition. Consumer attitudes and expectations data are not very accurate indicators of the future level of economic activity, but they are quite accurate indicators of the relative change from one time period to the next into the future. Thus, these expectations data can be tied on to the current sales-production data to develop better forecasts than straight extrapolation would provide alone.

Another anticipatory set of data worth collecting are product engineers' expectations on future performance characteristics of products. Product engineers cannot forecast surprise inventions, but most performance improvement comes from judicious extrapolation of the performance of existing materials, such as the heat resistance or tensile strength of metals, the power output of electronic tubes, break-strength of plastics, etc. For example, research engineers anticipated the improvement of laser beams years in advance through their knowledge of crystal physics and the probability of growing fractureless crystals. Similarly, the speed, capacity, and fuel consumption of future aircraft are roughly estimable, as is the range of radar, the speed and capacity of electronic computers, or the evolutionary development of synthetic carbon molecules. These data, approximate though they are, indicate future product performance for a company and its competitors.

A third set of anticipatory data is cost expectations for production. Production engineering departments can estimate rates of improvement in output per man-hour from capital equipment developments, learning curves in plant, and their own layout and production design plans. Similarly, the procurement department can obtain expectations of future materials prices from suppliers.

The difficulty with all this data, of course, is that they are not as neat, manageable, and programmable as the internal cost data from within the company. Hence, expectations data cannot be modeled as elegantly as internal cost data. Expectations data may be partly modeled, as in using consumer expectations to anticipate demand or production engineering estimates to anticipate cost. But beyond that, expectations data has to be treated judgmentally, by policy-planning executives, with subtle experiential models in the executive's mind—in short, by thinking; but that is what executives are paid for.

Resource Mobilization Requirements

The resource mobilization requirements of business give rise to numerous staff services, including human relations, procurement, facilities, logistics, legal, international, and public relations, which reflect outside interests from the social environment to the internal organization. The thinking side of management goes beyond working the operational decisions of enterprise, because business has many external interactions and clienteles as well. These many outside relations and interactions require specialized knowledge and thinking, which is provided by staff organizations. Line organizations are those that run the functional operations of the company. Staff organization are those that think about special problems of the firm originating in the social environment, or outside interactions of the business.

The personnel staff function deals with the human and labor relations of employees within the organization. The tasks of personnel are to assist the organization to define job specifications; evaluate job requirements; set up wage and salary levels; recruit candidates from the outside to fill job requirements; appoint personnel; administer salary and fringe benefit compensations; negotiate with unions on wages and benefits; advise employees about their compensation rights; counsel employees and supervisors on dissatisfactions and conflicts; act as ombudsmen or conciliators in severe conflicts; handle grievances; provide due process in hearing employee claims and rights; and provide for the orientation of employees, training, education, human development, and organizational development. The human relations function is concerned with thinking through all the interactions of the employee within the organization, and providing some procedure with which these interactions can be handled amicably.

This portrait of the personnel functions encompasses such a human range that it prompts several questions. For example, if human fulfillment and development is the final end of society, is not the personnel function doing the whole job? Is not personnel, in fact, *the* business or institution? Is not the personnel function the whole and end of management? Why is the personnel staff not managing the business? The personnel function is caught in the business dichotomy between the ends of the employee and the ends of the institution to organize tasks to produce output. The dichotomy is between the subjective and the objective, between employees as subjective ends, and products as objective ends, which is why business (or government) policy deals with "objectives"—management by objectives; who ever heard of management by subjectives?

That management is objective and personnel relations are subjective creates great difficulty in the positioning of human relations in the policy process. Most executives would say that their major concern, and most of their time, is spent on human relations, and that the personnel department is their agent in this endeavor. Yet, most of the decision making, policy, and planning effort of the executive is concerned with the "objectives" of the institution and arranging the tasks to deliver (objective) outputs.

The consequence of this dichotomy is that the personnel function is generally procedural rather than decision oriented. For the most part these procedural tasks can be clerically performed. Only when there is a labor strike or adversary labor negotiations does the personnel function emerge at the top policy level of the company. The adversary and procedural character of personnel functions causes the personnel department to deal with employees as though they were outsiders—that is, employees are objects from the outside to be fit into an organizational process inside. The organizational process inside is run by the operating departments (production, marketing, and finance) because they are the ones who assign the work tasks that make up the process. Once the employee is objectified as a part or machine who performs a task in the process; and since objects by definition do not have ends in themselves, the employees no longer have ends independently from the organization. The subtle semantics and rationalizations have now turned the personnel function upside down, and the human ends of employees have been converted into institutional means.

In short, the personnel function suffers from the same schizophrenia that plagues marketing or any people-oriented function of institutions. The people are there to be means, to consume and to work. The conscience of most personnel executives will not accept this subtly inverted concept. They strive hard to let employees be heard and to help their development; and they succeed within limits—within the constraint of maximizing objective output. The consequence is that most personnel departments in organizations play a very uncertain and ambiguous role, which for the most part is relegated to a procedural rather than a policy role in management.

Another staff function is procurement, or the buying of materials for the productive process. Since materials are objects, and objects can be maximized into outputs, procurement suffers from no ambiguity of mission, as does personnel. The only dilemma that the procurement staff has is the determination of who is in charge of final procurement decisions? The procurement staff has an expertise in dealing with outside suppliers: who they are, what materials they sell, what the performance specifications of the materials are, what terms of trade are prevalent in the market, what price trends exist, what contract options exist, and what constitutes an optimum procurement contract. These contracts can be delicate negotiations because a supplier is both an integral component of the productive system, upon which the organization must rely for performance, and at the same time an outsider with his own interests. As an outsider with his own interest (caveat emptor), the supplier must be treated as an adversary by the procurement function. As an insider of production as a system, the supplier can close a business down or damage its reputation by failing to deliver materials on time, on cost, or on specification. In short, the relationship of the procurement department to a supplier is rather like a love affair; they both need and want each other but they also want their own identity.

The procurement officer understands this subtle, human relation between himself and suppliers; and he seeks to maximize long-term relations with suppliers to keep a source of supply. Sometimes, this may mean "keeping" the supplier by agreeing to pay a premium for early delivery or during an inflationary period, or by guaranteeing the supplier's survival during a depression by long-term contracts. In these decisions, the procurement manager is compromising the short-term interest of his own firm for the longer-term relationship with the supplier. This is judgmental on the procurement officer's part; and it enables him to keep reliable sources of supply in the long run.

The production executives have little understanding or interest in the human relations ties between supplier and procurement. They are a cost center that wants the cheapest short-term price for materials on hand now. Moreover, they are in charge of the "make-or-buy" decisions. If the component materials cost too much or are not available on time, the production department often will make the components themselves. Many manufacturers make about half their own parts and purchase the other half from outside suppliers, but this split is optional and may change, depending upon suppliers' prices and their effect on profitability. Frequently, the production department will have comparative costs between their own cost to make and the cost to buy. If the cost to buy goes up relative to the cost to make, the production department switches to a "make" decision because their profit will increase. Hence, the "make-or-buy" decision sets up a stress between the production department, which wants to maximize its profits in the short term, and the procurement department, which must maintain reliable sources of supply in the long term. However, the "make-or-buy" decision rests ultimately with the production department, because they are the ones responsible for guaranteeing the delivery, performance, and cost of the final output. Hence, the production department is really the final authority over many procurement decisions, as they affect performance specifications or cost.

Other staff functions include facilities planning, logistic, legal, international, and public relations services. Each of these staff activities also have external clienteles to deal with in the social environment at large. It is beyond the scope of this book to describe the main tasks and dilemmas of each, as in personnel and procurement. The tasks differ because the clienteles differ, but the dilemma is similar. The dilemma is that the outside group or clientele has a separate interest from the internal organization. It is the task of the staff function to understand this outside interest and convey it to internal management. Thus, facilities planning understands and reflects the relationships with outside contractors and suppliers of capital equipment: logistical relationships with outside field service and transportation organizations; legal relationships with litigants and the courts; international relationships with foreign governments and foreign buyers; and public relations relationships with media and the public. These interests diverge from the interest of the internal organization, and the staff function seeks to establish as amicable a long-run relationship with its clientele as possible. In the final analysis, internal operating departments have a disproportionate impact on short-term decisions that affect outputs or profits relative to outside interests.

An uneasy tension persists, then, between staff activities and the internal organization as to whose interests shall be persuasive in immediate decisions. While a cynic might argue that the internal organization will always prevail on short-term optimizations, the staff function still has the role of adjusting these optimizations within a constraint determined by public acceptance that makes it possible to continue a workable interaction with outside clienteles in the long run. The final trade-off, between internal optimization and long-run interactions with outside clienteles, is a policy decision of top management. As a result, staff operations are most effective (from the outside view) when they are close to top management and they condition management thinking about outside relationships and constraints, usually in advance of decisions. With such conditioning, top management itself asks about the impact on clientele or external interests when operating departments make decision recommendations.

5 The Tasks and Process of Business

The functions of business tell us something about the main classes of work that must be performed in an enterprise and the considerations that go into the functional decision process. We saw that most decisions are a trade-off between performance and costs. The exact level of performance or cost depends upon the tasks, or the work to be done, and how the work is done. Therefore, decisions can be made more specific by inquiring into the detailed, or lower level, tasks within the organization to evaluate their cost-performance impacts.

Management is a very detail-intensive activity, which is one aspect of management seldom stressed. The glamour of making sweeping decisions, and the presumed exercise of power, have given the management role a policy coloration that is out of proportion with reality, at least in a time sense. Perhaps 5 percent of an executive's time is spent making decisions; and the balance of his time is spent trying to get sufficient facts and information to make the decision. This means that perhaps 95 percent of an executive's time is concerned with detailed facts and work arrangements. He may be getting facts about people's conflicts and human relations, about the profits of the business, or about what went wrong with sales. What he is seeking in this detail sifting is the work tasks he can alter, either to reduce costs or to improve performance. This cost-performance trade-off is always at the heart of the decision, and more detailed facts about the task environment of the problem are required.

The tasks in any business process are specifically related to the technology involved and the character of the market. Hence, the task environment of a business must be learned on the job; and all we can show here is a methodology for exploring tasks in any business sufficiently to extract the cost-performance detail required in decisions.

The method is to think of all the tasks, however detailed, as related to the functions of business and to its final output. This means that tasks must be viewed as networks of events; and these networks function concurrently so that work is divided and proceeding in parallel. The networks then converge work tasks into larger packages or subassemblies that, at the end, become integrated into a final output. The second aspect of the method is to examine the detail of a business process by means of network analysis, which is to view the sequences of parallel tasks in successively finer detail. Network analysis is sometimes used in operations research to mean the mathematical computation of the time, cost, and probability interactions of the events in sequence. Network analysis is used here more in its scheduling context—the analysis of the time, cost, and performance characteristics of tasks by level of detail. In this scheduling or informational system context, networks are said to have indentures (levels), a term which comes from the programming code numbers used to identify groups, functions, or batches of information. We might set up a code of numbering for functions and tasks that would resemble the following:

1.0 General management
   1.1 Finance
   1.2 Marketing
      1.22 Market sensing
         1.221 Field data gathering
            1.2211 Questionnaire design
            1.2212 Field sampling technique

In this example, marketing is seen as a function of general management; and sensing the condition of the market is one of its subfunctions (as discussed in the previous chapter). Within the subfunction of market sensing, a task of field data gathering may be identified; and one of the more detailed tasks of field data gathering is the design of a questionnaire or survey instrument. In this example, questionnaire design is at the fifth indenture level of tasks to be done in business in the field of marketing.

Network analysis, then, is proceeding to that level of detail or indenture of information about tasks that may be needed to acquire the data on cost-performance characteristics necessary for making a decision trade-off. To do network analysis in this sense obviously means that the investigator (the emerging manager) must have a general understanding of the whole business process, what functional indentures there are, and how far in detail into the indenture level he must go to obtain the decision information.

The previous chapter has already suggested that the first indenture levels are the functions of the business—policy and planning, marketing, finance, research, production, and control, with possible additions from staff services such as personnel, procurements, logistics, etc. The second indenture levels are the subfunctions. In the case of production, they are production planning, material assembly, work layout, facilities planning, processing, assembly, service, and control (see chapter 4). The third indenture level is made of major tasks, and the fourth of more detailed tasks, as in the preceding marketing example.

The total number of indenture levels of detailed information normally runs to ten or twelve. The University of California has ten digits in its accounting code, without fund numbers. A PERT (Program Evaluation Review Technique) network for a missile system would have about twelve levels of task detail and indentures for the engineering work to be done. Management decisions normally require a person to go to the fifth or sixth level of indenture to obtain sufficiently specific cost and performance data to make decisions.

In summary, there is a structure and hierarchy to the levels of information about costs and performance that are crucial to understand to make decisions. In this chapter, the first and second levels of indenture are illustrated in an input-output diagram to give a general idea of the whole business process. Then, twenty detailed tasks at the third indenture level in marketing are described to demonstrate how to proceed down the task levels to do network analysis. Obviously, these twenty tasks are not very far down the indenture level in detail, when one considers that there are over 2000 identifiable marketing tasks that marketing managers must seek to assign and control.

Business Process, Tasks, and Operations

The business process operates by allocating a coordinated network of tasks and work orders among the functional organizational units to achieve a final output. These work orders are allocated (as we have already seen in chapter 3) on the basis of capability, economy, and time. The capability resides first in the functional organization of business, such as in production, marketing, or finance. Within that organizational unit, capability further depends on the learning level of individuals (where they stand on the learning curve for a task) and the technological facilities or equipment available to aid the human task.

The management decisions to subdivide work into divisions of labor are often referred to as delegations of authority at the functional level of business, and as programming at the lower levels—that is, management will delegate to the marketing department those general work functions that have to do with market sensing, distribution, selling, delivery, and measuring demand. The functions and subfunctions are treated as a group; and authority, funds, and performance requirements are delegated to that set of marketing functions. At the lower level (within a department or function such as marketing or production) the laying out of more detailed tasks is often referred to as programming. Programming is a consultative planning operation, because the manager will usually confer with the working staff to see what tasks to schedule, how the work might best be done, how much it may cost, and at what time it may be scheduled for completion. The manager will be experienced enough to know the general network of task assignments that should be performed, but he will look to his supervisors and working staff to suggest in detail how the work should be done, since they are closer to the technology, the market, the worker skills, and the improvements in work that are possible. The detailed task network is thus a suggested list of work assignments from the staff, selectively put into a cost and time framework (the network) by the manager.

How does the manager know what sequence of events to put into the network and what to assign selectively (from the task lists) as feasible in time and cost? The manager generally knows this from experience; that is, he has an experiential or heuristic program in mind, based upon what he has found successful in the past, that he adapts to the future. He knows also the relation of his work networks to the rest of the company, and what time and cost targets his management (policy and planning) will find acceptable.

The manager knows, for example, that the total business process has a sequence that schematically resembles figure 5-1. In this illustration, we see the flow of activity throughout the enterprise, with management represented as the initiator of action through its planning and policy decisions, which are then programmed (implemented) with funds as assignments to the functional departments of the enterprise. These functions represent the first level of indenture of information—that is, the marketing function is a repository for information about the work it has performed, such as market measurement of demand, distribution, sales, and delivery. Production is a collection center for information on its work, which is work layout, programming, processing, assembly, inspection, and output. The solid lines in the chart represent work assignments and work flow. The dotted lines represent the informational feedback control loop. Management is the control, or decision center of the information loop, because it receives feedback information on budget, production, sales, and decision models from its controller unit. Management uses this information to correct its policy and planning—that is, to reduce or raise the levels and kinds of inputs.

Figure 5-1 depicts the interaction of the business functions to form a process, or input-output system. But the diagram does not carry the knowledge of detail about tasks much further than has been discussed previously. Therefore, we want next to see how the detailed tasks fit into the whole business process. This interconnection is shown in figure 5-2. Figure 5-2 represents a flow diagram of twenty detailed tasks relating to the subfunction of marketing labeled as "sensing" in figure 5-1. Figure 5-2 thus is a network expansion of one block (subfunction) in the business process flow chart. Figure 5-2 depicts a greater level of detail about what the work of market sensing is and how it is done. The tasks in sensing consumer needs in the market are made up of four major task assignments in figure 5-2: (1) to ascertain past consumer buying behavior, (2) to measure current buyer demand, (3) to measure consumer attitudes toward the product services of the company, and (4) to assess the general financial attitudes of consumers toward the decision to buy now.

Present behavior can be extrapolated from past buying behavior by a sales data base that contains information about past sales and past owners—who they were, where they were, what buyer ownership still exists, what buyer loyalty or repurchase rates have existed, and at what intervals or turnover rates past owners have repurchased. If these market-sensing tasks are performed, an estimate of current and prospective purchases of past buyers can be made by extrapolation. The current demand or buying pattern of customers can be analyzed in still further detail according to what models have appeal and what distribution channels are most effective. This information can be compiled from data on sales

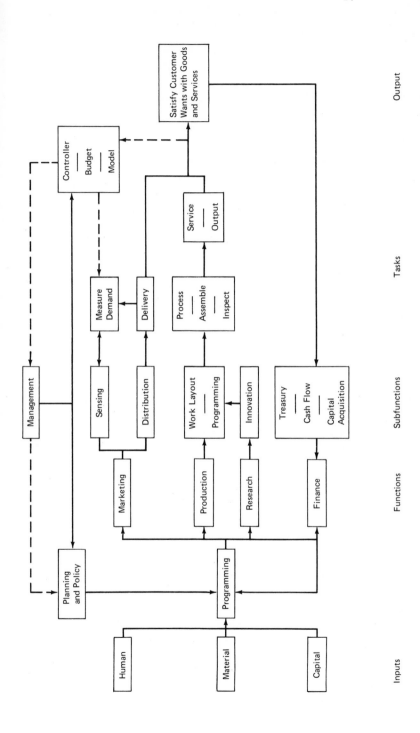

Figure 5-1. The Business Process.

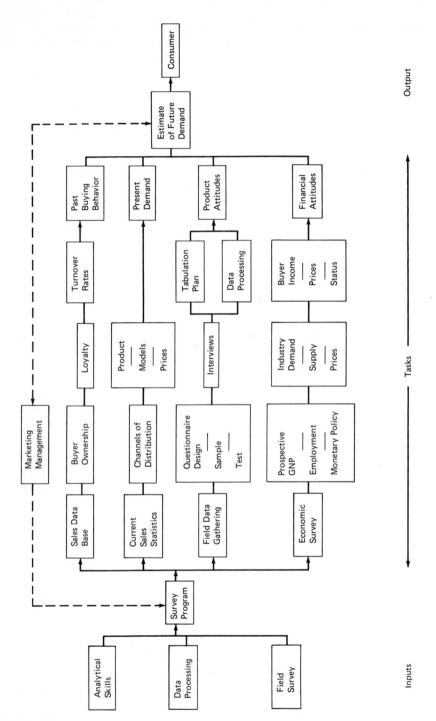

Figure 5-2. The Market-sensing Process.

by product models, distribution channels, and outlets, as well as data on the selling prices (figure 5-2). Prospective future demand can be forecast by conducting consumer attitude studies, which examine consumer satisfactions with products, style, performance, prices, and service. Such attitude surveys require detailed tasks in field sample design, questionnaire design, field test, field interviews, tabulation plans, and data processing.

Whether consumers buy a product depends on their general financial outlook—on whether they feel better or worse off financially. Their financial attitudes depend on the state of the economy; and the state of the economy can be estimated by tasks that gather information on sectors of the gross national product, employment, monetary policy, price trends, industry demand, industry supply, product prices, buyer incomes, the consumer price index, and buying power of the consumer (figure 5-2). If all these tasks are performed by appropriate inputs of human analytical skills, field survey, and data process capability, marketing management can obtain informed estimates of prospective demand.

The task network (figure 5-2) is at the third indenture level in this illustration. Any one of these tasks (for example, determining channels of distribution) could be expanded into a new network (or fourth indenture level) of its own if there is a need to do so. For example, distribution channels are a very costly portion of marketing operations; and for the purpose of making a marketing distribution decision (perhaps to improve the sales per outlet) a more detailed network (fourth indenture level) of tasks would have to be studied to obtain cost and performance data by outlet—that is, if the marketing manager wishes to improve his sales per outlet, he must know what sales performance and cost he is obtaining per type of outlet so that he may select (make a trade-off) the most effective sales outlets, and drop the effort (tasks) expended on the less effective ones. Marketing management is also the control (indicated by the dotted line), representing the feedback control loop. Thus estimates of future demand are compared with actual experience as time advances, and marketing management calibrates the similarities or differences between the estimates and actual data. If the estimates are off, marketing management initiates new survey research programs to investigate the demand factors causing the abberations.

Figures 5-1 and 5-2 together show the general business process by functions, and the breakdown of work flow by tasks. As such, they illustrate that the business process operates by allocating a coordinated network of tasks and work orders among the functional organizational units to achieve a final output.

Efficiency of Operations

The efficiency of operations is controlled by allocating resources proportionate to task efforts within organizational units. Management is then able to organize the activity and effort of a business by allocating tasks within functional departments to keep track of the performance of these tasks (control) through information about the delivery of work and outputs. However, while these allocations of tasks organize the work, they do not assure that the work will flow through the process.

Management therefore next seeks to regulate the process flow, much the same as instruments and valves control the process flow in an oil refinery. To regulate flow, management must have some concept of what constitutes an acceptable or optimum rate of flow. The rate of flow of work is governed by a concept of efficiency. The efficient rate of flow is one in which the final outputs are delivered on time, at the performance specification, and at minimum cost. Any other flow rate is unacceptable. If the output does not meet performance specifications, it lacks the quality and reliability needed for delivery to the customer. If the output is not delivered on time, it may cause a loss of sales among customers, who will not wait, or extra costs in selling and distribution. If the output is not produced at minimum cost, it will not be competitively priced in the market and it will reduce profits.

This efficiency test for the final output can be worked backward through the work flow process and applied to each task. Each task or work order has a performance specification, a time estimate within which it is scheduled to be done, and a cost estimate of how much the effort (man-hours X wages X equipment) will require in expenditures. The task network can then be scheduled in time and budgeted in cost according to these estimates. The performance is assumed to be fixed and determinable by inspection or usage. Then any slippage in time or cost is detectable by the human eye, a data processor, and an exception report. The data processor compares actual time and cost with estimated time and cost. When the actual exceeds estimate, an exception is noted, and this is printed out or flagged as a control action item for management. The manager who looks at this report notes where the tasks are failing to meet their targets and takes control action—that is, he investigates the reasons for the tasks not being accomplished as planned. He investigates by going back down the indenture list of tasks to find the ones that exceeded cost and schedule, then discuss them with the supervisor and the staff to discover what went wrong.

In many cases, there are good reasons for the exception—the estimates were not realistic in the first place. For example, suppose the marketing manager finds from an exception report that the task network on consumer attitude surveys toward product are running over on time and cost (see figure 5-2). When he investigates, he finds that the field survey team is attempting an in-depth psychological interview of a kind they have never done before, and the actual interview times are running twice as much as the estimates. The action of the marketing manager is to correct his time and cost estimates for the future to be more realistic. In another case, suppose the marketing manager finds that the analysis of sales by distribution channels (see figure 5-2) is costing too much in time and money. He investigates with the supervisor and finds that the person doing the analysis is new and unfamiliar with the distribution outlets of the firm; that is, the analyst is low in performance on the learning curve for the task and does not really know what he is doing. The marketing manager, with the supervisor, takes remedial action by intensive training of the analyst, exposing and orienting him to the variety of distribution outlets, so that he can perform his analysis more quickly and with more understanding.

Thus, the efficiency of operations is controlled by comparing (calibrating or instrumenting) actual versus estimated time and cost, and then taking remedial action to bring the two together, either by shortening the actual time of performance or lengthening the estimated time to a more realistic measure. Successive iterations of such feedback control continually improve the accuracy of both the estimates and the actual performance times, until the work flow process may be said to be optimized, balanced, or regulated. When this occurs, the management may then allocate resources proportionate to task efforts within organizational units with some degree of assurance and reliability that the time, cost, and performance targets will indeed be met. Such a condition constitutes a well-managed company.

Decision Process

We have seen how management organizes tasks into a network of work flows that make up the business process, and we also have noted how management regulates the work flow to a measure or concept of efficiency. Efficiency is not an end in itself, however; it is a means to the financial survival of institutions. The decision process seeks to organize the means of production and delivery, within a specified performance constraint, to achieve an optimized financial goal. Management has to be able to make ends meet, to gain enough revenue to pay all expenses, to manage the cash flow so bills can be paid, and, if possible, to make a profit. Executives frequently speak of this process of financial survival as making a profit, or maximizing profit. This shorthand expression for financial survival is so taken for granted by executives socialized into the economic profit that they assume that workers and consumers have the same appreciation of profits as they do. Quite to the contrary, consumers and workers frequently attribute the profit motive to be a self-declaration of greed.

The emphasis on profit as motive is a disservice to business because it attributes to executives the basest of intents for what is, in reality, a fairly complex motive-mission concept. There may not be much doubt that the executive as a person has a motive of self-enrichment in seeking a maximum profit, but the institution as such has a social contract to fulfill human needs and a requirement that its authority and continuance is based upon the allegiance of its clientele. The conflict of interest has emerged again, this time between the executive and the institution (we observed it before between the executive and customers).

This distinction between profit and financial survival is an important concept to consider, because the decision process, by definition, is going to optimize something. The decision process is designed to make a trade-off between two parameters, one monetary and one performance. The profit motive, as an explanation, declares that maximizing earnings is a trade-off between minimizing costs and some satisfactory level of performance (quantity of sales at an acceptable quality to consumers). The executive is willing in his decision to give up sales quantity (which means employment) or product quality (which means consumer satisfaction) to lower costs and maximize profits. However, many executives believe this *is* the decision criterion and act on it in the short run, getting rich themselves, thereby causing trouble for the business institution.

The short-term maximization of profit at the expense of employment and consumer satisfaction is the prescribed course for regulation or nationalization of the industry. The path has been followed by railroads, truckers, maritime shipping, broadcasting, utilities, oil, gas, medicine, hospitals, advertising, banking, insurance, real estate, accounting, pharmaceuticals, airlines, communications, securities, defense, personal finance, food, and coal mining—all of which were once relatively free market enterprises that now have some form of government regulation, licensure, inspection, standard setting, rate-making, or control over their performance. If environmental standards were included, the list would encompass all of industry. The public does not like short-term maximization of profit and resorts to the political arena to control it. This has been happening for one-hundred years, and business is slow to learn. It has become clear by now that simple profit maximization cannot be their sole decision criterion.

If the decision criterion does not optimize profit, then what does it optimize? In the long run, if the business is to survive and be independent of government control, the decision must satisfy financial survival within three constraints whose order of importance are (1) earnings (profit) equal to a competitive money rate for capital and management, (2) satisfactory product performance, and (3) reasonable employment stability. One may argue that this decision definition amounts to the same thing as maximizing profits. But consumers and employees do not contest the desirability of a business surviving; in fact, they depend upon it. They only object to being gouged. Short-term profit maximization leads to decisions of opportunistic gouging—recently, in sugar, wheat, meat, food, and oil; in the past, in all the industries that are now regulated.

The decision criterion for financial survival is to make ends meet, subject to a competitive money rate to attract capital, good products, and stabilized employment. The money market in this criterion takes care of the earnings, or profit rate. Formerly, such money rates, judged by price-earnings ratios on the stock exchange, were of the order of 10 percent. Since inflation, they have risen to perhaps 15 percent. The executive under such a criterion makes ends meet (balances income with expenses), allowing for a current money rate, with reliable products and reasonably steady employment. Judgmentally, he is devoid of self-interest and greed. He is making decisions that the following markets require of him: (1) the money market, (2) the consumer market, and (3) the employment market.

To summarize, then, management organizes work by allocating coordinated task networks to functional organizations and controls the task performance to a time and cost that enables the company to earn a competitive money rate, deliver satisfactory products, and maintain employment. This is the long-run decision criterion of business. Those who prefer to be regulated by government may try short-term profit maximization.

Decision Impacts on Allegiance

In the previous section, we treated the performance level of business with respect to product quality as fixed, to minimize costs sufficiently to earn a competitive money rate and maintain employment. This decision criterion is *intermediate* in time frame (not a short-term gouging decision, which brings regulations), a survival decision that brings in adequate funds from the money market in the intermediate (three to ten years) term. In a still longer time frame, over the life of the business (for example, ten to fifty years), a corporation needs not only to survive from year to year, but also to maintain its authority to retain the freedom of action it needs to adapt to changing times.

The railroads are now over one-hundred-years old, heavily regulated, and so constrained by authority that they can scarcely cope with their problems. The demise of the Penn Central and the prospective failures and consolidations of other railroads suggest an industry in desperate straits. Yet railroads are vital to the nation. A three-day rail strike in California nearly shut down the state's economy. How can so vital an industry have so little authority, so few degrees of freedom left in its decisions that it cannot cope with the present? The answer in part is that the railroads have few allegiances—people who support, trust, and grant authority to it. Early railroad history gave them a reputation for abuse of authority: high rates, shady land practices, hired gunmen, and the "buying" of state legislatures. Railroad regulation changed these practices, and in the process limited management discretion over its own survival needs—for example, in setting fair rates in competition with trucking. Now railroad management decision making is so limited that the railroads cannot get capital in competitive markets to maintain roadbeds.

The automobile industry, now seventy-five-years old, has somewhat similar problems. Although they do not have their rates and practices regulated, the automobile companies are now having to meet severe air pollution standards at a time when the changing petroleum supply also dictates higher gas mileage for consumer satisfaction. The automobile companies are protesting that these requirements cannot be met and are asking for delays in meeting air quality standards. The allegiances to the automobile industry are not great enough to provide strong public support for their claims. Indeed, allegiances may be moving the other way, as evidenced by the freeing of highway funds for rapid transit. In the long run, business executives need substantial freedom in decision making to meet the drastic changes that occur in technology, the environment, or their markets. Businesses who let their authority erode slowly, by maximizing their short-term interests, find themselves without the support or allegiance to maintain the authority needed for heroic change.

Authority is a grant of authority by those who give consent to a management to act in their behalf. Allegiance is a two-way pact: management acts on the behalf of its clientele, and the clientele support the decision-making powers that management needs to cope with change. In the short run these grants of authority by consent do not seem very important to some business executives, but in the long run they mean the difference between being regulated and not being regulated. The list of regulated businesses is very long. These are businesses with diminished authority over their own decisions. In some cases, the decision-making authority is so diminished that the business no longer has sufficient degrees of freedom to cope with current problems. This kind of business is in dire trouble, and there is no easy formula for giving authority back to the business, because authority comes from allegiance.

If the allegiances have eroded over time by the acts of the business, to a point where people no longer trust the decision makers, that trust cannot be recreated by a legislative act. The business brought the erosion of allegiance upon itself; and at some stage the erosion became irreversible. The satisfactions received from the business by workers and clientele are so minimal that they no longer care to consent to new authority grants. Decision makers need to reckon allegiances, year by year, in their decision criterion, so that fifty years hence their institutions will not be without authority to grapple with the issues affecting its survival—that is, the decision criterion used by management determines allegiances to business in direct proportion to the satisfactions received by its clientele and workers.

Social and Political Environment

We have been discussing essentially a social law of reaction applying to business decisions, similar to Newton's third law of motion, Buddhism's law of karma, or

Christianity's Golden Rule. Business earns its authority and its allegiances by its own acts; and acts that are not in the public interest bring an equal reaction in the opposite direction. The specific regulations of a business or industry are largely of its own doing. We cannot gainsay the reality of such reactions, even if we sympathize with the plight of the railroad industry at the present.

Beyond these specific reactionary regulations that a business brings upon itself, the social and political environment often place additional constraints upon business that are more general and sweeping in nature, such as regulations, standards, due process, and procedural requirements. That is, their cause is attributable more to social than business origins. Such policies as affirmative action, equal employment opportunity, social security, due process in administrative procedure, credit regulation, monetary constraint, labor arbitration and waiting periods, land use zoning, pesticide control, fuel and material allocations, radio frequency allocation, air traffic control, and some environmental controls (such as environmental impact statements) are basically social in origin, arising from blockages in the system where institutions do not work together.

Some regulations and constraints thus originate in the failure of interinstitutional interfaces to mesh. This is not the business decision maker's error or omission; he usually does not have enough information on the whole system to decide how his work flow will mesh with someone else's. For example, an airline might make very appropriate and rational decisions about its flight schedules, rates, services, consumer satisfactions, and employee satisfactions, and still could easily schedule a plane to take off just in time to collide with another. Hence, air traffic control is needed to monitor the performance of one airline operations schedule versus another. Each airline has suboptimized its own operations; but, not knowing all other flight plans, an air traffic controller has to integrate the work flow of the total flight system. Similarly, an individual business may be providing retirement benefits for its employees, but the total social system may still not be providing social security. Or again, a business may be conserving its use of credit, but the total economic system may be overusing credit, creating a need for government monetary constraint.

Thus the government is the controller of the social work flow of the whole society, in the same sense that business management regulates the work process flows within a company. As the regulator of the work flows in the total society, the government attempts to interface them by employing standards, procedural requirements, due process, constraints, or regulations.

Change Forces Affecting the Business Environment

We saw in the beginning of chapter 3 that change presents problems, problems require decisions, and decisions cause change. Hence, change is iterative. In chapter 3 we decided to enter the circle at the level of human problems, needs, or demand, because problems are a peculiarly human perspective. So we have explained, in chapters 3, 4, and 5, the nature of human needs, demand, business missions, business decision processes, functions, the allocation of tasks, the integration of task networks into outputs, the control of task networks by financial survival decisions, the effect of a decision criterion on allegiance, the effect of allegiance upon business authority, and the control of business authority by government regulation—that is, we have been once around the change loop, as visualized in figures 1-1, 5-1, and 5-2.

We now examine the entire loop and ask the question: What are the major forces causing change in business? This question is crucial to management, because to manage is largely to adapt to change. Change requires decisions. The decisions of management are made to deal with problems that are caused by the new events, alignments, causes, and impacts that occur with change.

The major forces of change in business are consumer demand, technological innovations, and social responsibility. Others could be mentioned, such as economic conditions, political events, wars, weather conditions, natural catastrophes, mergers, takeovers, and these can all have significant impacts. To some extent, however, they are outside events that management cannot easily affect. Moreover, the most common and regular forces of change that management can influence (at least in part) are consumer demand, technical innovation, and social responsibility.

Consumer demand is the alteration of consumer attitudes and purchasing rates for the products or services of a business. Thus consumer demand is a reflection of changing consumer needs and perspectives about themselves. Demand changes reflect, then, both the changing development needs of the individual, and society's changing attitudes toward life style. The sensing function of marketing is supposed to detect both attitudinal changes. The first set of demand changes, or alterations in the individual's perceptions of his development need, usually calls for some modification of existing products or services, such as improving the intellectual depth of television programming or modifying vehicles for more recreational usage. The second class of demand changes, perceptions of life style, may suggest that a company change its product lines—for example, change from the mechanical machine accounting business to the computer business or from emphasis on personal vehicles to generalized transit. Business has a great deal of trouble adjusting to either of these changes, especially the second, because businessmen see demand changes through the tunnel vision of their present product capability. Their ability to perceive demand changes is confined to minor modifications of existing products—a little more style here or advertising there. This tunnel vision causes some companies and industries to drop behind, or out of the growth areas in the economy.

The second major change force is technological innovations. The executive's perception of technical change is much more precise than his recognition of consumer demand, because technology is an internal perception with the force of organizational expertise and pressure behind it. The internal staff of technical specialists not only innovate change, but they actively promote it for the advancement of technology, the company, and themselves. The self-interest element in promoting technical change internally causes some management problems concerning the objective selection among the innovation possibilities (already noted in chapter 3) created by research and development. The prospective technical innovations available are many; a few have internal spokesmen pressing their case, knowledge, and interest. What about all the external technical innovations? Might they not be better options? For example, the Xerox process proved to be one of the greatest growth products of the 1960s, but the invention itself lay dormant for twenty years prior to its adoption because an outside inventor could not get a hearing.

Business decision makers generally have a low batting average in the selection of technical innovations. Some studies suggest that between 2 and 5 percent of technical innovations attempted in business succeed. Thus even in the best-run corporations, the odds are somewhere between twenty to one and fifty to one against the success of an innovation decision selected by management. Technical innovation decisions will always be risky; but the odds could be improved at least somewhat by avoiding the kind of tunnel vision that occurs in business, known as the "not-invented-here" syndrome. Management can attempt to look objectively outside, as well as inside, for its technical changes.

Social responsibility as a change force in a business originates as a reaction against its own decisions—that is, short-run decisions to maximize profit, at the obvious expense of consumers or workers, are short-sighted decisions. The public reacts by imposing regulations on it, which hobble business decision making permanently. This point was discussed earlier, but the question of what to do about it remains. The obvious answer is to look farther ahead in the decision-making process. One technique for doing so is war gaming, or business gaming. The gaming approach assumes that there is an environment that has interests and forces of its own, and what management does internally in decision making will inevitably, intractably, and indubitably set up some kind of interaction or reaction pattern in the socioecological environment. In other words, a decision creates waves; otherwise, it is not a decision at all. What are those waves? How do they affect the environment? What are the reactions and interactions that could occur? The gaming technique encourages a manager to think ahead and speculate about our interactions with the total social system.

A business-gaming management would make less short-sighted mistakes than are presently made, but the technique is seldom used. The reason is that most decision makers think of business as a closed system, where the enterprise is autonomous and decisions are essentially internal. An autonomous decision is an authoritarian one. Public officials do not make the same mistake in foreign affairs because they know there are other autonomous, authoritarian decision makers in the international political environment. Hence, in international policy, decision makers try to strategize and outguess our cohabitators of the globe in war games.

In business, the assumption is made that the objects in the external environment will remain as inert as those in the internal material processes, but they do not. They react as consumers demanding price controls, environmentalists demanding pollution controls, and citizens demanding government regulatory controls. Hence, controls come as a surprise to business decision makers, showing them that they have a social responsibility that was not obvious when the decision was made. The social responsibility is obvious only when the reaction sets in, regulation occurs, and the decision authority of business has been permanently curtailed—perhaps fatally, as in the railroads.

The dominant change forces affecting business have one thing in common: they all represent a form of myopia and tunnel vision, in which the decision maker is so focused upon his internal optimization of tasks that he sees only the internal world; and he fails to see the larger world in which his company and his decisions are only a small part of an environment (a social system) that will react with or against him, depending upon how his decisions affect broader social interests.

Forms of Business Ownership

All of these major change forces are also areas of accountability in business. Business executives know that they are accountable to stockholders for earnings and for the conservation of assets. What is not as obvious is that business is accountable for its market, technical, and social actions as well. The accountability is not established by the same financial statements that annually respond to stockholder interests. The change forces establish accountability by blows from the outside, by falling sales, by product (technical) or cost competition, or by new government regulations. These blows from the environment effect the financial statements by lowering earnings; but their first impacts are felt in sales, competition, or controls—that is, business exists in an open system; and the environment reacts to business decisions by responses which constitute new changes. The changes from the external environment take the form of new demands or controls that are a form of accountability, a correction for management mistakes, a feedback control for mismanagement. The social environment corrects a company for mismanagement the same way a father corrects a misguided son, or the police a misguided father.

The kind of correction a business receives is related to its form of ownership and size. There are three major forms of business organizations: sole proprietorships, partnerships, and corporations. Corporations are by far the dominant type of business ownership in the U.S. economy due to their advantages in capital accumulation and tax avoidance.

A sole proprietorship is the ownership of a business by a single individual as a person. Because the individual owns the enterprise as a person, the business and owner have all the liabilities and tax responsibilities of a person. A sole proprietorship has unlimited liability for all commitments and acts to the full extent of the wealth of the individual and all his future earnings as a person. A sole proprietorship also has the same tax liabilities as an individual. Sole proprietorships are normally organized by obtaining a business license under state and local law, notifying the public of the business's existence, its form, liability, and address. The unlimited liability of sole proprietorship, as well as the limited capital access of most individuals, means that such businesses are normally small. The owner is highly accountable, personally, for all his acts.

A partnership is a business owned by several individuals who have formed a contract or agreement among themselves, in writing, about the nature of the business and of each other's participation, both in terms of financial contributions and management. A partnership is also formed under state and local law by filing the partnership agreement and obtaining a business license. A partnership, being collective, is often able to aggregate more capital than a sole proprietorship. The partnership, as a group of persons, also has unlimited general and tax liability for its acts, to the full extent of the wealth and income of each and all partners. Partnerships exist mostly in personal service businesses, where the partners can have a professional and mutual relationship and trust among themselves, and where personal responsibility is the essence of the business, as in medicine, law, or finance. Beyond these personalized fields, the risk of one partner making business commitments or mistakes that may wipe out the entire wealth of other partners makes this form of legal organization unattractive.

Business corporations avoid the difficulty of partnerships by limiting the amount of liability only to the capital stock or equity (ownership interest) of the corporation. This means that businessmen can make mistakes without unlimited personal liability for the acts. Corporation income is also taxed on a flat rate rather than a progressive rate, as are individual incomes. An indefinite corporate life also enables corporations to hold assets or wealth indefinitely over the lifetimes of several individuals. These advantages have made it possible to accumulate large aggregations of capital, and therefore corporations have become large in size. Corporations are formed by obtaining a charter under state legislation that defines the purposes of the business and the financial structure of the investors and officers.

The high degree of accountability of sole proprietorships and partnerships has meant that fewer government regulations are aimed at them and their social responsibility. The regulatory controls or corrections directed at proprietorships and partnerships from the social environment have mainly been aimed at fraud or misrepresentation, but otherwise have been less than for corporations. Partnerships and proprietorships are also normally smaller in size than corporations, and, being smaller, they are often more personal and closer to the market, consumer attitudes, changes in demand, and shifts in life cycle. The product and service characteristics of smaller businesses are more sensitive and flexible than larger ones. Hence, consumer demands for regulation of business are often directed less at partnerships and proprietorships than at corporations. Partnerships and proprietorships, being small, also have less access to technology, due to barriers to entry and oligopolistic competition (see chapter 2). Hence, changes in technologies hit them harder than they hit corporations. The forces of change affecting proprietorships and partnerships that are the most severe are, therefore, technological competition and the death of an owner. Technological competition has put most proprietorships and partnerships out of business in mass production and mass retailing. Death of an owner requires the business to be reorganized.

The forces of change affecting corporations are, as stated before, consumer demand, technology, and social responsibilities. The myopia of corporations in these areas is at least partly related to their limited accountability for management mistakes, and to their size, which removes decisions from personal contact with the social environment.

Internal Organization

The legal ownership organization of a business is determined largely by comparative advantages in technological competition, and by avoiding liabilities and taxes. Once the legal form has been established, the internal organization of a business is determined by technology, human specialization, market structure, and size—approximately in that order.

Technology determines scale, frequently due to size of efficient capital equipment (particularly in manufacturing). Economies of scale are not as significant in trade and services; indeed, sometimes the human factor causes an inversion of efficiency with scale. In manufacturing, the minimum investment in capital equipment can be tens of millions of dollars. A paper-making machine, for example, is about a block long, costs many millions, and is not subdividable into smaller, efficient units. Economies of scale can change, however, with new technology. In the tire and rubber industry, for example, the minimum plant output used to be about 50,000 tires per day; this scale was determined by the size of the Banbury mixer, which mixed plasticized rubber with carbon black. Two technical innovations in the 1950s, however, lowered the minimum plant output to 10,000 tires per day by reducing the mixer size and automating the vulcanizing presses to cure the rubber. This change brought a new order of competition to the tire industry, specifically the private brand tires made by smaller plants. Thus the minimum technical size is at least partly a matter of design.

The human tasks required in a business are significantly related to its technology—that is, the technical content of work requires a corollary human specialization. The human tasks take their form from technique, and the internal organization is built up from technical specialties of like tasks into departments. We saw this occur earlier in this chapter, where management decisions allocated a coordinated network of tasks to be done, and then grouped the task networks into organizational units of responsibility, which are made up of similar task specialties and functions.

Market structure will influence internal organization in terms of the specialization of marketing tasks, the degree of personal service required in delivery, and in the form of distribution channels or outlets. Sales through mass discount houses, for example, require a marketing force selling to national accounts. Marketing through independent retailers takes a much larger sales force. Door-to-door sales or service requires a still larger force. Similarly, service calls after sale for repair or maintenance affect scale.

Size itself, whether from technical or marketing structure, imposes its own constraints. The larger the organization becomes, the more difficult it is to get information through the several layers of its hierarchy. Each organizational layer becomes a filter, changing or obscuring the meaning of messages, which causes interferences in the management information feedback system. Management tends to deal with this communications problem by decentralizing operations (perhaps by creating divisions), so that the communication links and decision links are shortened. This decentralization of management reduces the number of hierarchical layers within operating organizations, but increases the need for interaction at the policy and planning level, in effect dispersing authority over production, marketing, research and development, finance, and control (which are big data nets that can get fouled up by too many organizational layers) while tightening up the centralization over policy and planning decisions.

The integration of policy and planning decisions has been largely to assure the financial survivability of a conglomerate corporation. That decentralization has been a major management movement since World War II indicates that economies of scale are not the most critical determinant of size. Management authority is the most important determinant of size, as evidenced by the centralization of policy decisions. If preference concerning authority structure is the key variable in size, then the appropriateness of that authority preference to human ends comes into question (chapters 1 and 2).

Knowledge Requirements of Business Management

The knowledge requirements of business management are a depth of understanding regarding human relations and financial solvency, plus a general, adaptable knowledge of the business process. Business executives generally rise through the ranks of a corporation by performing well on the tasks assigned to them in some specialized department. As they advance, they learn to manage finances, make ends meet, and meet their earnings goals. As they get higher in the organization, they learn to deal with organizational behavior problems—human beings, their relationships, and outside clientele. The typical executive is a specialist first, a finance manager second, and a human relations manager last. The experiential origins of executives are reflected in the priority of their decisions, the actions they feel comfortable in performing, and, hence, the goals of the business. The low priority of human ends and relationships contributes to the three myopias discussed earlier, or the tunnel vision on consumer needs, technical options, and social reactions.

The knowledge requirements of a healthy business are in reverse order to those of the typical executive. A deep understanding of human relations, human ends, the social process, and the forces of change and social reaction is the most essential for the preservation of a business in the long run. A knowledge of financial survivability is the next most vital requirement. The third requirement is to know the business process as a whole and to have a methodology for probing the decision trade-offs (cost versus performance) in any network of specialized tasks.

A business executive has to start somewhere, of course, to learn from experience, because management is an art that can only be guided by formal training and must be applied on the job to be learned. This means that every executive must start in some specialized work, and, indeed, his understanding of task networks will be improved by such experience. The real problem for the young executive is not to be carried away by specialization, which he is often encouraged to do by the simplified mythology in business that his job is merely to optimize networks and maximize profits. This viewpoint, solidified by years of conditioning, is what produces the three myopias that rob businesses of their vitality and authority over time. The rising executive should learn and remember early that the knowledge requirements of business management are depth of understanding regarding human ends and the social process, financial solvency, and the cost-performance trade-offs within the task networks of the business process.

6

The Functions and Process of Voluntary Social Institutions

Voluntary social institutions are assumed, in this discussion, to include all nonprofit institutions other than governments. Such a definition includes a very wide variety of organizations, such as schools, universities, hospitals, health associations, counseling services, and community associations of all types. The activities performed by such social institutions vary considerably, but we concentrate here on the similarities of their management problems, rather than on the dissimilarities of their techniques or technical services.

The commonality among these nonprofit institutions is, first, that they try to provide a personal service in a social context (of other people) to meet individual needs. These services are not of a kind normally available from business, and they are too personalized (as opposed to standardized) to be provided by government.

Second, the service is made available voluntarily—that is, by the wish and initiative of the individual served. For this reason, we call them voluntary, even though some may be public institutions (such as universities) supported by the state. Still, the learning process provided by such institutions is dependent upon volition and participation by the client, or else nothing will be learned.

Third, the service is usually professional (or semiprofessional) and provided without profit. The motive of those providing the service is, then, usually dedication to a public need. The public service character of these activities also means that the participants try to comply with some standards of quality, either of a profession or derived from successful client experience in the past.

Fourth, the services are at least partially experimental, mainly for the reason that every individual is unique and needs a degree of individualized treatment. What may have been successful learning or health practices for the average population may need to be modified for a specific individual. Moreover, changes in times and social context may require innovation in the treatment or process, since education today is different than a generation ago, due to scientific discoveries and changes in the complexity of society.

And last, the services are adaptive—they change with differences in individuals and contexts. In other words, the sum of the experimental responses become part of the knowledge and practice for the future. Hence, the services evolve in an adaptive way with the changes in individuals and the social process.

In summary, voluntary social institutions differ from business organizations in the degree of individualization of services. Business seeks to provide generalized products or services at a profit to a mass market, while voluntary social institutions seek to provide unique or adaptive services to individuals without a profit (at or below cost). Thus, the two types of institutions complement each other.

Mission of Voluntary Social Institutions

The mission of voluntary social institutions is to develop a participative model for helping individuals explore and meet their own needs. Voluntary social institutions are essentially advisory in assisting an individual to explore some need or problem that he perceives. The mission is, then, that of the individual, rather than of the social agency. The social institution merely takes on the mission posited by the individual and then assists in its exploration. The social agency, in this sense, has no mission of its own, except as it identifies itself with a class or type of individual problem, such as health, counseling, or education. Hence, the mission orientation of the institutions takes its form from the method of assistance that it offers, as much as from the class of problems (purposes) with which it identifies itself.

The method or model of assistance used by a social institution can be characterized by its main form of communication by means of an advisory role. The personnel of social institutions are normally advisors, and the individuals or clients are advisees. The nature of this advisory relationship is some form of dialogue, and, hence, the relationships may be characterized by the flow and direction of communication—who is transmitting and who is receiving what. The basic communication relationships in voluntary social institutions are prescriptive, interactive, supportive, and receptive.

Medicine and the health service professions provide typical examples of prescriptive communication or advice. The role of the physician, with his expertise in medical knowledge, is to diagnose the symptoms of illness and prescribe a regimen of life habits and medication that will cure the illness. The physician cannot literally cure anyone; he can only advise the patient how to cure himself. The patient assumes that the physician, with his training and experience in clinical medicine, provides advice that, if followed, will help him to return to normal health. The patient's knowledge of medicine is so limited that he is unable to diagnose and prescribe for himself. Hence, the physician's prescriptive communication is usually taken as dictum that the patient follows faithfully, especially when beset with pain or death. The prescriptive advice of the physician often is not seriously followed when it is preventative and interferes with pleasures, such as diet, nonsmoking, or nondrinking. In other words, the following of prescriptive advice depends upon the motivation of the client, specifically as to the immediacy of the problem and his will to live.

Educational institutions try to use an interactive model of communications to aid the individual in learning. The interactive model assumes that the individual client or student wishes to learn. The school function, then, is to place organizing ideas before the student as intellectual seedings (similar to cloud seeding), and hope that the student's experiential thoughts will coalesce around the seed-idea. These seed-ideas are concepts, theories, formulae, principles, or hypotheses, which are intended to organize bodies of thought into a recollectable and usable framework of reasoning. Since reasoning ability is the main objective of education, the dialogue takes the form of the advisor (teacher) posing issues or situations in which a theory applies and then inquiring of the advisee (student) how he would reason out the extension of the theory or application. The interactive dialogue is a stimulus to learning, assuming the student has a motivation to learn, and the student has his own experiential base of thought to relate to the concepts. Frequently, neither of these conditions prevail, particularly in compulsory education. When the student has little or no related experience, the theory seems abstract and meaningless; and when the concepts seem meaningless, the learning motivation is minimal. Then the educational dialogue ceases to be two-way communication and becomes a one-way lecture—that is, interaction becomes prescriptive, transmitting facts and empty concepts. The immediacy of these concepts, and their relation to living (will to live), is obscure, as in the preventative medicine case. Hence, the advisee follows the prescription only as remembered or as is convenient in the future. The learning loss or inefficiency of education is thus directly related to its lapse into the prescriptive, as opposed to the interactive, mode.

A supportive form of communication is much more personal because it originates with the individual as the transmitter. Note that in the prescriptive or interactive mode, the advisor is the initiating transmitter. In the supportive mode, the individual initiates the transmission of ideas, and the advisor is the receiver or listener. This change in communication role immediately signals a change in motivation. The communication would not begin if the individual were not motivated to initiate it. Therefore, the dialogue begins with something of immediate and personal interest to the individual. Consider an example of marriage counseling, Alcoholics Anonymous, or a suicide prevention service. These voluntary social institutions stand by to receive calls for help. The individual who calls for help recognizes himself to be in desperate straits with which he can no longer cope. He seeks advice on how to handle a personal, emotional disaster that may be a marriage crisis, a drinking addiction, or self-destruction. The call for help is itself a statement of the problem that the individual is encouraged to elaborate on and ventilate to the extent he perceives his own problem. The advisor is initially passive, hearing the individual's self-evaluation and despair. The advisor then becomes supportive, identifying with the individual, establishing empathy, and demonstrating that the individual is not alone in his trauma. Others, too, have faced the trauma; perhaps the advisor was an alcoholic or near suicide. The feelings and emotions are shared. The advisor invites new emotions, things not thought of by the individual, based upon the experience of the advisor or others. Has the advisee considered what it would be like to be unmarried and live alone? Can the pain that leads to drink or suicide be alleviated in some other way, perhaps by talking about it or transferring pain and guilt from himself to the advisor? The new questions, the new emotions enlarge the problem, the options, and the hope. The advisor becomes more supportive, showing the advisee that the problem can be shared, that options do exist and hope is possible. The advisee begins the transference of some of his pain, and then he becomes more free to explore optional behavior that is open to him. The advisor may again become the listener, letting the individual find his own way among alternatives he perceives. In short, the supportive role is one where a person identifies with the individual and encourages (counsels) him to explore his own psychological being and options.

The receptive mode is even more nondirective than the supportive role. The advisor in the receptive mode is primarily a receiver of communication, and the individual is the transmitter. The individual again is motivated to convey some traumatic experience to another, to relieve himself of anguish or of guilt. The advisor establishes himself as noncritical and forgiving of any behavior, as in a religious confessional or psychoanalysis. The individual airs his guilt and despair, in the process transfers it to another, and learns from himself how to avoid repeated pain.

In summary, voluntary social institutions assume their mission in two ways: by identifying themselves and their expertise with a class of personal problems among individuals; and by the mode of dialogue that they choose to conduct with the individual. The success of the advisory function tends to be proportionate to the motivation of the individual to deal with a problem of immediate personal interest.

Functions

Voluntary social institutions have a number of functions common to all institutions that relate to their own maintenance and the production of a service. In this respect, a voluntary social institution may be said to have many of the aspects of a business, such as research, marketing, production, finance, control, and policy (as in chapter 4). The more highly institutionalized the social agency becomes (such as large hospitals or the multiuniversity), the more common these functions appear—that is, large social institutions tend to become business-like in direct relation to size. They must, because their services become more standardized and less individualized. The standardization of services causes production-like problems of how to deliver a specified quantity and quality (performance) on time and on cost. (The methods for the performance of these business-like functions can be reviewed by managers of social institutions in chapters 4 and 5 with little difficulty in seeing their applicability.) In other words, a voluntary social institution loses its distinctive character as such to the extent that it standardizes the delivery of its services.

We now concentrate on those functions which are distinctive among voluntary social institutions that maintain the individualization of their services. Such voluntary social institutions would necessarily inquire more about these functions and usually (but not necessarily) be smaller in size. A sense of inquiry is a necessary condition for voluntary social institutions with individualized services because every individual is unique. Inquiry must establish the uniqueness; and an adaptive response to the uniqueness of each person is the condition of individualized services. The sense of inquiry in voluntary social institutions gives rise to three unique functions: need analysis, voluntary participation, and self-learning.

Need analysis is the exploration with the individual, or in the community among individuals, of the unmet human needs with which the individual is unable to deal due to lack of knowledge or experience. Recall (from chapter 1) that a management function must be performed when an individual cannot meet his own needs, but must seek some form of group action to satisfy them. Voluntary social institutions perform that management and technical function in newly emerging fields of social change. Over the last one-hundred years, for example, the evolution of new social needs has brought into being the following types of voluntary social agencies:

Immigrant naturalization services
Boy Scouts, Girl Scouts, and 4-H clubs
Temperance associations
Travelers' aid
Red Cross
Legal aid
Community settlement houses
Tuberculosis association
Public health associations
Mental health associations
Preschool and child care agencies
Salvation Army
Delinquent assistance agencies
Food distribution agencies
CARE and international assistance agencies
Alcoholics Anonymous, Weight-Watchers, etc.
Marriage counseling
Venereal disease prevention
Suicide prevention
Pregnancy and abortion assistance
Cancer association

Heart association
Drug abuse assistance

These are only a few of the typical areas in which voluntary social institutions fill in the gaps of unmet needs that fall between government and business services, and the list appears to grow year by year, despite the rapid expansion of government. The burgeoning of voluntary social institutions is an indicator that the social process as a whole is not meeting human needs, and that unmet needs, growing apace, find no receptive recourse other than in voluntarism.

Beyond need analysis—or the constant alertness to the rising tide of unmet human needs—social institutions have a second unique function, which is the nature of voluntary participation. Not only is the individual client a voluntary participant in seeking the service, but those who provide the service in an advisory or assistance role are also largely made up of volunteers. Indeed, in many voluntary social agencies, the preponderant part of the service is provided by volunteer participation under the general guidance of a few professionals who supply technical, program, or management support.

The development of volunteer participation is a management art requiring a keen sense of motivation and recognition of volunteer effort. Indeed, it would be similar to having employees in a business who were so motivated that they did not seek compensation. If business management approached its employee relations problems the way a manager of volunteer social institutions cultivates volunteer interest in his institution's jobs, there would be many fewer employee complaints in business. Volunteer participation is often motivated by someone who has been touched deeply by the human problem concerned; for instance, many volunteers to the heart or cancer associations have lost family members or loved ones due to the disease. Similarly, those in alcohol, drug, or suicide prevention have often been victims of those illnesses. Volunteers are motivated by a profound interest in the human problem; and the management function in the volunteer social institution succeeds by giving them a worthwhile activity in dealing with the affliction, and by giving them recognition and appreciation for the work they do. These are good human and employee relations principles anywhere, but they are essential to the survival of voluntary agencies.

The third unique function of voluntary social agencies is to aid the individual in self-learning, or adaptation. Self-learning requires that the voluntary social institution find a way to help the individual search out his own identity, interests, purposes, and needs. This identity search defines the problem, to which the individual can pose alternative solutions. The individual then learns by making an experimental response to his problems by trying a plausible solution. If it works, he is rewarded with the satisfaction of feeling confident about handling such a problem in the future—the reward or satisfaction reenforces learning. In other words, the advisor helps the individual seek his identity, problems, alternatives, experimental responses, and reinforcement. These are the elements of adaptation and self-learning.

Task Organization

The individual client, coming to a voluntary social institution for assistance, is in a searching mode; that is, he tries to identify and solve a personal problem. To be of assistance, the social institutions must also engage in the inquiry and search; and, hence, their tasks become exploratory. Indeed, their expertise and techniques *are* exploratory; for example, medical diagnosis is an exploratory examination of symptoms and pathological condition. In education, learning is an exploratory methodology of advancing hypotheses and reasoning alternative proofs. In alcoholic or suicide prevention, the tasks are to explore the basis for neurosis and suggest empirical solutions.

The tasks of a social institution, then, are in the first instance exploratory—to help the individual identify his problem accurately. Once the personal problem is adequately defined, the next task is to examine alternative approaches to solution. These alternative solutions are drawn from experience, frequently from clinical experience where surrounding conditions are controlled to the greatest extent possible. However, individuals are variable in their physical and experiential make-up. Therefore, it is not fully predictable whether a past clinical treatment will correspond sufficiently to the psychosomatic state of the client, together with his surrounding control conditions, so that the solution is workable. The advisor then tries to make as high a probability match as possible between past clinical experience and the state of his client; but, ultimately, there is no test for the proposed solution except to try it out. The method thus is heuristic, which means that it is derived from an experiential model but proceeds by trial and error.

It is hoped that the clinical experience and expertise of the profession practiced by the social agency will yield a high probability of success after an early trial treatment. The trial itself is an experiment. The client individual is then encouraged to construct an experimental response to his situation. If the experiment works, the individual is rewarded by his own satisfaction and repeats the experimental behavior until it becomes reinforced and natural to him. Then, the individual may be said to have learned and adapted. The third major task of social institutions, then, is adaptive learning and reinforcement.

Performance and Efficiency

The performance and efficiency of social institutions are measurable more by clients than by management. Since adaptation of the individual is the ultimate objective of a voluntary social institution, the performance or output of the institution's services (assistance) is known to the client more exactly than to the institution. For example, a student knows whether he has learned more exactly than a teacher; a patient knows whether he feels well more accurately than a physician; and a husband and wife know more accurately whether a marriage is working than a marriage counselor. The teacher, physician, and counselor may, it is true, administer tests to try to confirm the adaptation. But the test will reveal only objective evidence; does the student know facts, does the body function normally when measured by instruments; do the measurable attitudes of marriage partners seem normal? These tests do not tell anything about how the clients feel, or how they function away from the testing site; and these are the only performance characteristics that count, since the clients came for help in the first place because they did not feel alright. Do they now feel alright? The answer to that question is knowable only to the individuals, and only by hearsay to a social institution's management.

The validation of the performance of voluntary social institutions can only be accomplished, therefore, by the organization of hearsay information. But the organization of hearsay performance is subjective; and the validity of testimonials, however broad, is always conditional upon environmental influences other than the treatment or service provided by the social institution. Thus, subjective validation of performance is not acceptable in an objectively oriented world.

Voluntary social institutions thus revert to a strategy of measuring the quality of their inputs rather than outputs as a means of demonstrating performance, and the quality of the inputs symbolically comes to represent the quality of the output. Therefore in education the quality of the students is a key measure of the performance of a school, as measured by input data such as past grade-point averages or test scores, which really say nothing about the contemporary learning performance achieved in the ongoing classes. Also, the quality of the school is measured by the publications and credentials of the faculty—again past input data that say nothing about what the student is currently learning in the classroom. Similarly, in medicine the quality of the medical service is symbolically represented by the credentials of the physicians. In mental health and psychological counseling, the quality of performance is measured by the licensure of its clinical staff.

The use of input measures as surrogates for an output measure is a nonsequitor, which is a cause of embarrassment to many social institutions, particularly in medicine and education. In these institutions, quality is a symbolic word of great emotional defensiveness, precisely because the basis for identifying quality is tenuous and ambiguous. The tenuousness of the argument that input measures justify performance causes such institutions to make input control a social drill in which credentials, publications, admission requirements, grades, diplomas, files, medical records, and documentation become fetishes. The larger the social institution becomes, the more important these fetish records are because they are used to justify performance to a third party (such as the government, financial source, or courts), which has no direct knowledge of the benefits of the services to the first party (client).

The smaller and more voluntary the social institutions are, the more they can avoid surrogate-symbolic justification, because the volunteers have firsthand knowledge of the service benefits provided to clients, since they also took part in ministering the services. In a sense, then, voluntarism is a key to valid performance measurement in personal service-type social institutions, because it equates the value of the outputs to the input effort in the minds of common observers.

Control

Because output performance in personal services is not readily measurable, management places its controls on inputs rather than outputs. The output is recognized only as a volume of work load, measured as case load, patient load, student load, etc. This measure says nothing about the quality of output, but satisfactory performance is assumed by controlling the nature of the inputs. Therefore, the management control focuses on the amount and type of inputs into the process.

The first main control used by social agencies is manpower control, which is a table of organization showing how many professional or staff positions are to be provided for a given work load. This manpower control table also specifies the credentials of the staff. The credentials plus the quantity of staff is thus an input control that is presumed to assure good performance at the output side.

The second main control in social institutions is programmatic or line-item budgeting of all other expense accounts (other than personnel). All material, equipment, facilities, travel, communication, and supply inputs are prorated and controlled proportionate to the work load. Thus hospitals develop their budget and controls around the number of hospital beds and patient days. These measures determine facilities, space, material, equipment, and supplies. In education, the inputs are controlled in terms of floor space per student and faculty, plus equipment, supplies, and expenses proportionate to student enrollments.

The third major control over inputs is in terms of cost accounting limitations. Each class of expense, and each organizational unit, is treated as a cost center; and each cost center has a total cost as well as line-item costs, neither of which can be exceeded. In a hospital, for example, a surgical tray of specified materials has a standard cost that is not to be exceeded on an average over the accounting period. Similarly, in education a department has a total budget, an academic salary, and expense-item budgets. The funds are not normally transferable among the line items, and the total is not to be exceeded.

The management controls in social institutions are consequently used to lock in the inputs, so that their discretionary use is minimal. This is one of the significant differences between social institutions and business. In business, the management controls are output oriented, because the output performance and quantity is more easily measurable. In social institutions, the performance of output is not measurable, and management seeks control by locking in the inputs, which in their minds guarantees the output and its performance. The controls are of three types: manpower, material, and monetary (budgetary cost center) control. Manpower will normally constitute 60-80 percent of the total cost of voluntary social institutions; hence, the controls are redundant. Budgetary control thus is also a control over manpower and material; but as a line-item (nontransferable) control in itself, the budget imposes an additional constraint on top of the manpower and material controls. The adding of constraint upon constraint in voluntary social institutions gives middle-level management very little discretion or flexibility, compared to middle management in business. Large social institutions tend to be heavily controlled from the top down, precisely because their measure of output is indeterminate and embarrassing.

Again, this heavy-handed input control is not as prevalent in smaller social agencies with a high proportion of volunteers as it is in large social institutions. Such social agencies as community relations organizations and the cancer or heart associations depend heavily upon volunteers. The manpower cost in these social agencies is therefore comparatively low; and the main management decision is the allocation of volunteer time as well as supplies and expense budgets. These voluntary agencies tend to control programmatically (very much as business does), which is to assign broad time allocations of volunteers to functions (for example, to cancer or heart screening clinics) and to allocate expenses proportionately to the number of clients served. In such agencies, the program managers and the volunteers have broad discretion concerning the use of funds in relation to client needs, because they are personally close to the clients and can judgmentally equate the value of the expenditures to the value of the service.

Finance

The mobilization of funds assumes more significance than control as a major management function in voluntary social agencies. The foremost function of the chief executive of a voluntary social agency is usually fund raising. This is true of presidents of universities (public and private), hospitals, health agencies, counseling agencies, or community agencies. The primacy of fund raising stems from the nonprofit character of the institutions and the fact that many, in seeking to fill human needs, charge less than cost for services. An institution that tries to operate on a less-than-cost basis has to make up its deficit elsewhere, usually from private donors or government appropriations.

The management of voluntary social institutions have the primary function of raising funds elsewhere than from clients, and this fund mobilization requirement drives them to justify their performance to third parties who have no personal knowledge of the service. Since there is no adequate performance measure of output, the fundraiser must establish the symbolic quality of the service by surrogates measuring the inputs—that is, the fundraiser attempts to prove the worth of the institutional service by displaying the credentials of its staff and clients or qualitative narratives of typical services performed (testimonials). These symbolic representations of the services an institution renders will tend to appeal to donors or legislators, since they relate directly to the giver's value structure. If the donor himself (or someone in his family) was a heart victim, he will be touched by the symbolic appeal of the heart association, which is to say that the values of the social institution correspond with his own. If the giver is a business executive who is a large employer of Harvard MBAs, the business school syndrome of case methods and research will correspond with his value structure and appeal to him. The fundraiser then tries to structure the service appeal of his agency to a corresponding set of values among donors. In essence, the fundraiser is dealing with market segments and market demand in the same sense as a businessman, except his market deals in tax-free philanthropic funds (or tax funds).

We can now begin to understand why the management controls in social agencies are symbolic even though tenuous. They have to be symbolic to raise outside funds; and raising outside funds is the primary function of management in a less-than-cost service institution. Hence, controls have to be shaped to support fund raising that may have little or no relation to performance outputs as perceived by the clients.

The Process of Social Agencies

The process of voluntary social institutions operates by allocating a coordinated network of tasks among volunteers and clients, as well as functional departments, to achieve a prescribed service that symbolically will raise funds to cover the cost of service. Voluntary social institutions mobilize resource inputs in the form of human skills, material, and capital into a planned program of interactive responses with clients for the purpose of delivering a personal service. The management problem is rather similar to that in business, which we observed in chapters 4 and 5 (figures 5-1 and 5-2) to be the allocation of resources to tasks coordinated to produce an output. The differences in the management problem for voluntary social institutions are that the resources to be allocated are largely human skills, time, and effort rather than materials and capital, and, moreover, the output performance is not measurable. These two characteristics change the allocation and control concepts, which are illustrated in figure 6-1.

That service delivery is made up almost wholly of human skills means that

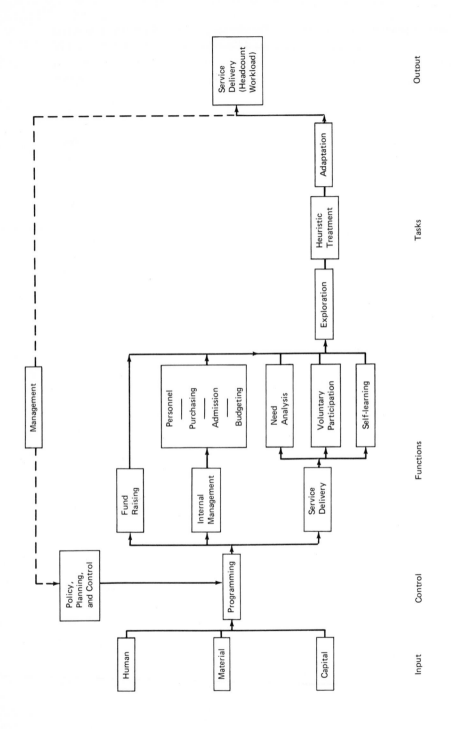

Figure 6-1. The Process of Voluntary Social Institutions.

the task allocation decisions of management are almost completely manpower and time allocations. This is shown in figure 6-1 in the form of the several functions feeding into the directive effort of exploration, heuristic treatment, and adaptation. That the service output is unmeasurable causes the control functions to be folded into policy and planning as a means of programming and controlling the inputs. In the business example (figure 5-1), planning and policy were forward-looking strategies used to develop a measurable output, and control was a postaudit check on meeting objectives. In voluntary social institutions, there is no postaudit check on meeting objectives (other than anecdotal or testimonial), because the output is not measurable. Hence, planning, policy, and control become one—merely controlling inputs.

Figure 6-1 also shows the primacy of fund raising in the mobilization of the finances need to support the service delivery tasks. Fund raising is the equivalent of the finance function in the business process model (figure 5-1), and service delivery is equivalent to the production function. The feedback in this process of social institutions is merely the quantitative work-load measure, which regulates the inputs. The quality of the output is symbolically assumed from the control of the inputs.

Figure 6-1 is mainly a functional description of the process of social institutions with a very broad identification of tasks. Figure 6-2 takes on the task block from figure 6-1, called a "heuristic treatment," and expands it into seventeen more-specific tasks related to learning in education. In figure 6-2 the inputs are the teacher, student, facilities, and materials, which are organized into a program of learning made up of curricula, discipline, observations (issues), and reasoning tasks. In approaching a teaching situation, the teacher bears in mind that the educational institution has a variety of subjects and disciplines in the total curricula that have a bearing on his class discussion; and the teacher then calls upon the students' related knowledge as it pertains to the classroom topic at hand. However, the teacher is most particularly knowledgeable himself in one discipline, which provides the teaching stance or framework of the lesson. The teacher's discipline has a body of literature, a theory of interaction, and a methodology for observing or measuring the interactions. The teacher tries to bring these disciplinary skills into focus, along with other curricula, to create a paradigm or model that the student can use as a framework for organizing his own thoughts, experience, and reasoning.

The teacher then poses an issue or set of observations, from which the student is supposed to discern a human or physical condition or state. As the state changes under observation, the student is expected to identify cause and effect relationships. The observations, state, and causality are then subjects of dialogue among the students and teacher in which they reason what the relationships are and what the alternative performances or solutions may be. To aid them in predicting performances among alternatives, they have the guidance of a paradigm or model drawn from their disciplinary literature, which guides

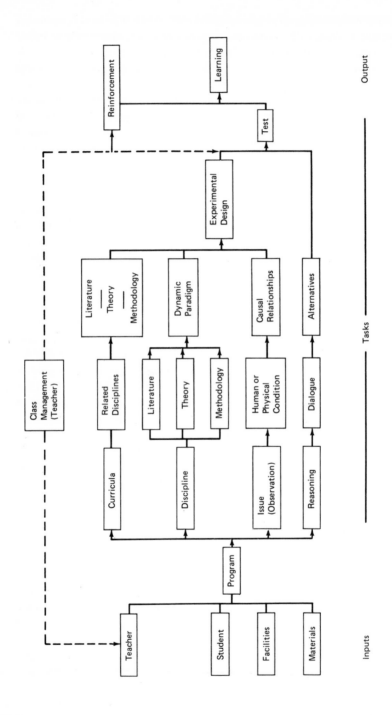

Figure 6-2. Task Network of Education Heuristics.

them on how to construct an experimental design. When they have constructed the experimental design, the students may then test the alternatives or hypothesis as to which meets the test of reality or provides the best performance.

The teacher will normally reinforce the reality testing to demonstrate the theory (paradigm) and to affirm learning. By this affirmation and reinforcement, the student acquires an adaptive behavior to apply in the future in similar cases. Meanwhile, the teacher, as class manager, has a feedback control that confirms the completion of the procedure, thus enabling him to start again with a progressively more difficult set of observations or paradigms. Although figure 6-2 is based upon a heuristic set of tasks from education, the same kind of task network might be constructed for a medical, surgical, and counseling procedure, or any personal service set of tasks.

In practice, the task networks are seldom as complete and objective in voluntary social institutions as they are in business management. The tasks in voluntary social institutions are thought to be within the professional competence of the practitioner, who resents any intrusion on his process due to the defensiveness inherent in the lack of a qualitative measure of output. Also, personal service tasks are usually limited to several interacting persons, and are not linked into complex parallel networks requiring scheduling control to produce a common output. In any case, the task network identification is normally subjective and in the head of the practitioner, if it exists at all. The lack of a clear set of tasks and procedures is one reason why personal services are widely variable, and sometimes quite ineffectual. Or, more bluntly, the absence of clear task networks may be evidence that the practitioner has not really thought through what he is doing. This is a quality control variable for which the management of voluntary social institutions have no regular feedback.

The Decision Process

We saw in chapter 5 that a business decision constitutes a trade-off between cost and performance. In social institutions the performance characteristic is ambiguous or immeasurable; and, hence, the rational trade-off between cost and performance is very difficult. The cost side of the decision can be rationally calculated; and, hence, part of the decision is minimization of cost. The decision process of voluntary social institutions thus seeks to achieve a prescribed (input-controlled) service at minimum cost within a political or bargaining context. Cost minimization is a significant decision factor in social institutions, because it is a companion skill to controlling the inputs, which is basically all the control the institution has. Moreover, it is important in an institution that must use outside fund raising to cover the deficit caused by charging less than cost for its services. Thus, cost minimization gives a sense of austerity to the operation that assists in the fund-raising appeal.

The other half of the decision parameter—what to do about an ambiguous performance measure—forces the decision into a political mode—that is, the adequacy or quality of performance has to be prescribed or agreed upon. This agreement requires consensus among practitioners, managers, donors, and clients. For the most part, however, clients come and go; and when they go, clients walk off with the only actual evaluation of the efficiency and performance of the service in their heads—the efficiency of performance is more known or measurable by clients than management. Moreover, if the client can be debriefed about his evaluation, it is subjective and testimonial, which does not stand up well in fund raising.

The quality of performance of the prescribed service therefore has to be agreed upon by the practitioners, managers, and donors. This agreement is a value judgment of a social group; and value judgment agreements are essentially political in nature. Moreover, the agreement is symbolic because its application is going to the control of inputs rather than outputs. Symbolic consensus requires a special kind of politics, which has been called insider politics (or the politics of a sacred community).

Iannaccone and Lutz[1] have pointed out that professions are likely to develop a process of sanctification of their work, because the diagnostic and remedial application of their special knowledge is probabilistic. They cannot be certain of their judgments or results due to variations in individuals or ambient circumstances. Therefore, the cloak of professional mystique (or sanctification) protects their self-image and their clients' confidence in the profession. The mystique and sanctification is maintained by establishing the condition that only those with special knowledge (insiders) are capable of judging performance. This condition gives rise to the politics of insiders, which Iannaccone and Lutz[2] describe as having these characteristics:

1. Governance resides in a board of elites or interest factions.
2. Semiformal consultation among the elites takes place before board (or management) meetings to establish consensus.
3. Debate is discouraged.
4. There is little loyal dissent, rather a show of unanimity.
5. Invisible politics takes place by informal agreements among the elites in the power pyramid.
6. Nominations to policy or managerial positions are controlled by insiders.
7. Management is a closed system.
8. The closed system produces crisis governance as an unchanging board encounters new forces from the outside (such as changing populations, needs, or finances).

By closing the management system and discouraging debate, the decision makers are able to achieve a consensus among themselves upon: a level of performance (however ambiguous), the nature of the input controls, symbolic sanctification of performance, creation of professional mystique, and avoidance of conflict or debate over results. The closure and sanctification of the management system through insider politics establishes a sacred community, which hopefully is immune from attack by outside forces such as "laymen."

The medicine, law, education, ministry, health services, and community agencies have been using this form of insider consensus as a main decision mechanism with considerable success over the years. It tends to break down to some extent during periods of rapid social change, when outside laymen (who do not recognize their place) intrude on closed management systems to voice and debate new needs. This forcing of debate creates crisis because the sacred community, being monolithic, has little conflict-resolution ability. Examples of conflict forcing itself on closed management systems in recent years have been the rising challenge of malpractice suits in medicine, the student demonstrations over relevancy in education, the election-financing laws and charges of illegal influence in law, and the ethnic demands for nondiscrimination in community agencies.

Insider politics is both the strength (cloak) and weakness of the decision process in professions and voluntary social institutions. It is a strength in protecting an ambiguous performance criterion, and a weakness in suppressing conflict resolution. In short, insider politics and output performance measures are an embarrassment in professions and social institutions that are not talked about openly in management decision making, with the result that the open conversation centers upon cost minimization.

Allegiances

The decision process in voluntary social institutions is insulated from client influence by the sanctification of the service through insider politics conducted by practitioners, managers, and donors. This insulation leads to the possibility that the prescribed service will diverge from the interest of the client group. If the interests and needs of the client group are not well served, allegiance to the social institution diminishes. Allegiance is a mutual pact in which individuals yield decision authority to managers who act in the individual's behalf.

Allegiance is measurable in social institutions by their personal and financial participation rates—that is, by the willingness of individuals to voluntarily seek or staff the services. Participation rates have been declining relative to population recently in a number of social institutions, such as educational enrollments, church membership, hospital occupancy, scouting, service clubs, community settlement houses, etc. Fund raising and volunteer recruiting have become more difficult even for those agencies with rising client participation rates, such as heart, cancer, and health associations. Some of these effects may be caused by competing services and interests. Nevertheless, they suggest the possibility of declining allegiances. If allegiances are declining, an alert management would at least explore whether its insider-specified services are still in line with current social needs.

Social and Political Environment

The social and political environment places few constraints on voluntary social institutions other than a general justification of their service and compliance with the dominant values of the community. Voluntary social institutions are assumed to fill the interstices of society where social needs fall between governmental and business services. Since social institutions are nonprofit and (for the most part) voluntary, they are presumed to need little regulation from the outside. The ultimate regulation is that individuals can cease to participate in their services if they choose.

When government becomes a donor or source of funds, however, regulation is established, as in the case of schools or Medicare. The regulations usually apply to the work-load measure (that is, student enrollments or patient days) and the compensation rates. Such regulation over quantity and rates also implies that the social institution must be prepared or able to justify the worth of its services. The government regulators, however, generally accept the definition of prescribed service performance that comes from the insider, professional consensus. Therefore the qualitative measure of output is seldom subject to regulation. The government and the public, however, do also expect the social institution to comply with the dominant values of the community. The punitive response by government and public to the student demonstrations in the late 1960s and early 1970s is an example of what happens when the social institution does not comply with the dominant values of the community.

Another reaction to deviance from community values is seen in the election of new members to governing boards, which initiates a struggle for governing power on the board, followed by a change in management. Iannaccone and Lutz have traced this process in the change in authority in school districts.[3] The traditional (sacred) community, with its closed-insider decision process, may itself become the deviant from changing values in a secular community made up of new people, new needs, and new coalitions. These new coalitions or power pyramids converge on the social institution through the election of new members to the board, the ouster of old board members of the closed sacred community, the formation of a new coalition, and a change of management.

Change Forces

The change forces affecting social institutions most sharply are new individual needs reflected in participation rates, and new values reflected in elections which rupture old coalitions. Declining participation rates by clients indicate a shift in individual needs. The institution may respond by broadening its service area, such as the tuberculosis association did by broadening into the entire field of lung and respiratory diseases. Another response is to change the method of treatment as exemplified by the abandonment of traditional curricula in some of higher education that have subsequently adopted the "open" or "university-without-walls" concepts. These changes in service—broadening or revisionist—are similar to changes in market demand in business. Voluntary services are a free market in the sense that participation is free; and those who wish to maximize participation are also maximizing demand. Social institutions generally have been weaker in research and product (service) development than has business. A changing society implies that social institutions have adaptive service-development capabilities.

The second form of external change affecting social institutions, besides changing client demand, is changing social values. The external pressure on institutions for affirmative action is an example of value change in the community. Nondiscrimination has become a significant social value through legislation and sentiment, brought partly by pressure from minorities and women, but partly by acceptance from a wider community. This community value change has been reflected in the initiation of new social institutions, such as community relations agencies, and in the changes in governing board membership of old social institutions to contain broader representation of minorities and women.

Internal Organization

The internal organization is determined primarily by expertise, volunteers, and size. Expertise governs the organizational configuration of social institutions because the tasks involved in service delivery (see figures 6-1 and 6-2) are crucially dependent upon a methodology, skill, or profession. Those who practice the skill have an organizational and participative voice in management because they alone can deliver the specified service output. The organizational structure of the practitioner element is usually large in the manpower allocation requirements and prominent in the decision councils of management.

Volunteers in a social institution also present a unique requirement for voice and representation because they are serving without compensation. Therefore volunteer attitudes and motivational interests must be given high priority by management to retain a willing work force to deliver the service. The volunteer recruiting activity will therefore normally be a specialized organizational function; and the manpower allocation of volunteer time (programming) will usually have organizational representation at a high management level to assure the volunteers' willingness to assume task assignments.

The size of a social organization is subject to the same principles of hierarchical layering and communication filtering discussed for business (chapter 5) and is subject to similar management information system requirements.

Knowledge Requirements of Management

The knowledge requirements for the management of social institutions are a depth of understanding of human participation, need analysis, fund mobilization, and insider politics. The participation of clients and volunteers requires motivational knowledge that recognizes human needs, interests, and the desire for recognition. The practical application of these skills, while enriched by a knowledge of psychology, is furthered mainly by a genuine interest in people as well as the practice of persuasive authority (chapter 3)–that is, persuasive authority is effective in direct relation to its personal application.

Need analysis implies an understanding of the changing social process and a research interest in the identification and measurement of attitudes and needs. Need analysis is very similar to the sensing or marketing research function in business (chapters 4 and 5; figure 5-2), with emphasis on the personal attitude research.

Fund mobilization is a financial fund-raising skill that implies knowledge of community social structure, programmed solicitation, and appeal motivations. The knowledge of community social structure is intimately tied with insider politics.

The art of insider politics requires a generalist rather than a specialist[4]–that is, one who can recognize and relate to a variety of diverse social values in a community and serve as a negotiator and bargainer among competing interests. The bargaining art is a delicate one, because the manager must take a firm enough stance on issues to project leadership, but not such a nonnegotiable stance that he loses face and leadership authority by compromising on an issue.

Notes

1. Laurence Iannaccone and Frank W. Lutz, *Politics, Power and Policy, The Governing of Local School Districts* (Columbus, Ohio: Charles E. Merrill Publishing Co., 1970), pp. 54-55.

2. Ibid., pp. 18-28.

3. Ibid., pp. 29-51.

4. Ibid., pp. 39-45.

7 The Functions and Process of Government

Government is the principal institution in the social system that is intended to act on behalf of all of the people. Voluntary social institutions and business have specific clienteles and services. Presumably, if business, social institutions, and individuals fulfilled all human needs, there would be little requirement for government. Government comes into being to settle conflicts and to fill in gaps that are caused by inability of business, social institutions, and individuals to meet human needs. The growing size of government over the past half-century, then, is a measure of the widening gap between human needs and the capability of existing institutions to fill them. The widening gap is an indicator of the mismatch between institutional activity and human needs, or the growing failure of the social system.

The government seeks to remedy failures in the social process by three main means: (1) providing the missing services itself, (2) redistributing income, or (3) reallocating authority in the social process. For example, the medical care services for the total population have been felt to be inadequate, especially for the poor; and government has increasingly been subsidizing medical care or providing medical services. The same situation has occurred in housing, transportation, food, urban development, research, agriculture, environment, energy, education, and social services.

When the provision of missing services is not a feasible remedy, the government seeks to redistribute income, which gives individuals the means to provide missing services for themselves. Social security and unemployment compensation are examples of income redistribution—that is, the transfer of tax revenues from those with higher incomes to those with lower incomes. Social security payments now constitute about 20 percent of the total cash receipts of the federal government; and these transfer payments are expected to grow substantially in the future, perhaps to a point where they are no longer politically or economically supportable.

The third method of dealing with the gap in human needs, when neither providing service nor redistributing income seems plausible, is to reallocate authority in the social process. The reallocation of authority takes place by authorizing legislation giving a new institution new powers to deal with a new problem. The creation of the Small Business Administration and the small business capital investment banks is such an example—that is, legislation created new public and private institutions that would channel investment funds into small, new enterprises. Another example is the Atomic Energy Commission, which created new public and private activities in the mining of uranium, in engineering, and in the development, construction, and operation of new nuclear power plants. The recently created Energy Research and Development Agency is currently attempting to accomplish a similar mission in the development of new sources of power, such as oil shale, coal gasification, and geothermal or solar energy.

The fact that the government uses three main modes to remedy failures in the social process (that is, the provision of services, the redistribution of income, or the reallocation authority) gives government functions some of the characteristics of business and voluntary social institutions. For example, in seeking to develop energy or new small businesses, the government is producing a goods or service the same as a business would. Its mission is production of business-type services. Hence, in this production mode, the government performs essentially the same role as business and uses the same decision-making techniques as business (chapters 4 and 5).

When the government provides social services on a stop-gap basis, such as welfare and health care, the government behaves in much the same manner as a voluntary social institution, performing similar functions in the production of the services and using similar management approaches (chapter 6). The main difference is that the government, in performing a social service, usually provides one, standardized, minimum option of service, rather than a variety. The result is that the individual has little choice, other than to take welfare services as they are or not at all. In this sense, government is an involuntary social institution providing missing services on a minimal basis.

The government's role in redistributing income and reallocating authority, however, is unique to government and not common to other institutions. The process of redistributing income or reallocating authority is political—it is a negotiated compromise among divergent interests. The unique aspect of government thus is its politics of negotiation, the confrontation of issues among differing parties. The politics of confrontation and negotiation is sometimes called pluralistic or outsider politics, to distinguish it from "insider politics," which we encountered in our discussion of voluntary social institutions (chapter 6). The government has its share of "insider politics" as well, particularly in its role as a regulator of business or as an involuntary social institution providing welfare services. However, the unique feature of government is its "outsider politics," or the politics of negotiation and compromise, which occur in the legislative process in attempts to redistribute income or reallocate authority. This chapter concentrates on these unique features of government—its income redistribution and authority reallocation role by negotiative politics—and assumes that the government's production of business and social services can be managerially understood by their similarity to those described in chapters 4, 5 and 6.

Mission of Government

The mission of government is the judicious use and distribution of authority in society. Justice as an ideal is commonly accepted by almost everyone. The problem is that the definition of justice also differs among almost everyone.

Political Definition. People often view justice as what seems fair to themselves and their own interests in relation to the interests of others. However, the individualizing of justice in this sense makes it a political definition, because it then becomes necessary to weigh the relative interests of one person or group against others.

Legal Definition. To avoid politicizing the definition of justice, the strict constructionists of the constitution would say that justice is equality before the law—that is, justice prevails if each individual has the right to a fair hearing, trial, and judgment by his peers on issues defined by law. The difficulty with this legalistic definition is that some persons do not have equal means to defend (or assert) themselves in the courts, which means that inequalities could develop due to differences in income distribution (rich-poor extremes). Another problem with the legalistic definition is that it assumes that the law itself is fair and representative of the general will of the people; but this assumption may not be true because some lobby groups have more wealth and power than others. Therefore, the laws may favor one group over another, which could also constitute inequality before the law.

Ideal Definition. Another definition of justice is an ideal one; that is, justice is those acts that are consistent with universal principles in the social and natural order. This ideal, advanced by Plato during very turbulent and unstable times, assumes that there is a natural order which is a reflection of ideal archtypes that are certain and absolute. The Absolute, or truth, as known to men of wisdom becomes the guide to justice. This concept of justice became embodied in medieval Christianity, but it has declined under the relativism of science. Moreover, the application of justice assumes that men of excellence and virtue govern human affairs, or that philosophers are kings. The scarcity of men with exceptional wisdom and virtue has, historically, caused governance to fall into less philosophic hands, with a loss in people's perception of justice in the process.

Utilitarian Definition. A more practical definition of justice has been the utilitarian one of Jeremy Bentham: justice is the greatest good for the greatest number. This form of justice is capable of practical democratic realization by voting. However, it assumes that every individual has an equal vote on matters that affect him, or that he can vote on specific issues. We saw in chapter 2 that in a representative republic, operating with lobbies and a two-party system, the voter does not have the opportunity to express a choice on specific issues, only on vague positions advanced by two similar candidates.

Economic Definition. A somewhat more elegant refinement of utilitarian justice has been called, in the field of economics, Pareto optimality, after the economist Pareto. The welfare or benefit of an economy are optimized, said Pareto, if no one can be made better off without making someone worse off. Better and worse, in this case, are defined as the next incremental benefit or cost of an action. This marginal benefit concept assumes that society (government) should take actions to improve human welfare as long as the next added marginal benefit to one group is greater than the marginal loss or cost to another. This idea gives rise to the benefit-cost concept of government services. For example, a reclamation dam providing irrigation water to farmers should have a higher net value of water over time (measured by the productivity and value of crops) than its cost of construction to the taxpayer.

Recapitulation. These several approaches to justice include, respectively, political, legal, ideal, utilitarian, and economic definitions. All of these concepts of justice come into play, to some extent, in the legislative decision-making process. Conservatives tend to favor the legal and ideal definitions; liberals tend to favor the utilitarian one. In practice, the political definition tends to dominate in governmental decision making, followed by the economic definition as next most influential—that is, legislative issues tend to be resolved first, by weighing and compromising the relative interests of various opinion groups, which is basically a subjective judgment; and, second, by rationalizing the decision in terms of benefit-cost analysis. In cases of doubt under either of these approaches, legal, ideal, or utilitarian arguments may be persuasive.

Justice thus is an empirical concept, wrought by rational and subjective arguments in a political arena to see who has the most votes (or money). As such, justice is close to being an alchemy of the social process, because a noble ideal is wrought from base materials. The ideal of justice is noble, whatever its materials, because it is the best means of resolving conflict that the decision process can devise. And out of this conflict resolution and compromise emerges the mission of government, which is justice in the use and distribution of authority in society.

Functions of Government

Order. The maintenance of social order is essential to decision making, so that settled patterns of behavior and response make decisions predictable. Chaotic social conditions make decisions unpredictable. Individuals and institutions alike need some framework in which they can take actions with an expected result. We saw in chapter 1 that social order is the sine qua non of individuality; that is, a person must have the routine affairs of living arranged as social habit before he can turn his personal decisions to more intimate and vital choices. The personal choices of intimate life and individuation are so critical to human beings that they will tolerate even the mismatch and mismanagement of institutions over long periods for the sake of order. Order is the highest form of security, because it enables a person to cope with his own problems and his own world. Nothing in government takes precedence over order as a priority; for without order, there is no governance.

Economic Development. The next highest form of security is economic security, especially that which can be created and controlled individually. The whole process of economic development, property rights, income rights, and capital expansion creates a framework for economic security by individual decision and effort. Chapter 2 was concerned with the private and public management of economic development, in which the government role is managing and providing fiscal and monetary policy, income distribution, capital flows, property rights, contractual rights, incorporation rights, technology, education, resource management, infrastructure, transfer payments, and the maintenance of consumption. These are the ingredients conducive to economic development and personal security.

Income Redistribution. Since about one-fourth of the population are excluded from the economic process, they cannot achieve their own economic security by productive work. The government redistributes tax revenues from high-income groups to low-income groups to maintain their subsistence and consumption. The implications of this point have already been covered in chapter 2.

Redistribution of Authority. As last resort, the government tries to create new public or private institutions with new authority to solve problems of unmet human needs (chapter 1).

Actual Government Allocation among Functions. The distribution of the federal budget for 1976 according to these functional responsibilities is shown in table 7-1. The detail shows the main functional elements of expenditures of the federal government as a percentage distribution (out of a total budget of about $350 billion). The maintenance of order takes about 30 percent of the budget, mostly for national defense. Income redistribution is the largest function of government, accounting for 54 percent of the budget, with the largest transfer payments occuring from income (social) security, health, and interest. Economic development in all its forms constitutes 11 percent of the budget. The portion

Table 7-1

Functional Distribution of Expenditures of U.S. Federal Government

Function	Element	Percent	
Order	National defense	27	
	International affairs	2	
	Law enforcement	1	
			30
Economic Development	General science, space, technology	1	
	National resource, environment, energy	3	
	Agriculture	1	
	Commerce and transportation	4	
	Community and regional development	2	
			11
Income Redistribution	Education, manpower, social services	4	
	Health	8	
	Income (social) security	34	
	Veteran benefits and services	4	
	Interest	10	
	Undistributed offsetting receipts	−6	
			54
Redistribution of Authority	General government	1	
	Revenue sharing	2	
	Allowances	2	
			5
Total			100

spent on general government and legislation for redistribution of authority is only 5 percent of expenditures. While relatively small in budget amounts, general government and the redistribution of authority is the most significant of all government functions in managerial or decision consequences.

Major Tasks

Social Choice, Bargaining, and Legislation. Social choice is the decision-making apparatus of government; and it occurs in at least three levels. The first is congressional legislation, which provides the basic and broad authority to perform functions or programs. The second form of social choice is the Executive Orders of the President, which set major objectives for operating departments of government. The third is administrative regulations, by which operating departments make rulings to govern themselves or private decision makers. The regulatory agencies make extensive use of administrative regulations to govern decision parameters in business. For example, the Federal Trade Commission, Federal Communications Commission, Interstate Commerce Commission, Federal Aviation Agency, Food and Drug Administration, Environmental Protection Agency, Price Control Board, to name a few, all govern business decisions through administrative regulations. Legislatively, then, social choice has three forms: congressional enactments, Executive Orders, and administrative regulation.

Politically, social choice occurs by direct voting, by congressional legislative bargaining, and by executive regulatory decision. Voting, particularly on referenda used in many states, is a form of direct democracy on specific issues. Congressional legislation is a representational form of social choice in which interested parties, lobbies, and, sometimes, voter groups influence a negotiated compromise in Congress. This form of congressional confrontation of interest groups may be called outsider politics, because it brings outsider groups together as coalitions for bargaining.

Executive regulatory decisions, the third form of social choice, are similar to "insider politics," coalitions, or consensus (discussed in chapter 6). Insider politics is characterized by elites who operate informally in closed sessions. Government regulatory actions tend to be elitist because special knowledge is often required to decide questions such as medical care, forest land use, space technology, scientific research, satellite communications, nuclear energy development, etc. These elite groups of experts tend to talk among themselves, exchange common data, and agree among themselves in informal consensus. Most of the operating data for these decisions are under the control of private business. Since business supplies the data and expertise for data interpretation, the opinion of business tends to become the opinion of the government regulatory agencies. By this process of supplying data and expertise, the regulated (business) tends to co-opt the decision process of the regulator (federal agency)—that is, the insider politics of informal consensus on common data and expertise supplied by the private sector influences the formulation of social choice in government agencies; and by this means, private decisions become public policy.

The task relationship of social choice, coalition, bargaining, and legislation to the government process is illustrated in figure 7-1. Governmental management (Congress and the President) selects policy areas in which deficiencies in the social process need attention. These policy and planning areas are effectuated through a budget, which allocates effort to the functional areas of order, economic development, income redistribution, and reallocation of authority. In all of these functional areas, the social choice process (bargaining, coalition, and legislation) permeates through all three levels of government—Congress, the President, and the Executive Branch—with increasing specificity at each level.

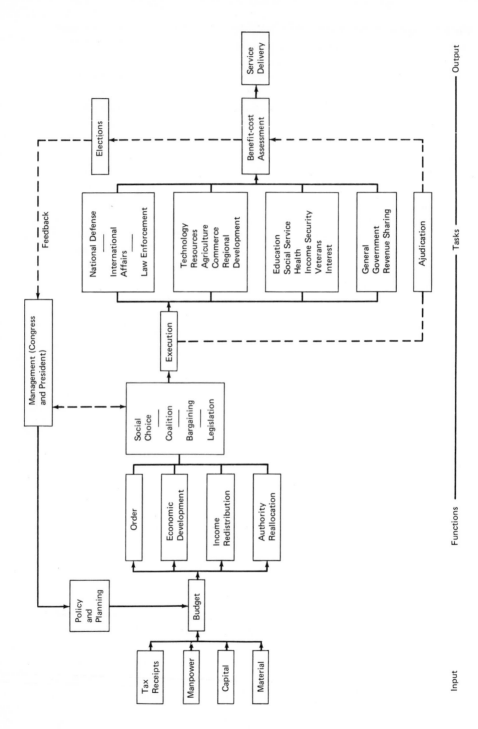

Figure 7-1. Major Functions, Tasks, and Process of Government.

When the decision criteria are settled at all three levels, the Executive Branch proceeds to execute or administer the program.

Execution. The execution of a program constitutes the service delivery of the function, such as health, education, veterans' benefits, space program, etc. (see figure 7-1). The means of execution are program management methods similar to those discussed in chapters 4, 5, and 6.

Adjudication. The execution of government programs sometimes causes conflicts in the course of operations, or a claim that someone's rights or property values were infringed. When these claims occur, a suit at law may be entered before the courts, either by the government, or by private citizens as plaintiffs against the government. The judicial branch of government then adjudicates the dispute before the courts according to precedents in law and interpretation of legislative intent. The opinion of the courts, either at the lower or appellate levels, are conclusive and enforceable in settling the disputes.

Finally, the delivery of government services causes an evaluation of the worth of those services by the recipients, citizens, and Congress (see figure 7-1). This evaluation of worth is some form of benefit-cost assessment, either formal or subjective. The question of whether government programs are worth their cost is decided in elections, where representatives are elected or defeated based in part on the programs and services of government that they espouse. The broad defeat of representatives on a question on price control services, for example, would tend to cause that service to be reduced or discontinued. Thus, elections are the feedback loop by which management (a new Congress and president) decide what policy and programs to support for the next electoral period.

Performance and Efficiency

The performance and efficiency of government is reflected in cost-benefit analysis or by citizen votes on specific issues. The performance and efficiency of government is difficult to measure because much of its activity is service oriented, value laden, and subjective. Government deals in the human ends of society, trying to make value judgments to remedy deficiencies and gaps in the social system. These subjective judgments are based on feelings and emotions. They are not easily quantified, rationalized, or converted into facts. The measures of government performance are attitudinal rather than factual.

Government is sometimes held up as inefficient, according to the business model; and it is said that business efficiency should be brought to government. We have already seen in previous chapters that business efficiency is achieved by maximizing economic growth rather than human growth, and by excluding or externalizing costs, thereby throwing the burden of social costs on the government. Indeed, this so-called efficiency is what has caused government to grow in size to provide remedies for the failures of business in meeting human needs. Government size and activity are measures of business neglect of or inefficiencies in the social system. Government can hardly use business decision criteria to correct failures that originate in business omissions. Government has to use a different and more subjective decision process, one that allows human feelings and emotions to confront the needs and failures of society. That process is politics, the politics of bargaining, interest parties, coalitions, pressure, negotiation, and compromise. The political arena allows the emotional flux of dissatisfied individuals to be expressed, specifically because this emotional flux has little voice or expression in the business decision process.

Nevertheless, attempts to objectify the government decision process continue, because in our factual and scientific culture the idea of subjective and emotional influences upon decisions is contrary to convention. The quality and ends of life are known mainly by feelings, which are excluded from the decision process. The process of means becoming ends in themselves is complete when the ultimate quality that determines human life is omitted from the decision criteria.

The attempts to objectify the government decision process have not been very successful. The closest analogy in government to the business "efficiency" criterion has been benefit-cost analysis. Benefit-cost analysis is the government analog to the rate of return on investment in business. In business, the rate of return is the value of earnings from a venture as a percentage of its investment cost. In government, the benefit-cost analysis is the value of benefits from a project as a percentage (or multiple) of its program costs.

The benefit-cost analysis works quite well for governmental public works investments, such as irrigation dams, which are similar to business investments—that is, the value of the water as a benefit to agriculture can be calculated in relation to the investment cost of the dam. Historically, public works have been justified before government budget hearings on a benefit-cost ratio for over fifty years. The difficulty with benefit-cost analysis emerges when the benefits are not easily summed up as dollar values. The value of irrigation water from a dam is easily measurable by its contribution to agricultural crop production. But the value of child care, subsistence to the aged, or even law enforcement is not easily converted into dollar benefits. Children, the aged, and peace on the streets have a value to be sure, but it is a humanly felt value rather than a dollar value. In many cases, these humanly felt values are more important than dollar values. If children and the aged die from lack of care, or if citizens die in the streets from crime and violence, the human ends of life are destroyed, which is more important subjectively than dollars attributable to a rate of return on investment.

Benefit-cost assessment therefore has its limitations when the human values of the benefit are subjective. Nevertheless, the government has tried to apply benefit-cost analysis where it can. The U.S. Bureau of the Budget made a study of five agencies to improve the government's productivity (efficiency) by using essentially a benefit-cost approach—that is, by trying to measure the value of the output versus the value of the input.[1] The productivity study was conducted on five different kinds of government. Two agencies were able to show measurable and strong increases in productivity. These were the Treasury Department in its check-writing operation, and the Veterans Administration in its insurance accounting, both very business-like production activities. Both showed large increases in productivity (value of output versus cost of input) because they were in the process of computerizing their operations—that is, they were using capital-intensifying means to improve their output by displacing workers. They were externalizing the cost of unemployment (the employees displaced by computers) just as a business would. The test of efficiency was the direct cost per unit of a premium collected or a check written. The benefit-cost analysis did not include the externalized social cost of unemployment of those workers displaced, which would have altered the results.

Two other agencies included in the Budget Bureau's productivity study were the Post Office and the Federal Aviation Agency. Both produce services that are labor intensive, and both had no new technologies during this time period. Also, they showed no increase in productivity. The Bureau of Land Management, the fifth agency, was unable to arrive at measures of output for its services of handling land and mineral claims and making cadastral surveys. These illustrations suggest that benefit-cost assessment is indeed a useful tool of analysis for decisions within government when the benefits are tangible and expressible in dollar terms. When benefits are intangible and subjectively felt, they are assessed mainly by the political process.

Elections are a means for voters to express their subjective feelings on the worth of government services. Unfortunately, voters seldom have the opportunity to make that expression on specific issues, because their elected representatives make the value judgments for them. The value judgments of elected representatives are not necessarily the same as those of citizens, because representatives want to be reelected, and they are influenced by the lobbies that can help them be reelected. They also can spend taxpayers' money to buy votes through new programs for new constituencies. The representatives have a built-in motivation to spend money or placate powerful interest groups. This conflict of interest in representative government is exacerbated by obscure accountability. The accountability of elected representatives is obscure because the responsibility for consequences is spread among a large group—that is, all the other legislators and legislative committees, as well as the executive. The negligible accountability in representative government is a major source of persistent inflation, wars, and poverty.

On rare occasions when voters can express themselves on specific issues, they often demonstrate willingness to take a tougher stand than their representatives. In California, recent elections have had as many as one or two dozen propositions on referenda, usually issues too controversial for the legislature to handle, such as election laws, mass transit, air pollution controls, and land use control. The public has generally shown itself to be tighter with expenditures and tougher in performance standards than the legislature is willing to be. Elections on specific issues thus are a form of accountability, often lacking in the present political process, which makes possible ultimate assessments of government services' worth.

Allocation of Funds

The truncated form of decisions (chapter 3) are a means by which institutions maintain themselves—that is, give institutional continuance in decision making higher priority than the human ends of society. Government bureaus are prone toward self-maintenance; and abolition of programs or bureaus is rarely attempted by the legislatures. The consequences are rising government expenditures as new programs are added while few are deleted.

A principal tool of bureaucratic maintenance is the budgetary process. Agency expenditures become established in a base budget, which is reappropriated perennially without critical reexamination. New budget requests are the principal focus for a decision—budgeting is an incremental process, largely confined to decisions on new money requests. The reason budgeting is incremental, rather than systematic, goes back to the difficulty of evaluating a program's worth in the first place. An existing program has (1) survived an original scrutiny of its worth in some previous budgetary examination; (2) has been justified by benefit-cost measures if possible; and (3) has survived legislative scrutiny, which gives the program presumption of electoral sanction. With such a history, the program is presumed to merit continuance in the base budget from year to year without undue reevaluation.

In fact, these three reasons are not logically sustainable year after year. Times and needs may have changed since the original incremental scrutiny. Benefits and costs may have changed. And the electoral sanction via legislative acceptance is dubious if representatives are not accountable on specific issues. Nevertheless, the fixity of base budgets enable bureaucracies to persist once they become established in the budget, with some question about how much more (or fewer) expenditures will be approved from year to year. Thus it can be said that the allocation of funds is the principal means for institutional and bureaucratic maintenance.

Control by Budgetary Process

Despite its limitations in reevaluating established programs, the budget is the principal management tool for control in government. Figure 7-2 shows a task

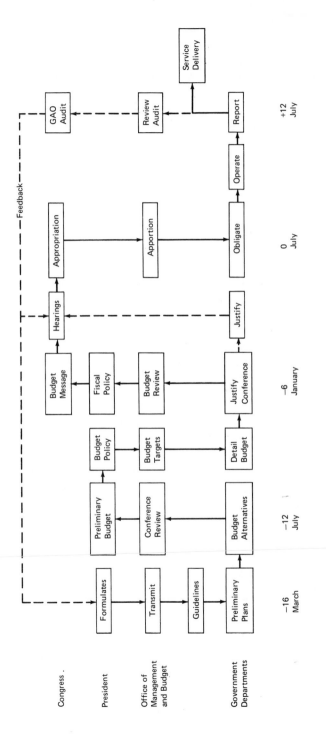

Figure 7-2. Task Network of the Budgetary Process.

network of the budgetary process, which indicates how management control is supposed to work. The figure illustrates the budgetary cycle, beginning sixteen months before the start of a new fiscal year. The budget is initiated by the President formulating a general policy on budget preparation, which includes decisions concerning the approximate size of the total budget, the program areas to emphasize or deemphasize, and alternative changes in revenues to cover expenditures.

This general policy formulation is then transmitted through the Office of Management and Budget to the government departments as a set of guidelines for agencies to use in the preparation of preliminary plans for their operations and expenditures some sixteen months hence. The departmental agencies consider activities and alternatives that they may pursue, as well as where to increase or decrease emphasis in light of the Executive guidelines. Perhaps energy programs should be expanded or emphasized in the coming year, while social service programs are deemphasized. The agency confers with the Office of Management and Budget on these priorities and alternatives to see which satisfy the objectives of the Executive the most. Out of these consultations on alternatives there emerges a preliminary budget, which then goes to the President for his review. The President examines the preliminary consolidated budget to see how it fits in with prospective economic conditions, revenues, and his impression of human needs. The President may revise some preliminary programs upward or downward, and these revisions become the substance of a budget decision or budget policy. The President's budget decision is then converted into more specific expenditure targets by the Office of Management and Budget, which then transmits the budget targets to the departmental bureaus.

The departmental agencies now make firm, detailed budgets, along with justifications, in keeping with the budget targets given to them. They confer with the Office of Management and Budget on their detailed budgets and submit their justifications, which are then cross-examined. The Office of Management and Budget, on the basis of its examinations, makes up a final budget with the President (along with the Department of Treasury) to supply revenue estimates. The revenue-expenditure package becomes the fiscal policy of the President, transmitted to the Congress as the budget message and request.

Congress holds hearings on the President's budget, calling for detailed justifications from the operating departments. Congress may alter the President's budget or act upon revenue measures. Then Congress makes appropriations to the government departments. The appropriations are "apportioned" by the Office of Management and Budget into quarterly allotments that may have some conditions attached to them concerning spending rates or objects of expenditures. The operating department then takes actions that obligate its apportionment. These actions implement the field work for which it was created—that is, the performance of services.

When the services are completed they are delivered to the public, and a report of completion (or accounting report) goes to the Office of Management and Budget, which reviews and audits the expenditures. The General Accounting Office, an agency of Congress, also audits expenditures and performance. These audits constitute the feedback that informs the Congress and the President what services and actions were executed. This feedback information then may be used to correct or change performance in the next budget cycle. While the budget cycle is highly organized as a control, the corrective feedback information is very slow as control loops go; that is, the corrective information on service delivery occurs two and one-half years after the budget formulation decision. Control theory indicates that slow corrective feedback allows systems to go out of line, or oscillate, between initial and corrective actions.

Process of Government

The process of government, as a flow of actions from initiation to delivery, has been generally described in preceding sections and especially in figures 7-1 and 7-2. For example, the President and Congress, as management, make policy and planning decisions on the relative priority of effort to be applied among the main functions of government: order, economic development, income redistribution, and authority reallocation (figure 7-1). These policy and planning decisions are then effectuated through a network of tasks forming the budget cycle (figure 7-2). The budget hearing, legislative, and priority process of choosing among government programs is political, and the social choices are resolved (figure 7-1) through coalitions, bargaining, and compromise. The process of government thus is managed by allocating a coordinated network of tasks by program among functional departments to satisfy benefit-cost criteria on the worth of services delivered.

The Executive Branch of government implements the Congress's and the President's policies by allocating tasks such as national defense, social services, technology, commerce, or health, among the operating departments (figure 7-1). Each of these programs is made up of large staffs of people, large expenditures, and a large network of activity allocated and controlled by bureau or department heads. This administrative staff directs the work (tasks) of approximately one-fourth of the American economy, if all staff, contractors, outside ventors, and participants are counted. The coordination of these task networks is a monumental administrative effort; and it is a credit to the administrative skill of federal managers that the government works as well as it does. Indeed, those who use their administrative skills to manage the task networks are less responsible for the breakdown in governance than those who control policy formulation and the government as a whole.

Decision Process—Multiplicity of Goals

The decision process seeks to satisfy a multiplicity of goals in a political bargaining process that tries to rank-order the goals and equate the human benefits or worth of services to their cost. The multiplicity of goals is peculiarly a government problem. By comparison, business operations usually have several products or services. Even in large conglomerates with many product lines, the number of product services is small relative to the government. Similarly, the voluntary social institutions concentrate on relatively few services in which they have expertise. The government, in contrast, solves the residual problems and performs the services of society that are not performed elsewhere. These services are multitudinous; and since people's wants are relatively insatiable, the requests for new government services and activities are ever present. The problem of the legislator thus is to decide which of these many service demands are most essential, and in what priority.

The prioritizing of services is the most difficult problem of government, because the value of the output is difficult to measure, or even to judge. As a result, the judgment is made on the basis of the apparent public support for one program choice versus another. A legislator has several ways to appraise this apparent support. One way is impressionistic—that is, his own impressions from meeting and talking with his constituents, or the impressions of his staff and advisors. Second, he may take part in or hold public hearings, in which various interest parties represent their views. Third, he can attempt some sort of public opinion poll, by constructing a survey or simply reading his mail. Last, the legislator may listen to lobbies who claim to represent large membership groups and who have money to help marshall convincing arguments.

The legislator typically looks at all these sources of information as bargaining groups with whom he attempts to make a reasonable compromise. Compromise is a difficult art, because a compromise pleases nobody. However, the object of the compromise is to find the least offensive solution, or the one that dissatisfies the least number of voters. The least dissatisfaction normally occurs when the benefits of the action help the largest number of people at the least cost. Legislators will thus try to arrive at a priority among the many goals before them by seeking solutions with the most benefits or least dissatisfactions at minimum costs.

Allegiance of Citizens

Voluntary social institutions measure their allegiance by participation rates, or individuals who seek their services. The government, as an involuntary social agency, measures its allegiance by nonparticipation rates—that is, people who deliberately seek to avoid government or to defy it. The allegiance of citizens to government is reflected in the degree of internal order, and the amount of participation in elections that provide a social choice.

The simplest way to avoid the government is not to vote, which is a passive way of expressing no confidence or no interest in what the government is doing or not doing. If the government's role in an individual's life is trivial (see chapter 1) or otherwise conducive to apathy, citizens find it easier to stay at home on election day, rather than search for reasons to motivate themselves down to the polls. During most elections, about one-third or more of the people fail to vote. The number of supporters for a majority candidate, winning by a narrow margin, is about equal to the number who have expressed no confidence or no interest in him by staying home. Under these circumstances, a winning candidate scarcely has a mandate from the people. Indeed, if nonvotes were counted in elections, the nonvote in some elections would come close to a majority, all declaring their nonallegiance. This is a signal to be read with some interest, because the next step may be conflict. A more violent way to declare nonallegiance to the government is to break its laws. The rising rates of crime in the United States for two generations are overt declarations of nonallegiance to the government by increasing numbers of citizens. Some violators break the law because government is not just in their view; and others may lack personal or social growth to be responsible citizens. As the number of lawbreakers and nonvoters increases, a reassessment of human needs and justice is certainly an obvious step in any attempt to maintain order.

The Social Environment as a Constraint

The social environment places constraints upon government decision making by means of a common sense of morality, and checks and balances imposed on the political system. The government is the regulator of society; but who regulates the regulator? The writers of the Constitution answered this question by establishing a system of checks and balances. The division of authority among the three branches of government was one attempt; others are a presidential veto of congressional enactments, Senate ratification of presidential appointments and treaties, House initiation of revenue measures, and Supreme Court rulings on congressional or presidential actions. Despite all these checks, the presidency has grown in authority relative to the other branches of government consistently for a half-century, which is an indication that the checks and balances are not working as they once did.

Another kind of check upon the presidency is a common sense of morality. President Roosevelt came close to outraging this sense of morality in his time by packing the Supreme Court, and President Nixon overreached the sense of morality in the Watergate cover-up. Each of these incidents has inspired new checks and balances to prevent abuse. Following Roosevelt, the presidential term was limited to eight years, and following Nixon, election laws have been strengthened further.

Change Forces Affecting Government

The change forces affecting the government most sharply are internal and external dissent, and technoeconomic change. Certainly the greatest threats and disruptions to the American society and the U.S. government have been wars over the past half-century. War is the outgrowth of failures in diplomacy or in the conflict-resolution machinery among nations. Neither the United Nations nor the League of Nations became effective international mediating agencies. Foreign policy continues to be bilateral in most cases, or it takes the form of power bloc coalitions. When different social objectives among nations cannot be accommodated, war results. After two world wars, two Asian wars, plus numerous smaller actions within one lifetime, the world still is not close to having permanent peace-keeping machinery. War is at the base of much of our internal disaffections, of inflation, and of the high cost of government. For the most part, wars are treated as exogenous, largely beyond influence and inevitable, because other nations are assumed to be the aggressors. By treating wars as inevitable, they become the inevitable, and are socially disruptive internally as well as externally.

The second most significant change force is internal dissent, or the threat from within, by nonallegiance. This dissent takes the form of apathy, nonvoting, nonparticipation, delinquency, crime, violence, confrontation, and senseless killing. These are signs of a social environment that fails individuals, and such failures need more remedy than mere policing (see chapters 2 and 3).

The third most obvious change force is technoeconomic innovations, which alter investments, markets, competition, and jobs. Business is reasonably well equipped to protect and maintain itself in dealing with technoeconomic change by reinvestment, new market development, and barriers to competition. The result is that the cost of technoeconomic change is unemployment. Technological unemployment is a no-cost option for business, and leads to capital intensification. Unemployment is small cost to government, in the form of unemployment compensation. The main cost of unemployment is borne by individuals, who have no part in technoeconomic decision making. Indeed, two of the greatest change forces in the society, war and technological unemployment, represent decision areas in which individuals have little or no voice. If the citizenry participated in the decision process on these issues, they could better evaluate the trade-offs they would have to make to avoid war or unemployment.

The third change force, dissent and disorder, is the only form of expression left to a society in which disaffection has become endemic. Nonparticipation is the residual means for expressing nonallegiance.

Internal Organization

Internal organization of government is determined primarily by information flows, pressure groups, and size. The internal organization of government departments is influenced by the number of layers of hierarchy through which information can flow. The limit seems to be about eight layers of bureaucracy; then the filtering effect vitiates the messages. The U.S. Department of State is an interesting example of communications limitations in management. Hypothetically (that is, based upon field decentralization principles practiced in business and government), one would expect U.S. embassies in foreign countries to have direct lines of communication through the country's desk in Washington to top policymakers in the State Department. During a crisis, the ambassador does have direct access to top policymakers in Washington. However, during the normal course of operations, the embassy communicates through written reports sent to the country's desk for review and analysis by the staff, concerning economic affairs, capital investment, consular, political, military, or immigration affairs. These functional bureaus read, store, and abstract the information, sending a digest of the state of affairs by country or region to the next higher level in the State Department. As the information floats upward, it becomes more and more abstract because of the many interpretations made by the desk-bound employees (many of whom have never been to the country they are analyzing).

The State Department, at the top, is organized regionally; for example, the Bureau for Africa, Southeast Asia, and Latin America. The regional bureau has a program office and a policy office. The policy office analyzes the political status and implications of the staff reports, and the program office considers their meaning in terms of budgets and future programs (networks of activities). The two offices advise the director of the bureau, who in turn advises the office of the Secretary. The Secretary's office also has a department-wide policy and program staff, which reconsiders the priorities and actions recommended by each bureau to form a departmental policy. The State Department policy is then reconsidered in the National Security Council, involving other governmental departments.

The communication distance from the lowest level recipient of information (analysis staff) in the State Department to the bureau level is approximately eight layers, plus the departmental policy staff and National Security Council on top of that. By the time the information has been passed up the line, it bears little resemblance to the on-site field information as seen at the embassy or mission level. Meantime, the country desk (which should be the field management) and the embassy or mission abroad have little direct influence or input on policy. Embassy and mission staffs are known to have spent as much as 60 percent of their time responding to requests from Washington for information that they have already supplied. Attempts to solve this information morass by using computerized data storage and strengthening the role of the mission and country desk have been defeated by the eight-layered bureaucracy whose jobs and perceptions would be altered by more direct data access.

The State Department is so formidable, according to an in-joke within the department, that it can defeat the will of any President. This is why every one of the last five Presidents have bypassed the State Department with their own form of personal diplomacy, which revolves around the White House staff, the President himself, or a Secretary who operates independently of the department. This form of personal diplomacy frequently fails because the policymaker was poorly informed of the real situation in the field.

The State Department represents the extreme of information management problems, but all the large departments of the federal government suffer from some of the same difficulties. The concept of the "new federalism" was intended to deal with the information filtering through the layers of large organizations by decentralizing government to the regional level and by sharing revenue with local governments. The regionalization of the federal government has helped unstop the information blockage somewhat. However, the regional office have never been made the decision equivalent of a corporate business division. Moreover, revenue sharing with local government tends to dry up under the monumental deficits and inflation generated by the federal government.

The second major determinant of government organization, besides the information problem, is the impact of pressure groups. The federal departments tend to become creatures of pressure groups. Thus the Department of Agriculture responds to the agriculture lobby, the Department of Commerce to business, the Labor Department to labor, the Interstate Commerce Commission to the railroads, the Maritime Commission to ocean shipping, the Federal Communications Commission to the media, the Aviation Board to airlines, and the Federal Power Commission to utilities. Because these agencies deal with common problems and data along with their private counterparts, their views and policies tend to merge.

The Department of Interior provides one of the more interesting examples of how pressure groups affect management. The Department of Interior manages national resources and the public domain, dealing in mining claims, land grants and land use, water resources, reclamation, irrigation, oil, gas, and coal reserves. These resources were historically the base for the U.S. economic development—the government's policy of underpricing resources when disposing of them encouraged capital investment. Most of these underpriced resources have been sold or given away, except for water, federal grazing land, and off-shore oil. The Taylor Grazing Act permits the Department to lease or allocate federal grazing land to ranchers, who thereupon treat it as part of their assets. For example, ranch land is sold on the basis of the number of owned acres and leased acres available, as though the federal land were a permanent entitlement—that is, the interests of the regulator and the regulated have become one.

Obviously, powerful political forces are at work, securing benefits from the

Interior Department in land, water, mining, oil, gas, and coal usages. The focal point for these political forces has been the Interior Committee in the House of Representatives, which is made up mainly of congressmen representing cattle, water, and mining interests. For many years, the Department of Interior has been one of the most politically run organizations in the federal government, in which the bureaus, responding to the House committee, have had more power than the Secretary. The Secretary of Interior has been reduced to a public relations rather than an administrative position. Thus, the Department of Interior's organization and operations are determined, through a direct linkage between Congress and the bureaus, by the political interest parties.

A third determinant of government organization, besides information problems and pressure groups, is size. The federal government is a massive organization with millions of employees. How does one ensure that they are all working effectively in the public interest? First, there is the information-filtering problem (for example, the State Department) to be avoided. Even beyond that, however, is the coordination of vast task networks of people and events, assuming the information problem is solvable.

The Defense Department is the largest management organization in the world and, interestingly enough, its worst problem is not information filtering as it is in the State Department. The Defense Department deals with its information problem by strong and direct lines of communication and command between Washington and the field. Thus the Chief of Naval Operations communicates directly with all field commanders, such as CincPac (Commander in Chief, Pacific Forces) and all field missions or stations. Similarly, the Strategic Air Command has direct information, communication, and command linkages with all strategic air or missile bases. The information is conveyed directly by voice, memoranda, and computerized data—that is, information handling is not the main management constraint in the Defense Department, even though it presents difficult problems.

The major organizational constraint in the Defense Department is the difficulty in programmatic decision making, or in handling the policy-control nexus. This is the same organizational problem faced by the President and Congress regarding the whole government. When organization size becomes huge as in the Defense Department, the selecting of priorities among multitudinous goals and programs lacking output measures of their worth becomes a decision process of political log rolling rather than a representation of either a rational or a public benefit choice.

The Defense Department's decision process is compounded by having three services competing with each other for funds; and within each military service, the field commands and the logistic bureaus vie with each other for funds. Moreover, they conduct this evaluation of priority and programs within a framework of "insider politics" (see chapter 6), in which only the professionals or military are presumed to have the expertise to make judgments. The shroud of mystique around military programs, plus the dire threats of the inevitability of war, are used to seek top priority for every and all programs from the Secretary of Defense, and by the Secretary from Congress. Of course, top priority for all military programs results in no priority at all, but merely in the claim that all military requests must be fully met.

A rich nation can, for a time, throw all of its surplus productivity into war effort rather than into human development. However, war effort is basically destructive of rather than nurturing of human potential. Eventually, the military lack of contribution to productivity and human development begins to limit the society. For example, most of the inflation-stagnation of the United States in the 1970s is directly attributable to the large war-induced deficits of the 1960s, on top of all the previous war costs. The lack of priority, or lack of resolving the policy-control nexus, is the principal organizational difficulty of inordinate size.

Knowledge Requirements of Management

The knowledge requirements of management in government are an understanding of policy resolution, information flows, and budgetary control. The most important knowledge requirement in government management is an understanding of human ends, goals, and their conflict resolution. Political or policy goals are multitudinous, competing, and conflicting. The conflicting goals must be resolved and put into a priority that is monetarily manageable. The means of resolution are hearings, coalitions, bargaining, negotiation, and compromise.

The second most important knowledge requirement is understanding information flows so that people can communicate effectively within government organizations to make them manageable, and among citizens and government organizations to make the government responsive. The responsiveness of government is the principal means for building allegiance and maintaining order, which is the primary mission of government.

The third knowledge requirement is understanding budgetary control, because it is the only effective control in government. The government lacks output controls because its outputs are not easily measurable. The main mode of control is on inputs, which means budgetary control. The prioritizing of multitudinous goals, through the policy evaluation process, allows program costs to be organized into a budget control instrument within the financial constraints of the economy.

These three areas of knowledge are not widely or deeply understood, either by elected officials, government executives, or academics. The result has been a crisis of government, or a question of whether the United States is governable in the sense of maintaining order, allegiance, or justice. The crisis of governance centers around political accountability, the priority of goals within social means, and making the connection (nexus) between policy, control, and accountability.

Note

1. *Measuring Productivity in the Federal Government* (Washington, D.C.:
U.S. Bureau of the Budget, 1964).

8 The Decision Process Inherent in Mission

Learning the art of management entails first, an understanding of the setting and activities that are the concern of managerial actions, and second, the reasoning process by which decisions are made. Chapters 1 through 7 have been concerned with the setting and activities of management, the social framework, the ends, means, decision structure, business environment, functions, tasks, process, institutional structure, functions of voluntary institutions, and the functions and process and government. These are the surroundings in which management operates. The surrounding conditions provide the framework within which a decision is made, but they do not show how a decision is made.

This chapter is concerned with how a decision is made, the reasoning process, the information content, and the convergence upon choices. Previous chapters have also dealt with decisions, but in a different way. Chapter 3 was concerned with the structure of a decision, or the logical form in which a decision should be addressed. It also provided a typology of kinds of decisions and their place in the structure of choices. Chapters 4 through 7 described the institutional decision criteria of business, voluntary institutions, and government in the context of functions, performance, costs, and trade-offs. These are all part of the environment within which an executive finds himself when faced with a decision.

Next, we want to inquire, given this background information, how does the executive think about a decision? We are interested in what goes on in the manager's mind, as he sits alone knowing the institutional and social setting, and knowing the facts that the institution knows. What does he do with what he knows? The manager starts thinking by sorting his knowledge of a situation— assessing, evaluating, and structuring it. He sorts out his observations from his assumptions, those which are measurable from those which are not, and those which represent human needs or ends from those which do not. His mind also sorts out that information which is relevant to the problem. The sorting procedure is a process of elimination by which the manager attempts to isolate the key causal factors that he can alter to change present circumstances toward more desirable ends.

The desirability of ends is not easily agreed upon by everyone, as we have seen (chapters 1 and 7). The executive needs to have a model for a decision in his mind that approximates some known consensus of human wants and ends. The approximate consensus is the decision criteria, which the executive uses judgmentally for sorting. In the end, what the executive does is to use a process of elimination to arrive at the least undesirable choice based upon the decision criteria—that is, he wants to satisfy as many people, or dissatisfy as few people, as he can in the institutional setting. Or, in the more elegant terms of Pareto optimality, the manager's decision is to make some people better off as long as he does not make others worse off. The marginal gains of the decision should exceed the marginal losses.

The less elegant form of this decision approach—using a process of elimination to find the least undesirable choice—has a certain practical advantage to it. The dissatisfied people are always more vocal than the satisfied ones, and, thus, the least undesirable choice is the compromise decision that encounters the fewest complaints. The fewer the complaints, the more latitude and apparent allegiance the decision maker has. As a practical matter of holding together a coalition of followers, whether they be stockholders or customers or voters, the least undesirable choice provides the strongest base for the decision-maker's support.

Even in its simple, practical, and inelegant form, the decision approach of using a process of elimination to arrive at the least undesirable choice contains some very profound epistemological issues—How does the manager select information? Whose desires (or undesires) enter the choice and how are they known?

The use of a mental sorting technique, or the process of elimination, implies that some information is selected out of a vast array of information to make a choice. That selection process is at the heart of all scientific and managerial inquiry. In system thinking, everything affects everything else, which is to say that every decision affects everyone else, no matter how indirectly. This has been dealt with partially in chapter 3, when we discussed the decision makers. How does a manager decide who his decision will affect? This is a selection process, again, of sorting out the affected parties. And how does he know how they will be affected? The selection of information, both as to the objects and subjects of a decision, is the crux of the decision process.

Information Selection

Consider the executive as one who looks at the information content of the world. He may take, at the extreme, two viewing postures. One viewing posture is through a tunnel at what is directly before him, such as the present profit of his business. If he takes that viewing posture, all information other than the current revenue-cost data is immediately screened out. He may then make a trade-off of ways to change marginal revenue against marginal costs and resolve the decision. Having solved the decision in this way, the executive may have improved the institution's current profit, but done nothing about human development in the business, continuance of the satisfaction of customers, allegiance of constituencies, long-run maintenance of authority of the business, avoiding government intervention or regulation, maintaining the environment, or the human ends of society. The tunnel-viewing posture thus suboptimizes on a short-term goal and may be to the detriment of the long-run interests of the business or society.

At the other extreme, the executive may take a wide-angle viewing posture. Consider the executive sitting at home on his patio on a clear summer night, looking at the stars and wondering what problem he should solve and with what information. He looks up at the stars and his surroundings trying to see everything; and he is overwhelmed by his awareness of all the events of the universe, mankind, society, government, and his business. What information should he try to sort out—even to decide if there is a problem? Such a viewing posture is overwhelming; and it can be made tractable only by considering what it is possible to know or do anything about. There are some things, many things, that the executive cannot do anything about, at least immediately, such as natural forces. He cannot change the food chain, the ecology of the earth, the availability of exhaustible resources, the hydrologic cycle, the absorbed radiation from the sun, the weather, the calorie requirements for human subsistence, the number of people, human nature, human needs, or the present resources of the economy. The executive accepts as given those natural events that constitute his environment; and this first process of elimination greatly narrows the range of his information selection.

A large amount of information still remains, however, from which to select; and the executive looks at these events probabilistically. What is the probability that the observed events will occur, and what is the probability that they will affect his decision? This viewing posture requires that the executive adopt a probabilistic model of what to enter into his decision. The balance of this chapter is concerned with successive eliminations of information to arrive at the most probable events delineating a decision.

What we have been considering thus far in the selection of information is the use of deductive versus inductive reasoning. Deductive reasoning is the act of taking away, reduction, differentiation, or making an inference in which the conclusion follows necessarily from the premises. Deductive reasoning is the analytical slicing up of smaller parts from larger wholes, or the Aristotelian binary logic of not this and therefore that. The executive considering his profit optimization is engaging in deduction. The premise is that one of the goals of business, profit, is deficient. From this premise the conclusion is deduced that revenues must be raised, or costs cut, by some managerial decision. That deduction suboptimizes on the subgoal of profit, and ignores the other goals of business and society, such as allegiance to business, authority of business, long-term maintenance of business, human ends, etc.

Induction is the act of reasoning from parts to the whole, from particulars to the general, from observations to principles, from the individual to the universal. Induction looks for similarities rather than differences, synthesis rather than reductionism. The executive on his patio at night using his maximum vision is trying to assemble all the observations that illuminate the whole of his decision. The more observations he includes in his decision, the more whole and complete it becomes. But all observations and events cannot be known with certainty, so the manager must make probabilistic estimates of their effects. In practice, of course, the executive has to use some deduction to narrow the sphere of observation to manageable dimensions within his mind, and then use induction to comprehend as large a decision parameter as he can assimilate from all the relatable observations.

This chapter thus uses deductive and inductive reasoning together, deductively to narrow the field to the necessary and desirable conditions of the decision, and inductively to comprehend as large a decision as possible.

Necessary Conditions for a Decision

The necessary conditions of a decision are first determined by environmental constraints limiting the choice of missions and means available to the decision maker. The environmental constraints are the natural forces presenting limits or obstacles to what an executive might choose to do. Consider a decision maker who lives in a desert. The absence of water is an environmental constraint, and any decision made must take cognizance of how much water is available, and where. The establishment of a sugar mill in the desert, for example, is highly improbable because sugar requires gallons of water per pound in production and refining. By contrast, use of camels for transportation between wells or water storage areas is a probable alternative, because the water requirement is low.

Similarly, government and business policy in the United States must now take cognizance of the limited supply of low-cost petroleum available within the country. Cheap oil and gasoline are no longer valid decision assumptions in planning future products, future transportation, and industrial power sources, or in the U.S. balance of payments. Energy and oil have become major environmental constraints. Other environmental constraints are the absence of about twenty minerals necessary to the U.S. economy, (e.g., need to import most supplies of nickel, mercury, tungsten, platinum, sulfur, aluminum, asbestos, lead, vanadium, and zinc), deteriorating water quality, deteriorating air quality, rising prices of food and fiber, price and toxicity limitations on synthetic carbon compounds, limited fertile land, removal of arable land into urban uses, destruction of land productivity by strip mining, and rising levels of carcinogens in the food supply. The executive may observe these events merely as rising material prices, but unless he considers the sources, causes, and amelioration of these events, he will not be able to judge how fast or far material prices may rise.

Still, the executive can make some deductive estimates of his decision boundaries by considering the long-run availability of supply for those materials which he needs for his product or services. Indeed, the availability of long-run supply at a probable price is one of the first requirements of an investment decision. The supply-cost parameter determines what missions are possible and what means are feasible. For example, the mission of producing large, internal combustion engine cars for mass personal transportation is no longer a feasible mission, given the limited gasoline supplies and rising prices; and, thus, the automobile manufacturers are moving toward a mission of producing smaller cars that use less gasoline. Similarly, the availability of medical services in the United States, either by government or voluntary institutions, is limited by the supply of physicians and medical skills. The cost of increasing the supply of physicians has become so large that a reduction and change in the composition of services is in process, shifting some medical services to lesser skilled workers, limiting personal access to physicians in terms of their time or house calls, etc.—that is, the knowledge and laboratory requirements of physician production and usage has become a limiting environmental factor in making medical care decisions. The necessary conditions of a decision are determined by environmental constraints and limits, which may be initially thought of as the supply limitations of a problem.

Desirable Conditions for a Decision

Every manager lives within the milieu of conventional wisdom. This folk wisdom, being a convention, applies as a norm to ordinary events and cases. Conventional wisdom expresses ordinary values, mores, custom, folklore. As such, it is a guide and a restraint upon the executive in making a decision. The desirable conditions of a decision are thus determined by the value-judgment constraints on the manager derived from his socialization or the idea boundaries of his institution.

The conventional wisdom in business is that the executive's goals is to maximize profit in the short run; and if the executive makes a decision in keeping with this ordinary value scheme, he need offer no further justification or explanation. But we have also seen that short-term profit maximization can in some cases cost the business its authority, allegiance, and long-run survival. When the executive sees this possibility (when using his wide-angle vision rather than his tunnel vision), his decision needs to be an exception. He must then present a rationale to justify the exception, or why he is acting differently from conventional wisdom.

The same situation applies in government and voluntary agencies. In schools, universities, hospitals, medical services, the military, and social services, the conventional wisdom is that the "quality" of service is ascertainable only by the "professionals" who are knowledgeable about the technique and mystique of the service. Moreover, this quality mystique is determined by input controls and credentials. As long as an executive makes decisions in voluntary institutions based upon "quality," input controls, and credentials, he need not explain his decision further because its justification is obvious to the profession. But if he wishes to make the decision on different grounds (for example, based upon clients' perception of the service delivered), then he must justify the exception by a rationale which shows that what he proposes relates to quality and past exceptions in professional practice.

Similarly in government, the conventional wisdom is that a compromise should reconcile the interests of the strongest lobbies to appear on the scene with petitions and money. A politician who makes a compromise among the apparent interest parties need not offer further explanations of his acts because that is the conventional wisdom. If the politician decides to make a decision based upon the public interest of the "silent majority," then he needs to present a rationale to explain this exceptional act and how he identified the majority despite its silence.

The point is that decisions are normally made within the boundaries of accepted, commonplace values that the decision maker and his followers have been socialized to accept as desirable. These slogan values provide a convenient reason for deciding ordinary cases; but they constrain and delude the decision maker in the extraordinary or unusual cases. In fact, the decision maker is not worth his pay unless he can discern unusual cases, because anyone with ordinary intelligence at ordinary wages can decide ordinary cases. The executive is an executive because he has extraordinary judgment for unusual problems and unusual cases. The executive exists to take exception from the conventional wisdom as he sees the problem from a broader perspective than most people. In effect, this means that conventional values are a convenient rationale when he can use them to explain his action, but, for the most part, conventional wisdom is a constraint on the executive from which he must depart—and justify his departure—in the extraordinary situations that he sees in a broader light than most people perceive.

The extraordinary situations the executive perceives are the human needs that are beyond conventional values and, by observation, have gone unmet. These unmet needs are opportunities for the manager to create a broader decision framework. Unmet needs of the type discussed in chapters 1 and 2, for example, present new opportunities for business and government, and they call for unconventional decisions. The desirable conditions of a decision, therefore, are those value judgments of common currency that the executive relies upon for justifying ordinary decisions, plus those new desires and goals of extraordinary decisions justified by the fulfillment of unmet human needs—that is, an executive who is worth his pay is not constrained by the idea boundaries of his milieu. He must shape the value judgments of his followers and peers as he sees opportunities to develop a more holistic view of human needs.

Method of Decision

The method of inquiry by which the decision is to be resolved is determined by the institutional mission that the executive is attempting to fulfill; that is, the decision method is inherent in the mission. The mission of an institution dictates the terms of the decision method. The mission of business is to produce goods and services, which are objective products. The decision method thus deals with objects and is objective, quantitative, as well as a rationale for the minimum utilization of objects to meet human need. The decision method is a cost-minimization model accounting for the objects in the process flow of functions and tasks in business (chapter 5).

The mission of voluntary social institutions is to provide personalized services to individuals at or below cost. Personalized services are subjective. The decision method, then, deals with individuals and subjects, and is subjective, nonquantitative, emotional, as well as a method for enhancing the felt-response of individuals served. The measurement of felt-responses is tenuous and testimonial; and subjective testimony is not acceptable in an objective culture. However, the inputs are objective, such as skills, human credentials, equipment, materials. Therefore, the decision method is symbolic, a credentials demonstration model, in which the means of demonstration is consensus by in-group politics.

The mission of government is justice. Justice is subjective and variously interpreted by different groups of people. The decision maker therefore must consider those groups of people who have differing interests, whose interests are subjective, emotional, nonquantitative, diverse, and conflicting. The decision method is a negotiated compromise model by which confrontation politics seeks to resolve conflict by arriving at the least undesirable choice.

The mission of an institution thus is a statement of purpose, a norm, and, as such, a statement of the problem. The decision method is inherent in the problem, because the problem is definitive of objects, subjects, feelings, issues, data, and measures. The decision is inherent in the mission. Decision methods of one institution are not necessarily applicable in another—that is, the business decision method is not appropriate in government (except in business-like operations); and the decision method of government is not appropriate in business (except in political issues of interest party conflicts). The decision maker must understand the milieu in which he is operating and adopt the appropriate decision methods inherent in the mission.

Performance Goals of Decisions

The goals of a decision are determined by the functional performance requirements of the system. Every decision has a performance characteristic—that is, a minimum level of accomplishment which must be achieved. Decisions are used to direct work; work has goals; the sum of the work delivers a product (or service) to users to satisfy a human need. That utilization requirement is the functional performance of the output. The work function of an automobile is to deliver personal transportation at a specified speed, convenience, style, and cost. The functional performance of an appendectomy is to deliver a body free of the ailment, appendicitis. The functional performance is the specification of what the user wants; it is the specification of the human ends of the work.

The performance goals of a decision are therefore oriented toward fulfilling human ends. Human need and ends are numerous; and the executive can only specify the performance requirement in the context of some plausible solution or system. The system is a collection of technologies and means that perform work for the user. An automobile is a system made up of power train, carriage, wheel assembly, gasoline stations, highways, highway patrols, hospitals, and insurance companies, all of which make personal driving possible. The automobile system does work for the driver by moving him from place to place at high speeds compared with walking. The definition of the automotive system gives a performance requirement as to how much speed, convenience, and cost will meet a human need. The same human need may be met by another set of technologies (or alternate system), such as dial-a-ride-transit or helicopters. For any alternative system, the performance requirements would be much the same—that is, mass transit cannot meet the convenience and manipulative requirement of human needs; and helicopters cannot meet the current cost requirement. Thus the automobile remains the sole contender among these alternative systems as being the only one currently able to meet the performance requirements of human needs. However, human needs may change. For example, human needs may come to include clean air quality, which the automobile currently is unable to meet. Then another alternative technology may become the system that delivers personal transportation with the functional performance requirements of speed, handling, cost, and air quality. The decision maker thus needs to make a careful assessment of the performance specifications of human wants, because these criteria screen out those products or services that cannot meet human needs based upon cost, convenience, utility, or quality.

To recapitulate, we started by looking at the starry sky of the universe with wide-angle vision to see what problems should be solved or what decisions made. The information flow from the universe is overwhelming, so we began as managers to sort out information by the process of elimination—that is, we were faced with an information selection decision. We have used deductive reasoning to select information by three sets of screenings. First, we screened possible decision information by examining the necessary conditions imposed upon us by the environment, such as the lack of resources, environmental capability, or supply. Second, we screened information based upon the desirable conditions of the decision—that is the conventional or unconventional wisdom of what people want (or value). And third, we screened information more selectively by examining the performance goals of what people want specifically from a particular system. These successive screenings have narrowed the information requirements for a decision to manageable proportions, because the work functions can be identified as performance requirements for meeting a human need. We have arrived, by deduction, at an ideal system specification. We know, for example, in personal transportation what speed, convenience, cost, and air quality are required. We know in the case of appendectomies that the pain may be excised by surgical, medicinal, or psychological means within a time-cost parameter.

Now, as managers, we may switch from deductive to inductive reasoning and ask: If these are the performance requirements of an ideal system to meet human needs, then how can we next arrive at a feasible (buildable) system by observing all the alternative ways in which the performance requirement can be met? Or, by observing all the technologies, means, and cost, can we make a decision to build a personal transportation unit that meets the performance requirements better than the internal combustion automobile? Or, can I, by observation, find a better alternative for excising the pain of an appendix rather then by surgery?

Induction is the act of reasoning from observations to principles. We wish, as decision makers, to observe all the alternative ways by which the performance requirements of a system can be met, using the parts to know inductively the whole. The parts are the observable means. The whole is the performance specification that meets a human need.

Technology and Learning in Decisions

The purpose of a decision is to take an action. To do, to act, is to work. Decisions are made to organize work. Decisions are concerned with work design, the arrangement of tasks, the assignment of tasks, the creation of task networks, and the coordination of concurrent task networks into an output at a particular time and a particular cost with a specified performance (see chapter 5).

Work is designed around a technique; and, hence, the first information needed for task organization is what skills, crafts, or technologies are available to meet the performance specification of the system. The sorting, screening, or evaluation of technical alternatives is sometimes called technology assessment. Technology assessment begins by the manager's inductive observation of all the ways a performance requirement can be met, his survey of the state of the art (literature and practice), and his estimate of what research discoveries are potential if resources and effort are applied to them. This assessment yields the currently known ways to carry out the mission, with some rough estimates of their probability and cost.

The second information problem is to assess what learning requirements are implied in the technologies under review—that is, what human skills and human learning must be accomplished to be able to perform the tasks in the networks of work assignments? These learning requirements may include research discoveries, scientific advancements, engineering design, manufacturing development, capital equipment, and human operator skills. The sum of all these learning requirements constitute the labor costs of the development.

The executive proceeds to observe inductively all of the technical alternatives by which a performance requirement may be met, and then he assigns costs to the alternatives by estimating the labor input needed to learn (develop) the technique. By assembling the technical and learning requirements of a system, the executive has the elements of a decision about how to organize the tasks of work to be done.

Data Requirements

We have seen that the decision or inquiry method is inherent in the mission. When the mission is objective, as in business, the inquiry method is objective. When the mission is subjective, as in government or voluntary institutions, the inquiry method is subjective. The data requirements of a decision thus are determined by the inquiry method being used.

The data requirements of an objective inquiry method are objects—that is, materials, events, costs, sales, prices, man-hours, dollars, numbers of customers, numbers of workers, tons of steel, and ton-miles of transport. These objective facts can be assembled into pro-forma income statements, balance sheets, flow of funds, and rate of return on investment calculations (chapter 5). Also, the technology assessment and learning requirements are objective, since they are made up of equipment, experiments, man-hours, and capital. Hence, the task organization networks for new products or development can be priced out as objective estimates of rate of return. The information input for these factual inquiry methods is the assemblage of objective data, inductively, from the observations of experience in the present.

The data requirements for a subjective inquiry method are subjects—that is, persons, their feelings, emotions, values, attitudes, relationships, agreements, conflicts, coalitions, and differences as individuals and as groups. The feelings of individuals can neither be assembled nor known definitively. Their attitudes can only be approximated as well as words can express them. Their expression can be assembled to the extent groups have shared values and confront other interest parties with issues. Subjective inquiry then seeks to identify individual attitudes expressed in words, group values expressed as issues, and conflict among groups by analyzing differences on issues. Subjective inquiry is an approximation of the expressed feelings on human needs. All the participants in the inquiry are likely to project their own feelings into the queries or responses—that is, the subjective content of response messages is continuously transmuted by the feelings of the participants, such as the sender, receiver, analyst, hearer, and the decision maker. At any state of inquiry, subjective data may become a garble of many inputs that are difficult to decipher. The manager, in making a decision, needs to screen out emotional projections from intermediaries (including his own, if possible) and get back as close to the source of transmission (to the feelings of the user) as possible.

One of the problems a decision maker faces in a scientific and objective culture is the difficulty of treating subjective, emotional data as valid evidence. Yet feelings are the ingredient that ultimately determine the goals, values, and norms of a decision. The decision maker frequently feels pressed to use objective inquiry methods to make subjective data more cosmetic and acceptable, often with the result of having meaningless sets of data. The decision maker should frankly identify (at least to himself) the subjective as well as the objective contents of decisions, and should then recognize that the inquiry method used determines the data requirements of the decision.

Alternatives

The alternatives of the decision are determined by the operational capability of the institution. Existing organizations have a capability built up over the past to fulfill their mission. This capability is made up of technologies, equipment, and the functional skills of people in research, marketing, finance, engineering, production, control, policy, and planning. These skills and techniques have all been shaped and honed to a particular use in an existing institution, such as building television sets, houses, and refrigerators; teaching arithmetic; treating respiratory diseases; or counseling marriages. Those trained in counseling marriages cannot easily build television sets, nor vice versa. Thus the capability of the organization shapes the decision maker's choice. A manager can only decide on new sets of tasks that are reasonably similar to or adaptable from existing skills. Otherwise, the decision poses a new set of learning requirements, which for practical purposes may mean a new and different organization.

Executives seldom decide in favor of building new and different organizations because they often do not know enough about the capabilities of a new organization to minimize their risks, and the existing organization will oppose a drastic change. We saw in chapter 1 how a leader has to maintain a leadership base and have a group of followers and supporters to do his work and will. Existing organizations do not like to be faced with new sets of capabilities because it makes them obsolete, and hence expendable. Therefore the executive is usually constrained in a decision to build upon the existing organization, adding new skills, perhaps modifying the organization, adapting it, but surely not abandoning it. Therefore, the alternatives that an executive effectively considers in a decision are those which are adaptable to an existing operational capability.

Control Parameters

The control parameters of a decision are determined by the evaluative capability of the institution. Control requires a feedback loop from the output to the input having three elements: (1) an instrument or measure that detects the quality and quantity of the output, and whether the output characteristics meet the performance goals of the decision; (2) a control unit, which may be mechanical or managerial, that compares the measured output with the performance specification of the decision to see if they are identical or different; and (3) an adjustment valve or gate that regulates the flow of inputs to make a correction, causing the work to conform to the performance specification.

In business production where the output can be specified in quantitative, economic, or engineering terms, a measure can be made of a product's performance. When output measures are instrumented, a control loop can be established, and frequently the operation can be automated. When the output cannot be measured (as in some cases of government and voluntary institution activity), two elements of the control loop disappear—the output instrumentation, and the control unit comparison. All that is left is an input control at the gate, which is subjectively or symbolically operated.

Of course, output measurement is not an all or nothing option. Most events are at least partially measurable, if one wants to try; and few things are fully measurable, even physical objects. For example, the endurance and performance of a physical product such as an inertial platform, stable gyroscope is very difficult to measure because of the fine tolerances, complex interfaces, balance, momentum, and centrifugal forces of a rotating mass. On the other hand, subjective human attitudes are at least partially measurable in such cases as learning progress in education or pathological recovery in medicine, if one is willing to put credence in verbal appraisal of feelings by the client, whose option is closer to the source than that of the observing expert.

Control is a matter of willingness to utilize the best measures available. The evaluative skill of many personal-service organizations is low because they prefer to rely on professional assessment (mystique) rather than subjective measurements of clients. An executive can, in such organizations, press for better measures, even subjective ones. To do so assures an output closer to the performance requirements of the clients. In other words, improving the evaluative capability of an institution improves its responsiveness to human needs and strengthens the allegiance of its users—its the evaluative capability thus determines the control parameters of a decision.

Knowledge Requirements of Management

In this chapter we have considered the proposition that the nature of information selected by a decision maker determines both the definition of the problem and the definition of the answer. Indeed, there are no problems and no answers except those dictated by the choice of information. Information selected therefore is the ultimate management decision. Consequently, the knowledge requirements of a decision maker are (1) to know how to select meaningful decision data from the welter of information in the world; (2) to select data by screening it through information specifications, first deductively then inductively; and (3) to know when to depart from conventional information.

The approach to information selection suggested in this chapter has been to screen decision data by eight sets of specifications or parameters, first deductively then inductively, according to the following pattern.

By deductive reasoning:

1. The necessary conditions of the decision determined by environmental constraints.
2. The desirable conditions of the decision according to conventional values and unmet needs.
3. The method of inquiry that is inherent in the mission.
4. The performance goals from human user requirements.

Then, by inductive reasoning:

5. The alternatives of the decision determined by technology and learning requirements.
6. The data requirements derived from the inquiry method.
7. The alternatives allowed by operational capability.
8. The control conditions determined by evaluative capability.

Example. Consider that we are managers in the automotive industry or any industry concerned with personal transportation. We wish to examine the need for making any new decisions relative to new products or services in personal transportation. We proceed by defining our mission and then selecting information relative to the mission by the eight information specifications shown earlier.

Mission. To provide personal transportation for individuals that maximizes their convenience and personal freedom of movement at an acceptable cost.

By deductive reasoning:

1. Necessary conditions:
   a. Conserve energy and petroleum, which is in limited supply, to an equivalent of less than one-fifteenth of a gallon per mile (or more mileage than fifteen miles per gallon).

b. Reduce emissions of nitrogen oxides and other pollutants by 90 percent of 1970-1974 emission levels (these are Environmental Protection Agency standards).

c. Reduce space occupancy requirements or roads and parking (that is, arable and urban land is getting scarce).

2. Desirable conditions:
    a. Make earnings from the manufacture and sale of personal transportation at least equal to the money market rate for capital.
    b. Sell the personal transit service at monthly payments not more than one-sixth of the average family income (about the present level of total transportation expenditures).
    c. Provide door-to-door travel convenience.

3. Method of inquiry:
    The object of the service is personal movement within a time and cost constraint; therefore, the method of inquiry is objective, to measure movement characteristics within time and cost limits.

4. Performance goals:
    Individuals are accustomed to personal movement by automobile and equivalent performance requirements are expected of alternative systems.
    a. Personal access to transportation at the time and will of the individual.
    b. Not more than ten minutes or one-fourth of travel time spent in queues (that is, traffic jams, congestion, waiting curb-side, walking to or from parking, etc.).
    c. Door-to-door service, or at least walking no further than from typical parking lot.
    d. Through-transit or rapid connections, if any.
    e. Speeds to 55 (70?) miles per hour.

By inductive reasoning:

5. Alternative technologies:
    a. Technology assessment of probable alternatives, such as improved internal combustion engines (with afterburners), stratified charge engines, rotary engines, gas turbines, car pools, dial-a-ride bus, guideway automatic bus, pneumatic trains, helicopters, jet-thrust platforms, etc.
    b. Learning requirements for developing alternate technologies (development and operating costs).
    c. Capital requirements for alternate technologies (capital costs).

6. Data requirements:
    a. Objective data as to engineering performance and cost of alternatives.
    b. Subjective data as to consumer attitude toward alternative means of personal transport.

7. Alternatives allowed by capability:
   a. This assessment depends upon site of decision maker—whether in automobile, aircraft, mass transit, or government institution; that is, the information selection is a screening of what that institution is capable of building or designing.
   b. The decision maker would next assess how far he could adapt the existing institution by hiring new people and getting new facilities.

8. Control conditions:
   a. Control over production would be as to size, speed, fuel consumption, emissions, space occupancy, and cost of the output—all measured objectively and fed into a control loop.
   b. Control over marketing or the go-no-go decision would be based upon attitudinal surveys of the expressed feelings of customers (or test markets), whether they would buy the alternative forms of personal transit, given price and performance specifications.

Admittedly, this example is an abstract of how successive screening could be used to select information for a decision. More complex cases would be posed by personal services, such as medical care or psychiatric care, where the subjective content of the information selection process would be much greater. The higher the subjective content, the more probabilistic, ambiguous, and risky the decision becomes. Nevertheless, in principle the information selection for framing the problem and solution would proceed in the same way.

In the preceding discussion and example we have thus seen how a decision maker selectively moves from arrays of information toward specific decision information by using successive information filters. He arrives at his decision by a process of elimination, in which the final choice is a test among the alternatives of their comparative performance versus cost (which is a trade-off of marginal gains versus marginal costs). Nevertheless, we must recognize that some of this information selection has been judgmental—that is, some of the decision information may be looked upon as "hard" data and some as "soft" data. The hard data are:

1. The necessary conditions set by environmental constraints
2. The method of inquiry
3. The data requirements inherent in the method
4. Operational capability
5. Control capability

The soft data are:

1. Desirable conditions of the decision
2. Performance goals
3. Alternative technologies

The decision maker should know when to depart from the implications of a decision, based upon the information that has been selected. The decision maker generally departs from the soft data and not the hard data, based upon his own intuitive perception of the probabilities of the data being accurate. That is, the soft data in the decision are subjective evaluations either by the customer or the design engineers; and their evaluations tend to be retrospective, based upon past experience. The intuitive leap of the executive is to estimate the probability that a new technology is possible, or that it would induce a new set of user attitudes. That kind of decision is a high-risk guess, but most growth industries are based upon such a guess. Thus the executive, having been as rational as possible in the screening and selection of information for a decision, at some point has to make an intuitive guess about its probabilistic meaning. The executive therefore departs from the information in a rational decision structure at the final assessment of significance, probability, and risk.

Part II
Decision-making Methods

9 Economic Decisions

Decisions have a mission and purpose that are derived from the ends of society and of individuals. These purposes establish a framework for institutions and their decisions. Thus framework was discussed in Part I, with regard to the structure, form, and types of decisions; the functions of business, government, and social institutions; and the selection of information for decisions (chapter 8).

We now wish to consider (given the purposes and data of decisions in Part I) how the decision is made. What is the criteria and method of resolution by which decision makers make up their minds about one alternative versus others? Decision-making methods are derived from a number of fields and disciplines, including economics, political science, mathematics, and behavioral sciences, as well as from experience and intuition. These decision-making methods are the subject of Part II.

Economics has made a major contribution to decision making and provides an appropriate beginning for one class of decisions in business and government. Economics assumes that decisions are made rationally by individuals with perfect knowledge of the market. Perfect knowledge is, of course, ideal; and economics treats the convergence upon sufficient knowledge for a decision as an information cost. These information costs are included in the transaction along with other product costs. One of the problems, as we later see, is deciding how much information and information cost is sufficient for a rational decision. This cost becomes very high for intangible types of decisions, particularly in government and in the assessment of social costs. Nevertheless, we start with economic decisions because they constitute much of rational decision making.

Beyond the rational decisions of economics are other forms of decision making (discussed in chapters 10 and 11) that are empirical, behavioral, and social choice methods. These several approaches, taken together, lead to quantitative and systematic decision methods (chapter 12). Part II then surveys the spectrum of decision methods to help a manager clarify which approach is applicable in different cases. The economics, political science, and mathematics of decision making are whole disciplines in themselves warranting depth of study; and, obviously, this survey cannot go into depth on the theories, proofs, and formulae that are found in these disciplines. Rather, the intention here is to summarize the main decision rules or concepts that a manager might use in a sequence ranging from the tangible to the intangible human ends—that is, the approach is inductive. We are observing a spectrum of events, from tangible to intangible human needs, to see which decision methods and data will help resolve a problem or choice.

Economics deals initially with discrete goods or services that can be separately identified, produced, sold, bought, and priced. Economic goods thus represent discrete units that make them tangible, quantitatively manageable, and rationally treated in decisions. Most of the concepts in this chapter are derived from applied microeconomics, the theory of the firm, and managerial economics, for those who wish to pursue their methodology in greater depth.[1]

Basis for Economic Decisions

The basis for economic decisions is to equate incremental costs with incremental revenues or benefits. Economic decisions deal with the net change in costs of revenues from one time period to the next—that is, the decision making is incremental. Incremental decisions assume that the existing institutions, or the existing system, serve appropriate missions but may need corrective adjustments to improve costs, profits, or benefits in the economic process. Economics is concerned with managerial decisions that bring markets into equilibrium and, as such, is a feedback control concept for economic adjustment.

Incremental decision making may be contrasted with holistic, or system, thinking. A holistic approach looks at a system as a whole and inquires what its purposes or missions are, and then it proceeds to examine ideal and feasible alternatives for carrying out the mission. Part I of this book is a holistic or systems approach to society, individual needs, and the ends of management—Part I does not assume that the existing economic or social system is the only alternative way for the United States to develop itself. Incremental decision making, by contrast, does assume the existing economic system to be appropriate and continuing, and merely inquires whether it is currently functioning in a satisfactory or unsatisfactory state in terms of being in equilibrium. In other words, a systems approach looks at events anew to see what managerial methods will achieve the mission and purposes of human beings most effectively; incremental decision making looks at the existing state or system as it is, to see what adjustments would make it work more smoothly. Incremental decision making is a concept for "fine tuning" the economy.

Most executives in business, government, and voluntary institutions are incremental decision makers, and several are holistic decision makers. The reason is twofold. First, incremental decision making is simpler. It only requires selective adjustment of one or two variables out of myriad possibilities; that is, it is management by exception. Second, the executive assumes that his existing institution is the system. We encountered this form of tunnel vision in chapter 3 in the truncated institutional decision, where the decision maker is concerned with himself and the continuance of his institution, rather than with the fulfillment and ends of human beings as a whole. Therefore, what he sees is the need to "fine tune" the economic adjustment of his existing institution rather than adjust to broader human ends; and this causes the decision maker to suboptimize on his own goals.

Be that as it may, incrementalism is the dominant form of decision making in society, and every potential manager has to know what it means and how to do it. That is the concern of this chapter. Incremental decision making is based upon a broad principle that has many corollaries. The broad principle is that economic decisions equate incremental costs with incremental revenues. Incremental means the last added events, or the net change, involved in the decision. The term "incremental" is sometimes used interchangeably with the word "marginal." Strictly speaking, marginal changes are always expressed on a per unit basis, while incremental changes may be expressed either as a total (that is, total cost or total revenue) or per unit. Incremental thus is a broader term than marginal.

Table 9-1 presents a form of incremental or marginal analysis frequently used in economics. Suppose a producer of woodwork cabinets sells in a market with a demand schedule similar to that shown in columns 1 and 2. Demand means the quantities that will be purchased at various prices; and, hence, demand always implies a schedule that relates prices to quantities. As the quantity of goods increases in the market, the price declines. The seller may use this demand schedule to calculate his revenue, by multiplying the amount he can produce (shown in intervals of 10 units) by the market price. This calculation (column 1 X column 2) gives him his total revenue prospects at various prices (column 3). He may then subtract his total costs (column 4) to arrive at his profit (column 5). Thus far, we have produced an income statement of the total dollars the seller may realize in revenue, cost, and profit at various volumes.

Table 9-1
Illustration of Incremental Analysis

Demand Schedule		Total $ Income Statement			Incremental or Marginal	
1 Quantity	2 Price	3 Revenue	4 Costs	5 Profits	6 Revenue	7 Costs
10 units	$130	$1,300	$1,600	$−300		
20	110	2,200	2,200	0	$900	$600
30	100	3,000	2,700	300	800	500
40	90	3,600	3,200	400	600	500
50	80	4,000	3,600	400	400	400
60	70	4,200	4,000	200	200	400
70	60	4,200	4,500	−300	0	500

The incremental analysis is shown in columns 6 and 7, and this data is the crux of the decision making. Column 6 is the net change in revenue (column 3) as the quantity increases. Similarly, column 7 is the incremental cost (from column 4) as quantities increase. At that point where incremental revenue equals incremental costs (at a quantity of 50 units in this illustration), profit is at its maximum—that is, as long as the net increase in revenue is greater than the net increase in cost by adding units to production, the seller will gain by increasing output; and, similarly, buyers will be better off by having more goods at the lowest possible prices.

The basis for economic decisions is to produce or sell added units in the market to that point where incremental revenues just equal the incremental costs, because at this point buyers and sellers are best off. Or we might say, the welfare of both buyers and sellers is at an optimum. This general principle of equilibrium, at a point of maximum general welfare, has a number of corollaries that help explain the economic forces at work; namely, the motivations affecting the sellers and the buyers. We first look at the producer's, or seller's, options.

Diminishing Marginal Productivity

A decision maker will add a production factor to increase output, (as long as marginal revenue exceeds marginal cost) to that point where he encounters diminishing marginal productivity. The factors of production are land, labor, capital, and management. When combined, these factors form a production capability. The manager must decide how to combine these factors and in what proportions. Economics defines the best (most efficient and profitable) combination of factors in the law of variables proportions, which is also called the law of diminishing returns or the principle of diminishing marginal productivity. The principle is as follows: If the quantity of one productive factor is increased, while the quantities of all other productive factors remain constant, the additional increments will reach a point of diminishing marginal productivity. For example, if the quantity of labor is added incrementally to a shop with a fixed amount of equipment, space, land, and management, output will increase to a maximum level, followed by diminishing marginal output. This may be illustrated graphically (figure 9-1).

In figure 9-1, the total output or product increases as additional labor is employed with a given amount of capital investment to point d, where output begins to decline. Suppose, for example, there are five sets of milling machines and shaping equipment in a cabinetmaker's shop. Each added employee from one to five (or perhaps six) would increase the output. But at some point—perhaps seven or eight employees—the workers would get in each other's way, have no equipment to use, and interfere with the work flow. At that point, total output would decline. The marginal product is the net change or increase in

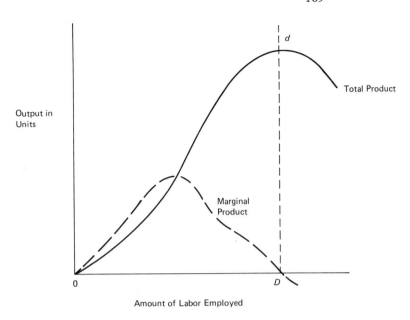

Figure 9-1. Illustration of Diminishing Marginal Productivity.

output, shown as a dotted line on the graph. It increases sharply at first and then diminishes, until at point OD the marginal product becomes negative—that is, after point OD, each increment of labor causes a net loss in production. This is the point at which the decision maker would cease to add labor. He would add labor as long as there was any net gain to be achieved in output (and as long as marginal revenue exceeded marginal cost).

The ratio of the output to the units of labor is called the marginal product of labor. The same approach may also be taken with other factors of production. For example, the amount of labor, land, and management may be held constant, and capital equipment may be added in increments until it, too (as in figure 9-1), reaches a point of diminishing marginal productivity. The ratio of the output to the units of capital equipment is called the marginal product of capital.

The principle of diminishing marginal productivity illustrates that there is a preferred or optimum mix of the factors of production that the decision maker seeks to maximize efficiency and profit—he will add any one factor of production to a given set of productive capabilities until that point where marginal output diminishes is reached.

Diminishing Marginal Utility

We next examine the buyer's circumstances to see what economic motivations affect him. These are stated in the following corollary: *The diminishing marginal utility of additional units to the buyer causes market prices to vary inversely with the quantity of goods.*

Consumer demand is influenced by the use any particular product has to the buyer. Individuals become satisfied through consumption, and they have limited capacity to consume added units. One loaf of bread may be essential to life. Two loaves may be overly satisfying; and three loaves may cause a stomach ache. The consumer may pay a high price for one loaf of bread, a low price for the second, and require a negative price (bribe) to take the third if he had to eat it. Thus the market price that the consumer is willing to offer is a factor of the use—or lack of use—he has for specific goods. This utility declines with quantity, so that each added (marginal) unit is worth less. Thus, the consumer's marginal utility diminishes with quantity, and the diminishing marginal utility is reflected in a declining price.

Demand is the relationship between price and quantity that reflects this diminishing marginal utility. We noted earlier that demand always implies a schedule relating price and quantity. An example of a demand schedule was given in figure 9-1, columns 1 and 2. The seller used this demand schedule to calculate his total revenue. Total demand in the market, then, reflects all buyers' diminishing marginal utility for a given product (or service) by a declining schedule of prices that buyers as a group are willing to pay for all quantities.

A demand-price schedule is a useful decision tool for both buyers and sellers. It helps a buyer estimate what price effects will occur if shortages or increases in supply take place. It helps a seller estimate his marginal revenue from added production, which he wishes to equate with his marginal costs.

Maximizing Earnings

Earnings are maximized when marginal costs just equal marginal revenue from the last added units to the market exchange. This corollary is similar to the first incremental proposition, except that it is specifically phrased as a decision rule for the private businessman wishing to maximize his profit. (Another corollary of this same marginal concept is applied to the pricing of public goods later in this chapter.) The business decision maker, wishing to maximize his profit, will increase production to that point where his marginal costs equal marginal revenues. The calculation of marginal costs and revenues was illustrated earlier in this chapter in table 9-1. A graphic illustration of profit maximization is shown in figure 9-2.

The demand curve is shown slowing downward from left to right, showing the buyers' diminishing marginal utility by an increase in quantity. The demand schedule (quantity times price) is also a total revenue for the supplier. The marginal revenue is the net change or difference in revenue from one quantity interval to another, and it slopes sharply downward from left to right under the

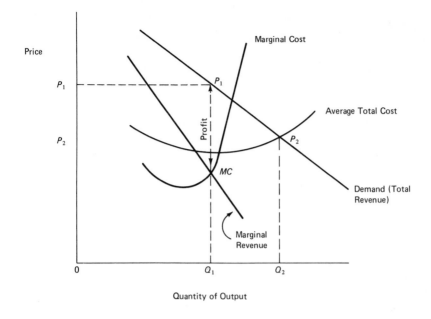

Figure 9-2. Maximization of Profit.

demand curve. The average total cost represents the cost of production for the quantities offered at varying prices. The average cost curve intersects the demand curve at P_2. P_2 represents a price at which the seller recovers his costs but at no profit. The marginal cost curve is the net change in average total cost with each increment of quantity. The point of maximum profit for the seller is at quantity Q_1, where the marginal cost just equals marginal revenue. At quantity Q_1, the selling price is P_1. The profit is the difference between price P_1 and the marginal cost, marked as MC—that is, the profit on the graph is $P_1 - MC$, and this is the maximum profit position for the seller.

Figure 9-2 illustrates the price that would prevail under conditions of monopoly, when one supplier can restrict production and control the quantity to hold up the price and get a maximum profit. Under conditions of competition, any supplier with a similar cost structure can gain some incremental profit by increasing output as far as to price P_2. It is thus argued (hypothetically) that free competition tends to drive price down to a profitless equilibrium. Whether this happens depends on whether businessmen recognize their self-interest in keeping price and profit above a competitive equilibrium. Means for avoiding competition include (1) product and brand identification, which segments the market into noncompetitive units; (2) following a price leader who maintains a profit margin by limiting output; and (3) by combination, merger, or price collusion.

The extent to which businessmen use marginal analysis as a decision tool for arriving at profit maximization is uncertain. A questionnaire survey by Hall and Hitch[2] found that a majority of firms did not attempt to equate marginal revenue and marginal costs, but, rather, arrived at pricing by applying full cost, plus a percentage markup for overhead, plus a percentage markup for profit. Earley[3] made a study which indicated that many large, well-managed firms were moving to accounting systems that were capable of identifying marginal costs, and that executives were employing marginal concepts. Case studies by Kaplan, Dirlam, and Lanzillotti[4] indicated that companies stress full cost plus margins, which are related to target returns on investment. Companies showed preferences for stable prices, following price leadership, and adjusting their margins to market conditions and maintaining market share. In a study of small firms, Haynes[5] found little evidence of adoption of incremental accounting techniques; rather, price was a subjective evaluation, by trial and error, in attempts to maximize profit.

There is some question, then, whether business executives approach pricing and profit determination as rationally as economists might think, based upon incremental analysis. The advent of computer accounting systems does make it easier to tabulate marginal cost data, provided the account classification sets up cost centers that identify fixed and variable costs by product. Such accounting systems are fairly costly, and their use for marginal choices requires analytic skills and a strong commitment.

Executives often show more interest in the firms' profitability of the firm or its organizational divisions, rather than its product or product line. A person who has lived and worked with business executives is likely to experience conversations dealing with pricing in terms of full cost or average unit costs plus markups for overhead and profit. However, new products, or existing products in trouble, are sometimes viewed in terms of their "contribution" to profit, which is a form of marginal analysis—that is, it may be that marginal decisions are the exceptional cases, and that full cost plus margins (along the lines of the Hall and Hitch, or the Kaplan et al. studies) are the more common perspectives of decision makers.

Cost Allocation

One reason why executives may not pay more attention to marginal cost analysis is that costs themselves are arbitrary and ambiguous in many cases. The ambiguity of costs may be contrary to popular impression, because individuals often think of their own costs and expenditures as hard and certain numbers. This is true because most consumer expenditures are direct, current costs. The direct and current costs of business or government are also hard figures. But business and government have many indirect or overhead costs that are allocated according to accounting rules and conventions; and it is these conventions that make costs arbitrary and sometimes ambiguous.

Cost estimation and cost allocation distribute indirect costs, applicable to multiple time periods, to units in current production. Direct costs are the costs of labor, material, supplies, electricity, and other current expenditures of business, not unlike those of consumers. Overhead costs are that portion of capital investment or other indirect costs assigned to a current time period. Capital investment is the investment in land, building, and equipment; and these are sometimes called fixed costs. Land lasts indefinitely, but its use-value may extend only over the life span of the productive facility placed upon it. Buildings may last from twenty to one-hundred years, and they are customarily written off or depreciated against current income at some rate acceptable to the Internal Revenue Service, frequently twenty to thirty years. Similarly, equipment investments are charged off or depreciated against current income over shorter periods, often ranging from five to fifteen years. Businessmen also usually have the option of whether they want to charge off the investment in equal annual amounts (called straight-line depreciation) or at more rapid rates during the early years (called accelerated depreciation). Since both the time period and the rate of depreciation are variable and subject to discretion, the consequences can be wide variations in estimates of costs or profits. The same judgmental allocation of costs pertains to other indirect costs, such as research expenditures or the portion of general management expense allocable to a particular product.

In many manufacturing companies, half or more of the costs are indirect and allocable—that is, the amount of these indirect costs to be charged is a matter of judgment. Therefore, the total cost is not more than an estimate. The following example shows how much cost estimates may vary by different allocation assumptions. Consider a situation where a small manufacturing company makes two kinds of control valves, A and B. Valve A is a common industrial model selling for $34 each at current market prices, and valve B is a more finely machined precision model which sells for $50. Both are produced in a common plant structure, which is valued at $1,000,000, and which has an additional investment of $1,000,000 in equipment. The company spends $50,000 per year on research and development (R&D). General administrative expense (GAE) for management is another $50,000.

How should management decide to allocate costs among the two products? Their practice is to allocate fixed cost on a thirty-year straight-line depreciation for plant and a ten-year straight-line depreciation for equipment. Research and development expenditures are treated as an asset and spread over three years, which is the same as the company's product cycle period for revising valve designs and tools. The direct labor and material expense for valve A is $100,000; for valve B, $140,000. Each are produced in volumes of 10,000 per year. Valve A is estimated to use 60 percent of the machine time in the plant, while B uses 40 percent. The costs and profits are estimated as shown here:

Case 1. Thirty years depreciation on plant, ten years on equipment, three years on R&D.

Overhead costs:

Plant depreciation charge	$ 34,000
Equipment depreciation	100,000
R&D	16,000
GAE	50,000
	$200,000

By allocating 60 percent of the $200,000 overhead to product A and 40 percent to product B, the following profit statements result:

	Product A	Product B
Sales	$340,000	$500,000
Less costs:		
Direct	100,000	140,000
Overhead	120,000	80,000
Profit	$120,000	$280,000

Next, we assume that the management, on the advice of the company's accountant, decides to depreciate the plant over twenty years instead of thirty, and to depreciate equipment over five years instead of ten. Plant depreciation charges would then be $50,000 per year, and equipment $200,000 per year. The profit statement for case 2 would now be reported as:

Case 2.

	Product A	Product B
Sales	$340,000	$500,000
Less costs:		
Direct	100,000	140,000
Overhead ($316,000)	190,000	126,000
Profit	$ 50,000	$234,000

The accountant now advised management to consider accelerated depreciation, such as the sum-of-the-digits method, which enables the depreciation charges to be raised to $400,000 in the earlier years, and reduced correspondingly in the later years. The income statement again revises the profits downward, this time to a loss on product A.

Case 3.

	Product A	Product B
Sales	$340,000	$500,000
Less costs:		
Direct	100,000	140,000
Overhead ($466,000)	280,000	186,000
Profit or loss	$–40,000	$174,000

The income statement from case 3 causes management concern, because product A is now losing money. They consider abandoning product A until they realize that its "contribution" to overhead costs is $280,000, without which product B would also be a loser.

An industrial engineer in the plant makes a study and discovers that although 60 percent of the number of machine hours are devoted to product A, these are in fact all simple and inexpensive machine operations. Product B, on the other hand, is built with the expensive precision equipment. If the "value" of machine hours is used to prorate cost rather than the "number" of hours, the ratios are reversed and product B takes 60 percent of the value of machine time. The accountant also recommends that research and development be written off as an expense each year, rather than prorated over three years. He refigures all the cost allocations as follows:

Case 4. Plant depreciated over thirty years, equipment over ten years, straight-line.

	Product A	Product B
Direct costs	$100,000	$140,000
Overhead costs	80,000	120,000
Profit	$160,000	$240,000

Case 5. Plant depreciated over twenty years, equipment five years, straight-line.

	Product A	Product B
Direct costs	$100,000	$140,000
Overhead costs	140,000	210,000
Profit	$100,000	$150,000

Case 6. Accelerated depreciation.

	Product A	Product B
Direct costs	$100,000	$140,000
Overhead costs	240,000	360,000
Profit	0	0

In our example, management has found six different ways to allocate costs, all in keeping with accepted accounting practices. The differences in profits are startling, as the recapitulation below demonstrates:

	Product A	Product B
Products under:		
Case 1	$120,000	$280,000
Case 2	50,000	234,000
Case 3	−40,000	174,000
Case 4	160,000	240,000
Case 5	100,000	150,000
Case 6	0	0

Which of these profit estimates is "right?" They are all right, and they all are correct by accounting practice. The point is that costs are an estimate, and hence profits are also an estimate. Within limits, management can make profits anything they want them to be by their cost allocation methods. A management that wants to make a strong profit showing to stockholders, and to pay out dividends, might choose cases 1 or 4. A management that wanted to avoid paying federal corporate income taxes and maximize its internal cash flow would select case 6. Compared with cases 1 or 4, for example, case 6 avoids paying $196,000 in federal income taxes, and increases the internal cash flow by $216,000. This internal cash flow can be reinvested for the expansion of the business. A growth-minded decision maker would obviously choose the cost allocation practice, leading to case 6.

With cost allocation being an effective tool for manipulating profits to meet management objectives, it becomes clear why marginal analysis is not more seriously regarded by executives. Marginal analysis assumes that costs are definitive. Management practice demonstrates that costs are, at best, a rough estimate with a wide range of possible outcomes.

Break-even Analysis

A break-even point is achieved at that volume which absorbs fixed costs, as well as variable costs, at current market price. To break even means to come out of a loss position into a profit position, the break-even point being zero loss and zero profit. Regardless of its cost allocation and estimation methods, management is concerned about breaking even, because failure to break even is an indication of management incompetence. Break-even analysis is, therefore, a serious management interest.

Case 6 (in the preceding section) illustrates a product just breaking even. A

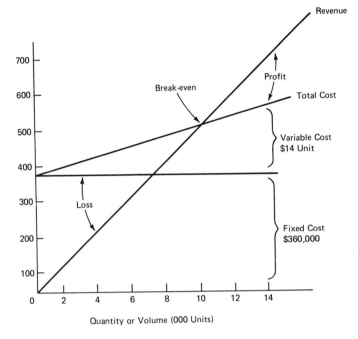

Figure 9-3. Illustration of a Break-even Chart.

typical break-even chart for product B is shown in figure 9-3, using $360,000 as the fixed cost that must be spread over the quantity of units produced. The direct cost is $140,000. This is also called "variable cost" because it varies directly with the number of units—that is, $14 per unit. The product price is still assumed to be $50, which, multiplied by the number of units, gives the total revenue.

The product in this illustration has a very high proportion of fixed costs. The result is that the loss is very large at volumes below 10,000 units. The loss is indicated by the difference between the total revenue line and the total cost line. Similarly, the profit expands very rapidly after 10,000 units is reached and all fixed costs are absorbed. Indeed, when the entire fixed cost is covered after 10,000 units, the entire revenue (less $14 per unit variable cost) is clear profit. Management has a very high incentive, with such a product, to drive the volume as far beyond 10,000 units as possible, either by vigorous marketing efforts or by pricing tactics. To decide whether a change in price of product B would result in large additional demand and profit, management needs to know something about the slope of the demand curve, or of the price elasticity of demand.

Price Elasticity of Demand

The price elasticity of demand is the relative percentage change in quantity of goods sold which accompanies a percentage change in price. Price elasticity of demand is a measure of the steepness of slope of the demand curve; and this is useful for management to know because it enables them to decide whether a change in pricing will improve their volume and profit. For example, suppose a 1 percent change in price is accompanied by a 10 percent change in volume. The demand is said to be highly elastic, and the 10-to-1 ratio indicates that the demand curve is very flat near to the horizontal. The price elasticity of demand in this instance is 10. Next, assume the opposite—that a 10 percent change in price is accompanied by a 1 percent change in volume. The elasticity of demand is 0.1, or highly inelastic, and the slope of the demand curve is very steep near to the vertical.

These two illustrations represent very extreme elasticities, but let us see how they might be useful for decision making in the case of product B discussed in the previous section. Product B breaks even at 10,000 units of volume at a price of $50 per unit; and we also know that beyond 10,000 units, the incremental profit is very high. As management, we wish to reduce prices to go to a larger volume to capture the high incremental profit, but only if the price for product B is inelastic, so that a gain in total revenue accompanies the price cut. Table 9-2 demonstrates what happens to profit for product B with a price elasticity of 10 and 0.1, compared with the original case 6. (We assume that management makes a 2 percent price reduction from $50 to $49 per unit.)

When demand is very elastic ($E = 10$), a 2 percent reduction in price to $49 is accompanied by a 20 percent increase in volume, from 10,000 units to 12,000 units. Total revenue is increased to $578,000 ($49 × 12,000). Variable costs increase ($14 × 12,000) to $168,000; but overhead costs remain the same. Thus,

Table 9-2
Illustration of Price Elasticity Effects

	Original Case 6	Elastic E = 10	Inelastic E = 0.1
Price	$50	$49	$49
Volume (units)	10,000	12,000	10,200
Revenue	$500,000	$578,000	$499,800
Less costs:			
Variable @ $14	$140,000	$168,000	$142,800
Overhead	360,000	360,000	360,000
Total cost	$500,000	$528,000	$502,800
Profit	0	$ 50,000	$ −3,000

total revenue has increased faster than total costs, and the increase in profit is $50,000. When demand is inelastic (as in illustration of $E = 0.1$), a similar calculation shows that total revenue declines while variable costs increase, with a resultant loss of $3,000. Given the cost structure of product B, management would make a decision to reduce price if demand is elastic to increase profits. If demand is inelastic, the decision would be not to cut price to avoid potential loss.

Pricing Decisions for Private Goods

Pricing decisions for private goods, under conditions of competition, reach equilibrium when the average total cost of the least efficient producer equals the market price. When a market is supplied by several producers who compete with each other, each producer will seek to test the price elasticity of demand and to arrange his cost allocations to maximize profits. The cost structure or allocation practices of various firms may differ, due to differences in efficiency because of technology, marketing practices, or management skill and judgment. The more efficient firms supplying the market will have lower cost structures than the least efficient. The efficient firms will tend to produce until their marginal costs equal the market price. The least efficient firm will produce until its average total cost equals the market price. The market will come into equilibrium when the average price offered by buyers and sellers is equal for a given quantity of goods. These tendencies can be illustrated graphically as shown in figure 9-4.

In figure 9-4, the market is in equilibrium at price OP, where supply and demand are equal for quantity OQ_3. The point of intersection represents equilibrium in price and quantity. The supply is made up from three firms of varying efficiencies. Firm 1 has the lowest average total cost (AC); and it will tend to produce to quantity Q_1, where its marginal costs equal the selling price, because this is its point of maximum profit. Similarly, firm 2, which is next lowest in efficiency and average total cost, will produce to quantity Q_2. The least efficient, firm 3, supplies the balance of the market demand by producing to point Q_3, where its average total cost equals the market price. At this point firm 3 is able to cover all its costs, including a normal return (market cost of money), but it is realizing no extra profits as are firms 1 and 2. This figure illustrates a short-run market equilibrium. If other competitors can enter the market with efficiencies similar to those found in firm 1 or 2, prices will be driven down by competition over the long term. Theoretically, if all managements are equal, and if all factor prices (cost of production) are equal, prices would be driven down to P_t in some future time period. Then all firms, being equally efficient, would produce to the point where average total costs equal the market price P_t at the much larger quantity Q_t.

In fact and practice, differentials in efficiency and profit margins do exist

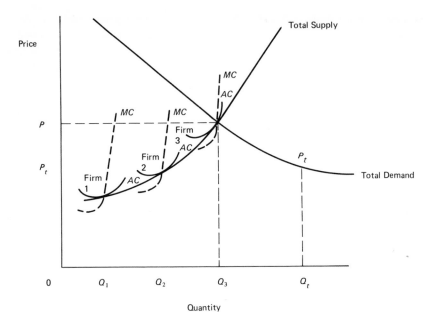

Figure 9-4. Equilibrium Pricing in Price Markets.

over long periods of time, due in part to management ability and in part to barriers to entry (chapter 2) erected to keep out competition. As a matter of practical intelligence, an executive needs to know where his firm stands within the industry in terms of efficiency and costs. An executive in firm 3 would be very foolhardy to cut prices as a means of increasing volume, unless he found means to improve his cost efficiency, because firms 1 and 2 could drive him out of the market in a price war.

Pricing under Limited Competition

Under conditions of limited competition among a few producers, pricing decisions realize a surplus profit by restricting supply to the point where marginal costs equal marginal revenues for all but the least efficient among a select group of firms. When competition is limited to a few firms, the executives of the few are roughly knowledgeable about their relative efficiencies and costs, merely by reading each other's published income statements. They can compare their own rate of return with others in the industry. If a decision maker knows that he is the most efficient producer in the industry—for example, for firm 1 in the previous illustration—what should his behavior be? Economic theory of pure competition assumes that firm 1, or other efficient competitors similar to firm 1, will cut prices and expand production, eventually driving firms 2 and 3 out of the market, until price falls to P_t and quantity Q_t. The motivation would be to gain the incremental profit as long as firm 1's marginal cost is below the market price.

In practice, industrial executives do not behave this way. Differential costs and profits have existed over long periods of time in such industries as automobiles, rubber tires, chemicals, electronics, steel, communications, and many more. Indeed, the entire stock market valuation scheme is built around price-earnings ratios that value differential profits according to the apparent efficiencies and long-run growth prospects of companies and managements. The leader (most efficient) firm does not cut price for at least two reasons. The first reason is to maintain an excess profit margin, such as in the example of firm 1, which is a very comfortable position in which to remain. The excess profits enable management to finance such security-building mechanisms as barriers to entry, technological and competitive superiority, and high personal incomes. The second reason is that driving out competitors brings the threat of antitrust action for unfair price competition in restraint of trade. Why risk treble damages or even dissolution while resting comfortably on a surplus profit margin?

Differential costs and profits can exist, practically, over extended time periods by limiting competition among a select few. Who selects the few? In a sense, the few are selected by the Justice Department by foregoing prosecution under the antitrust laws. Oligopolistic industries have evolved by slow erosion of the many high cost competitors, with the leading low cost firms limiting competition and restricting supply just short of a prosecutable case against themselves. Or in another sense, the few competitors are selected by leading business executives' notion of where the trade-off is among (1) maximizing profit, (2) building barriers to entry, and (3) avoiding antitrust prosecution. This trade-off is highly judgmental; and sometimes executives make mistakes that threaten to reduce profits, open competition, or invite prosecution. For the most part, however, executives understand the decision rules well enough to know that competition among the few is an easier life for themselves and their companies than either pure competition or governmental retribution.

Social Rate of Discount

Individuals have a preference for income in the present rather than in the future, which is reflected in a social rate of discount. Individuals prefer income in the present because it gives them options and choices as to current use; and, thus, current income has more utility or value than future income. This preference for current income is expressed by the discount rate, which equates the present value of future income with money in hand today. There are two forms of interest or discount rates. One is the market rate of interest used by lending institutions such as banks and insurance companies to make commercial loans. The market interest rates tend to fluctuate according to the supply and demand for funds; and the short-term money rate has varied in recent years from 6 to 12 percent.

A second type of interest rate that expresses the preference for current income is called the social rate of discount. This is a more theoretical rate expressing the idea that individuals have a marginal utility curve that shows their trade-off preference for a dollar now versus a dollar in the future. Perhaps the closest practical measure of this preference is found in the long-run savings rate at which individuals are willing to forego current consumption to put their money into savings. This social discount rate appears to be in the range of 6 to 8 percent.

The reason for distinguishing between the market interest rate and a social discount rate are twofold. The market interest rates fluctuate, first, according to central bank policy to inflate or deflate the money supply, and second, according to individuals' expectations about inflation. The money market rate of interest is an appropriate measure of the present value of future income for short-term, private business decisions, because that is the going rate business will have to pay for funds. The social rate of discount is thought to be fairly independent of inflationary-deflationary expectations, and, thus, it expresses the long-run social preference for current income. The social rate of discount is, therefore, appropriate to measure time preference in long-run public or social projects.

The government has historically used lower discount rates than the private sector, particularly in determining the present value of public works and reclamation projects. Many dams and irrigation projects have been justified on grounds of their income potential, using low discount rates such as 2 to 4 percent. These same projects would have been economically unjustified at rates closer to the market interest rates of 5 to 7 percent.

An argument against using different and lower discount rates in the public than in the private sector has been made—that such a differential presumes a capital market for public funds that is separate from, and lower in interest than for private funds. Such differential capital markets do not appear to exist in the real world. For our purposes in illustrating decision making, we assume that the discount rate used in private decisions is the long-term money market rate for borrowing at any point in time, thus reflecting their actual borrowing cost. Such a market rate will reflect monetary expectations concerning inflation and deflation, as well as supply and demand conditions for funds.

The social discount rate is assumed to be a long-term average of the market rate, over ten or fifteen years, which comes close to the savings rates at which individuals have actually foregone current consumption to save money. Such an average long-term rate has fewer inflationary-deflationary expectations reflected in it; but, since government both borrows and taxes over long time periods, the long-term savings rate does reflect the cost of money to the government for public purposes. In summary, we assume there is only one capital market serving both private and public uses for funds, and the cost to the private sector is the long-term money rate at which one must borrow, and the cost to government is the *average* long-term money rate.

The reason for making this distinction is that 1 or 2 percent can often make the difference between a feasible or infeasible project. The present value of money is expressed, as a formula, in terms of the future revenue divided by 1 plus the interest rate, or:

$$V = \frac{R_n}{(1 + i)^n}$$

In this expression, V is the present value of money, R is the revenue to be received in the future, i is the rate of interest, and n is the number of years elapsing before receipt of the revenue.

For example, the present value of $100 at 8 percent, to be received ten years hence, is $46.32. The present value of $100 *per year*, to be received over the next ten years at year end at 8 percent, is $671.01. When a flow of income is to be discounted, the discount formula is applied year by year and cumulated. The simplest way to use discounted values in decision making is to refer to present value tables available in mathematics or managerial economics texts.

The most frequent use of discount rates in decision making is in capital budgeting for either private or public projects. We turn to capital planning decisions next, first in terms of alternative or opportunity costs, and second in terms of selecting discounted income flows from among alternative choices.

Opportunity Costs

The cost of a decision is commonly thought of as the amount of an investment that has been made, in a family car, or in a new business machine. However, such a view describes a benefit that has been received. The real cost of a decision is the sacrifice of alternatives, or opportunity costs, caused by committing resources to the decision made. Thus, the opportunity cost of the family car may be the college education that the child did not receive, or the corrective surgery that the father gave up.

Opportunity costs are alternatives that were sacrificed, or opportunities denied by committing resources to the choice actually made. Opportunity costs are funds tied up in an individual's own business that could have been invested profitably in other ventures. The value of the opportunity cost is the difference in earnings (corrected for risk) among alternative investment choices. Thus in capital investment decisions, the decision maker will look at the different rates of return of alternative ventures. These differences describe his opportunity costs.

Capital Decisions

Capital budget decisions discount the prospective earnings for alternative choices and select the investment which has the highest marginal opportunity rate of return above the market cost of capital. Suppose a business executive is considering four technical alternatives for modernizing his plant, each having different sets of productivity. The market rate of interest at which the business would have to borrow is 8 percent per year, and the executive has made arrangements with the bank to borrow $671,000. We have seen previously that $671,000 is the present value of $100,000 a year of revenue for ten years at 8 percent. Therefore, the alternative investments will have to produce at least $100,000 in net revenue per year to be preferable. The net revenue produced per year for ten years by each of the four modernization options for an initial investment of $671,000 is:

	Income per Year	Discount Rate	Marginal Return
Borrowing rate in market	$100,000	8%	0
Investment 1	108,000	10	$ 8,000
Investment 2	119,000	12	19,000
Investment 3	134,000	15	34,000
Investment 4	150,000	18	50,000

Clearly, the executive would make a decision to select investment 4, because it has the highest marginal return above the market cost of money. Investment 4 produces $50,000 per year more than the borrowing cost, and yields a profit of 10 percent above all costs, including the cost of money.

Any other choice would involve a sacrifice or an opportunity cost. Suppose the company looked at only one option, investment 1, because it was preferred by the engineering staff on technical grounds. The justification for investment 1 is that it pays $8,000 per year in profit above the borrowing rate for funds. However, once the $671,000 is committed, all other investment options are opportunities lost. The opportunity cost of investment 1 compared with investment 4 is $42,000 per year, or an 8 percent profit differential. This is a sacrifice that a decision maker would not knowingly forego, if all alternatives had been reviewed by discounting prospective earnings and selecting the highest marginal opportunity rate of return.

External Economies and Diseconomies

The rate of return used as a basis for capital budget decisions in business is derived from the flow of net revenues—that is, revenues after all costs. Now we may wish to ask how good were our cost estimates in the first place? What did they include and what did they not include? Unless the decision maker is clear on which costs were included and excluded, the significance of the rate of return on investment is clouded.

We have already seen that costs can be allocated and estimated in various ways, which produce greatly differing results in net revenue or profit. Indeed, management can manipulate cost allocations in such a way as to produce, within limits, the profit it wishes. Moreover, in the earlier demonstration about the arbitrary nature of cost allocations, we dealt only with fixed and overhead costs that are tangible expenditure items in business accounts. The arbitrariness of the cost allocation was produced merely by the time period over which management chose to allocate the cost.

The direct and overhead costs of a firm are all internal costs in the sense that they are contained and internal to the accounts of the business. They are costs that the firm recognizes, internalizes, and includes in its accounts. There are also costs which firms exclude from their accounts, such as unemployment costs of employees laid off, or costs of cleaning up effluent from a plant which it discharges into a stream. These excluded costs are external to the firm, not recognized in its accounts, and therefore become social costs to someone else. Such exclusions from business costs are called external diseconomies.

External diseconomies are costs or damages that accrue to others outside the firm. Examples are health damage from air pollution being borne by citizens generally, or fish kills from mine acid run-off into a stream. External diseconomies tend to become government costs, borne by the taxpayer, to the extent that public expenditures attempt to correct the damages excluded from private enterprise accounts. External economies are also uncompensated benefits accruing to others outside the firm. For example, a business may build an access road, connecting two highways, to its plant and open it for public use. Then the public acquires a benefit of additional roadway for which the firm is not compensated.

The external diseconomies that firms exclude from their cost estimations are very large in the unemployment, welfare, and environmental fields. Because they are large and cannot be borne solely by individuals, they tend to become social costs of government, and they increase the size of government (see chapters 5 and 7). If one were to allocate back to business the social costs from the gross national product accounts that may be reasonably regarded as external diseconomies, business overhead costs are underestimated by perhaps 25 percent. Capital investment decisions would be greatly altered, in terms of a marginal opportunity rate of return above the market cost of capital, if overhead costs were revised upward by 25 percent to internalize what now are regarded as externalities, or external diseconomies.

Social Costs

External diseconomies are social costs, or pricing failures, that can be corrected by equating marginal cost of damage reduction to the marginal benefits to society. Consider a sugar mill that discharges effluent into a stream with a high biochemical oxygen demand (BOD). The nutrients in the stream will cause a loss of oxygen in the water as the nutrients are decomposed by bacteria. The loss of oxygen can cause fish kills, foul-smelling water, and eutrophication, making the water unusable downstream. A sugar mill without effluent control is treating the stream as costless water to itself. The stream is a common property of all the people; it is part of the hydrologic cycle of the whole ecology, consisting of circulation of water through transpiration, precipitation, stream flow, and transpiration again. A sugar mill, discharging BOD into a stream, overexploits the common property, because water is free or underpriced, to the detriment of all species whose life support depends upon the stream.

The corrective action is to charge the sugar mill a sufficient amount for the water to remove the nutrient and the biochemical oxygen demand, thus returning pure water to users downstream. This effluent charge would be equivalent to the marginal cost of damage reduction (that is, the cost of removing the nutrient), and it would correspond with the marginal benefit (that is, restoring pure water) to the downstream recipients.

Solutions to Externalities

Solutions to the externalities problem include standards, prohibitions, voluntary payments, damage charges, taxes or subsidies, sale of pollution rights, transfer of property rights, and regulation. The effluent charge is only one of many methods for recognizing uncompensated costs to others outside a business firm. Other methods are simply prohibition, such as the Water Quality Amendments of 1972, which prohibit any discharge into streams. Another form of compensation is voluntary payment—that is, the sugar mill pays downstream users for the opportunity cost of the water (the value of the water denied to them), and the downstream users can go and buy water they need elsewhere. Taxes or subsidies would levy costs upon the sugar mill to purify the water or subsidize its purification by the government. The downstream users might sell their rights to pure water to the sugar mill—in effect, selling pollution rights. Or, alternatively, the downstream users might sue the sugar mill for liabilities for impairing their property values. Again, the government might regulate the amount of water and pollution permissible on a permit system. All of these are ways in which the external costs of business can be imposed back upon it, by making them some form of internal charge to the firm.

Pricing of Public Goods

The pricing of public goods requires cost estimation of direct, indirect, and external costs to ascertain that the marginal gains and marginal losses to society are equal. The pricing of public goods provided by government follows in principle the economic decision making for private goods. The cost estimation and cost analysis is the same—that is, the sum of direct, indirect, and social costs. The difficulty comes in valuing the benefit. In private markets the buyer values his own benefit by his willingness to pay the market price, and presumably this balances the marginal utility or satisfaction to the buyer with the marginal cost that the buyer pays.

In public goods, however, there is no market price, and, hence, the valuation of the benefits presents special problems. When the income flow from public works projects is measurable in the same way as for private industry, the same methods can be used. For example, reclamation projects have generally valued the flow of income from sales of electric power and irrigation water in the same way that a business would. Suppose, for example, a dam produces 10 million dollars per year in electric power and irrigation water sales over thirty years. The present value of the income flow at 8 percent is $112,580,000, which is the amount the government could afford to invest in the dam construction to pay off the cost of the dam at a social rate of discount of 8 percent. The same figures can be expressed as a benefit-cost ratio, which would be expressed as:

$$\frac{\text{value of benefits}}{\text{cost}} = \frac{\$112,580,000}{\$112,580,000} = 1$$

When a government program does not generate an income flow in dollars, the valuation of benefits becomes more difficult, and it may be necessary to impute value to the benefits. For example, New York City is said to have 10,000 excess deaths per year from air pollution. How much could the government justifiably spend to reduce the death toll? The benefit of life is beyond price to the individual, but at least, at minimum, the lives could be valued at their discounted earnings potential. Suppose the earnings loss on early excess deaths from air pollution average ten years of longevity at an average earnings of

$10,000 per year for the 10,000 people. Discounted at 8 percent for ten years, the earnings potential has a present value of $671,010,000. If the social benefits of abating air pollution are $670 million, the government is warranted in expending (or initiating charges upon the private sector) at least up to that amount to equate marginal benefits to society with marginal costs.

Notes

1. For more explanation about economic decisions, see the following references listed in the bibliography: Haynes and Henry, *Managerial Economics*; McGuigan and Moyer, *Managerial Economics*; Reynolds, *Principles of Economics: Micro*; and Simon, *Applied Managerial Economics*.

2. R.J. Hall and C.J. Hitch, "Price Theory and Business Behavior," Oxford Economic Papers, no. 2 (May 1939), reprinted in T. Wilson and P.W.S. Andrews, *Oxford Studies in the Price Mechanism* (Oxford: Clarendon Press, 1951).

3. James E. Earley, "Marginal Policies of Excellently Managed Companies," The American Economic Review (March 1956).

4. A.D.H. Kaplan, Joel B. Dirlam, and Robert Lanzillotti, *Pricing in Big Business,* (Washington, D.C.: The Brookings Institution, 1958).

5. W.W. Haynes, *Pricing Decisions in Small Business* (Lexington: University of Kentucky Press, 1962).

10 Empirical and Behavioral Decisions

The economics of decision making deals largely with market effects of management actions that are observable as prices, costs, or estimates of costs and benefits. Market effects are observable when goods or services are discrete, separately identifiable, tangibly produced, exchanged, and valued by an exchange price. These characteristics of economic decisions apply more directly to things (goods and services) than to people. Thus economic decisions deal with only part of the management problem, because management must also consider the motivations and interests of people, either as buyers or producers, in making a decision. The job of the executive is to make decisions that cause other people to act; and people's actions depend upon their interests and motivations.

In addition to the economic effects of decisions, management thus is concerned about the behavioral influences that condition decision making. The behavioral aspects of decisions have been under serious study for about a generation; but executives have been making decisions for centuries. The practice of decision making by executives over the years has been based upon experience, trial and error, custom, example, and lore—that is, practical decision making has been empirical and learned by the executive in the practice of management.

In the past generation, this empiricism of decision making has been studied by the behavioral sciences through field research, data analysis, theory, and experimentation in attempts to explicate the concepts of executive practice. This chapter seeks to meld the concepts of decision making as they have emerged empirically and have been paralleled by the development of behavioral theory. Empirical and behavioral decision making, starts with executives' thought and action processes. The thought process of executives is then abstracted, approximated, and simulated in sets of rules or theories that appear to account for the behavior.

Empiricism and Intuition in Decision Making

The logical place to turn for knowledge about decision making is to the executives who do it. However, with a few exceptions, executives are singularly inarticulate about how they make decisions. Many executives in attempting to explain their success relate anecdotal experiences of events in their lives, rather than their thought processes.[1] Others are remarkably candid about their inability to explain their decision process. Several company presidents indicate that they do not know how they make decisions—they just do it.[2]

If the men who make decisions do not know how they do it, how can it be learned by someone else, or how can anyone else know? This has been the dilemma of management education. Management is experiential: it is learned by doing, not by analysis of business situations. Management is similar to Zen: those who know do not speak; those who speak do not know.

Yet much is spoken about Zen, as well as management. The learner must assume that any words spoken to him about management are only guides to start his own experience, from which he will learn by practice (that is, by deciding and managing) rather than by listening or reading. Management is a process or a way of experiencing life, as described in the *Tao Te Ching*. According to Lao-tzu, the process is made up of insights and images that are blurred and indistinct. These images are collages of experiences and things dimly seen conveying mental power, truth, and confidence. The decision maker hardly needs anything more, for the mental power comes from subconsciously making order of the world as he has perceived it. However, imagery in the mind of the executive can only be acquired by experience, seeing activities in practice, what people want, feel, and do. These experiences constitute perception, internal recall, feelings, and impressions, which are the materials from which the decision maker works. As we see later, the behavioral sciences have generally tried to approach decision analysis by documenting the perceptions and cognition of the executive—that is, what he perceives, knows, feels, and thinks.

Although most executives cannot explain their decision process, a few exceptions among managers have articulated at least part of an executive's approach to thinking, the most notable being Henri Fayol, Alfred Sloan, Chester Barnard, and Marion Folsom.

Henri Fayol (1841-1925), a French industrialist, tried to develop rules and principles of management from his experience. They have become widely used today in planning and organization. His book (1916) contained principles, such as authority should be commensurate with responsibility, and unity of direction requires one head and one plan for each activity.[3] The practical procedures for arriving at an implementable decision included five elements: a plan or program of action, organizational assignments, direction of work, coordination among divisions, and control based upon clear accounting information.

Alfred Sloan, of General Motors, made his contribution to the decision process by explicitly defining the division of organizational structures into divisional and decentralized units with a two-way flow of information within the organization.[4] Much of the recent decentralization movement into divisional operations by most major U.S. corporations followed the Sloan-General Motors pattern that had been set up in the 1920s.

Chester Barnard, an executive of New Jersey Bell Telephone, was among the first practicing executives to see and emphasize the behavioral content of decisions. In *The Functions of the Executive,*[5] Barnard stressed that an institution is an interacting system, with the needs of all participants (employees, management, investors, customers, and suppliers) entering into a decision that seeks to integrate these interests. He saw the organization as informal activity among small groups as well as hierarchically arranged from the top. He developed his ideas further in *Organizations and Management*[6] to show that one cannot understand a specific act of a human being without knowing all about the organizational environment in which the act functions as a part. If this sounds abstract, Barnard states in essence, you learn to deal with people effectively by learning their point of view and what influences their behavior. Perceiving the views and motives of others is easily said but difficult to realize without a *concept* treating the behavior as simpler than it is.

In this Lao-tzu-type statement, Barnard reveals the essence of the decision process: it is to conceive an image or abstraction of the interacting influences of people's behavior. This art of conception, abstraction, or imagery treats the real world as simpler than it is, but nevertheless the abstraction is an essentially accurate description of key (human) relationships. By treating the real world as simpler than it is, the executive has solved the information-selection problem and is able to see or encompass the problem with his own limited and bounded rationality.

-    How does the executive know what information to select for his abstraction? Barnard does not explicitly say how the decision maker selects an image simpler than the world is. He says that such selectivity is almost impossible to comprehend, or rationally think about; and this is why management is an art difficult to learn. Like any art, the abstraction comes from an individual's experience of that which is constant, important, enduring, true, predictable, revealing, and insightful. The executive observes humans in actions and comes to his own understanding of that which is universal about their behavior upon which he can build a decision. This observation impresses a kind of experiential programming upon the executive's mind, which becomes a knack, hunch, intuition, or nonrational perception. A New York theater wizard said of himself that he acts spontaneously because, when he thinks, he makes a mistake.[7]

Another dimension to the decision process is suggested by Marion Folsom, treasurer of Eastman Kodak and later Secretary of the U.S. Department of Health, Education, and Welfare. He specifically addresses the information selection problem by the use of executive staff personnel to study and learn how constituents think, feel, and act.[8] In 1914, Folsom noted, the president of Eastman had no staff assistants and President Wilson had only five, whereas today the Eastman staff corps is in the dozens and the President has hundreds of staff assistants, almost to the point where they form the decision apparatus to the exclusion of the operating department heads (Cabinet officers). Each presidential assistant specializes in information about the feelings of the interacting participants in the system. Hence, there are presidential assistants for labor relations, public relations, human relations, community relations, consumer relations, political relations, congressional relations, and foreign relations—every constituency has its sensor of relations. The images (conceptions) that a president must now have of all his relations are so huge in number that he needs assistant image makers to help him visualize (abstract) all the interactions that he has to engage in.

If the images of the human relationships of an interacting system become so immense that one decision maker cannot comprehend all the images, but has to have subimage makers feeding into his picture tube, how does the president of a nation or a multinational corporation know that his image or conception simulates the real world? Are the conceptions real or merely the subjective bias of his subordinates? Thus, the decision process has come full turn to Lao-tzu—within it are images that are indistinct and blurred.

What is the "right" conception among these many images? And if there is no right conception of the human interrelationships, there can be no right decision. Supreme Court Justice Felix Frankfurter addressed this issue in a letter to Marion Folsom, in which he observed that there are no available measures by which one can obtain a right answer. Confidence in a judgment comes, rather, from how the decision was reached—that is, whether various viewpoints were obtained and considered in a deliberative process and by disinterested inquiry.[9]

Justice Frankfurter's view of decision making is a legal one—that the process is all-important precisely because the judgmental aspect is indeterminate. This idea is imbedded in both constitutional and administrative law as "due process of law." Governmental agencies, in making decisions, must follow due process, which means adequate notice, definition of issues, hearings, evidence, precedent, and appeal procedures. Something similar to due process is embodied in business decision making in the procedural form of the planning process, which again defines the means of marshaling evidence or facts in relation to objectives.

The procedural approach to decision making—that is, the due process or planning process approach, is not an evasion of the judgmental issue in decisions. What due process assures is that the decision maker will have marshaled before him all the necessary information, human relationships, needs, feelings, interests, and images of the issue before he decides it. Due process is the video tape that stores up the decision maker's picture tube. It is, in management terms, the collection of information to define alternative choices. In legal terms, it is the building of a case.

The Case Method

The case method is a form of empirical decision making by analogy, which presents critical issues having options open to choice. The case method is more of a teaching device in management than a decision method used by practicing executives in real situations. Executives do, of course, reason by analogy, and they frequently make decisions based upon what has worked in the past. However, the normal course of corporate operations does not produce the documentation of issues, facts, and decisions in business cases in the same orderly fashion as in legal cases. Business decisions are arrived at more urgently, informally, verbally, and prospectively than in the courts, where cases are deliberate, formal, written, and retrospective. The essential difference—that business decisions look to the future, while legal cases decide issues of damages in the past—alters case content significantly; it is much more difficult to document the future than the past. The anticipatory, and hence speculative, element of business decisions is the main reason why the case method is not an operable decision method for practicing executives.

The case method has proved to be a useful learning device for management decision making. However, even its teaching use in management differs from that in law. In law, the case becomes the focal point for structuring a form of legal logic with which a person can learn to reason the likely decision outcome for a given situation by an analogous case serving as a precedent. The essentials of case analysis in legal logic are (1) to identify the facts and issues of a preceding case, (2) to examine the reasoning and intent of the decision or precedent in that case, (3) to analyze the similarities and differences of a pending case compared with a predecessor, and (4) to reason whether the similarities and intent of the precedent apply in the pending case. Law cases thus are decided by reasoning from analogy.

Business cases are compiled from past experience in actual situations by an observer who is not party to the decision as in legal proceedings. Moreover, in business cases there is no precedent or governing decision. A business case is an actual decision that is illustrative of one actual choice; but business decisions are seldom right or wrong in the sense of complying with precedent. Rather, they are exercises in the available options, and, as such, are less rigorous than legal logic. The rigor of legal logic stems from a final arbiter, the Supreme Court, with whom, by custom, the legal profession is willing to comply. In business, there is no final arbiter of a right decision, and, hence, the conventions of logic are not as applicable.

Business cases are therefore used primarily to reason out alternatives and to marshal evidence in favor of preferred alternatives. The case method in business follows much the same pattern as any planning decision methodology—that is (1) define the central issues or objectives, (2) organize the facts and evidence supporting the issues, (3) determine the alternative choices, (4) evaluate the alternatives, and (5) substantiate the decision. Consider the following abbreviated case example as an illustration of the case method.

The Hagenschaft Valve Company

The Hagenschaft Valve Company makes two valves, products A and B, whose sales, costs, and profits are as previously given in chapter 9. The Company was founded in 1880 by A.J. Hagenschaft, who invented the original valve designs. The company president is now Horace Hooper, who has run the company for twenty-five years. His policy (decision) has been to maximize profits by cost estimation practices of case 1 (review chapter 9), and to pay out 60 percent of earnings as dividends. Mr. Hooper owns 2 percent of the stock and has the support of the public stockholders because of his dividend policy, and the old-line employees because of the stable and secure employment he has provided over the years.

Recently, a young member of the family with controlling interest (30 percent of the stock) in the company, A.J. Hagenschaft III, has become vice president for operations. He is imaginative, a product development engineer with new product ideas, and a driving personality. A.J. Hagenschaft III has collected around himself a cadre of bright, ambitious young people who want to build the enterprise into a growth company. A.J. III advocates shifting the cost estimation to case 6 (chapter 9), eliminating dividends, federal income taxes, or any show of profits. Rather, he urges that the internal cash flow be maximized and plowed back into the business to develop new products and the capital required to build them.

The issue goes to the board of directors, who support President Hooper. The board members are stockholders who want a high dividend payout, and they charge that A.J. III wants to convert the corporation into a private investment fund for his own capital appreciation. The young staff supporting A.J. III tells the board they will pull out of the company and start their own enterprise if they are not funded for product innovation and development. Most of the technological knowledge about current production methods, as well as computer knowledge relating to accounting, is tied up in the young staff. It is not clear that the older employees could run the company if the young staff pulls out.

Partial Case Analysis. The principal issues of the case are:

1. Cost and profit estimation practices, case 1 versus case 6
2. A dividend pay-out policy versus a profit plow-back policy
3. Stable employment versus a growth enterprise
4. The competence of President Hooper versus A.J. Hagenschaft III
5. The competence of the older employees versus the young staff
6. The ultimate workability of human relationships among the two factions, the board, and the stockholders

Of the six issues, the most crucial is the last one—whether the organization can be kept together and made to work again. The company is in danger of being torn apart. Its survival is at stake. Many facts pertaining to earnings, costs, and the prospects for new products are pertinent to the case. But the ultimate question is whether the people can be made to work together. This is a political question of whether the interests of the contesting parties can be resolved. The facts in the case would have to be greatly expanded about the human relationships and interactions to be able to decide it. Indeed, the feelings and interactions of the people can only be appreciated by meeting the people, observing their behavior, talking to them, and sensing their feelings. The solution lies in what Chester Barnard called getting the people's point of view and what influences their behavior, which is more easily said than comprehended. It can be comprehended, says Barnard, only by a conception or series of images that show how these human relationships can be made to work together; and that conception has to be of the essence, an abstraction—simpler than the situation really is, but true to its character.

Of course, this abbreviated example of the case method will seem quite inadequate to many, because there is no right answer nor even enough information. That is the deficiency of all cases to a greater or lesser degree, which students complain about, unless that case is a purely factual account of costs, profits, and sales prospects (such as issues 1, 2, and 3). The result is that the case method tends to overwork the analytical manipulation of data to satisfy students that they are coming to a right answer, while slighting the ultimate decision issue about conceptualizing and visualizing a feasible set of human relationships when there are conflicting interests. The conceptualizing of human relations is the part of management that can only be learned by astute observation and sensitivity in real emotional situations, and to which there is no right answer. There is only the right question, posed by Justice Felix Frankfurter, of whether the decision is being reached in a deliberative and disinterested manner in which the conflicting interest parties can have confidence.

Heuristics

Heuristic models attempt to simulate empirical decision making by describing the process in terms of decision rules, procedures, and their sequence. The word "heuristic" means to discover or serve as a guide, which is valuable for empirical research but which is unproved and unprovable. The heuristic approach is one of trial and error, and it is a valuable adaptive means when an executive does not know the structure of the problem—that is, heuristics is a method of search.

Consider, for example, that we have been asked to observe the game of tictactoe and to discern what decision rules cause a player to win. The game is played on a three-by-three grid, with nine cells, in which the object is for a player to place three of his ciphers or marks in a row in any direction. If we watch two players long enough and mark the rules of procedure by which they play, we could come up with the following heuristic guide of decision rules for playing tictactoe:

1. Start by placing mark in corner.
    a. If opponent counters outside of the center, mark a second corner, then a third (game won).
    b. If opponent counters in center, mark opposite corner.
        (1) If opponent counters in third corner, mark the fourth corner (game won).
        (2) If opponent counters in side midsection, block opponent on opposing side. Then if opponent blocks our two marks in a row, mark corner (game stalemate).
2. Start by placing mark in the center.
    a. If opponent marks corner (game stalemate).
    b. If opponent marks side midsection, mark adjacent corner (game won).
3. Start by placing mark in side midsection.
    a. If opponent occupies center, mark adjacent corner (game stalemate).
    b. If opponent occupies corner, mark adjacent side midsection; and if opponent marks corner or a side midsection, choose the center (game won).

What have we learned by this observation? And what was heuristic? As a novice, we have documented a basic set of decision rules by our observations that will enable us to compete on equal terms with most experienced players. If both players follow the same heuristic guide, or course, the games won will tend to be equal.

What was heuristic? Our ability to discern a set of decision rules, a procedure of play, and a sequence was heuristic. We mentally learned to simulate the alternative choices available in the game. We acquired, in one short, experiential session of heuristic observation, what Chester Barnard called conceptualization of the game relationships, and what Lao-tzu called the "mental power" and the "confidence" to play tictactoe. The heuristic rules given in the preceding paragraphs also are, as Chester Barnard said, almost incomprehensible unless we experience tictactoe either by playing or observing it. The heuristic rules are an abstraction, an image, a "conception" of tictactoe, that are simpler than the game is.

What is important about the heuristic approach? Gordon[10] cites a number of characteristics:

1. When information is incomplete, the heuristic method allows the executive to make tentative moves or decisions to try to *understand* the structure of the problem.
2. He learns to *perceive* the conditions of winning combinations.
3. The executive learns what change in *relationships* or choices will produce different results.
4. He learns *promising pathways* for solving a problem by trial and error.

5. He learns the *order and sequence* of events by *notation.*
6. He learns the redefinition of *decision rules* that lead to winning combinations.
7. The executive learns a *perspective* of the effect of differing sequences on the likelihood of winning combinations.

That is, the heuristic approach helps one to understand the structure of the problem, perceive winning combinations and relationships, discern promising pathways, see order and sequence, approximate decision rules, and obtain a perspective on the alternative choices. In short, the heuristic approach enables us to learn the *process.* The process of life is the Tao, and the process of decisions is management.

Seen in this light, the heuristic approach is experience or the practice of management. The only difficulty with the heuristic approach is that it is difficult to follow in many-variable games or situations. The heuristic approach has been used in management as a means of simulation. Simulation is most commonly thought of as the computerized documentation of decision rules that enable an executive to observe the essentials of a management situation. Manufacturing plant operations have frequently been simulated to show the production flow and throughput of products in various assembly or processing lines. By varying the rates of processing or assembly, the executive can see (empirically or heuristically) how to improve the efficiency of output. Simulation has been applied to such problems as transportation, flow processes, inventory stocking, telephone queueing, retail reordering, and missile trajectories to "discover" the most effective process.

Yet heuristic models and programming have their limitations, which are mainly encountered when there are too many indeterminate variables. The game of tictactoe has few variables. A factory production line has more variables, but they are for the most part determinate. The game of chess has innumerable variables and permutations, the outcome of many of which are indeterminate unless linked into long sequences. A computer program to simulate the complete set of decision rules of chess has not yet been written, even with adaptive learning in the program, which can beat an expert human chess player. Why is this so? The computer program cannot anticipate long in advance, the way a human player can, the potential relationships involved in a strategic series of plays. The human chess player "sets up" the game in his mind long in advance, by alternative series of moves before they are made. He has, in Barnard's words, a "conception" of the play in all its relationships, which are something beyond decisions rules. They are conditional probabilities that change with every move, actual or psychological; and these are what the computer does not read or sense in addition to its heuristic decision rules. If chess cannot be programmed successfully to beat a human player, imagine, then, the complexities of a political game—for example, the nomination of a presidential candidate—where there are thousands of actors, feelings, motivations, and conditional probabilities. Field studies in politics, which are heuristic in approach, can identify some of the main decision rules but not all of them.

We may summarize by saying that heuristic observation is the closest thing to executive decision experience itself. By being "next best," heuristics will discover some main decision rules, but not all of them.

Behavioral Models

An executive, or any person, can easily make a decision in a vacuum based upon his own desires—tomorrow the sun will shine, or tomorrow inflation will be stopped by asking people to roll back prices. Such choices are easily made, but they are not really decisions because they cannot be implemented. The sun and the weather are not linked by any causal relationship with the decision maker. Simiarly, the President has been unable to stop inflation because he has been unable to establish a causal relationship that would influence citizens to allow a rollback of prices or wages.

A decision is, above all, an implementable and causal action which influences the behavior of other people in a desired direction. Thus, decisions are behavioral. And the "conception" Barnard speaks about, is a conception or image of what influences and relationships will cause people's behavior to change. Behavioral models anticipate the human motivations essential to implement decisions and generally show that the situational environment is more influential in decisions than executive style or factual data. That is to say, a decision must be acceptable to those persons who will implement it; otherwise nothing will happen. Chester Barnard[11] has set forth four conditions for acceptance of a decision by associates:

1. There is effective communication.
2. The decision is consistent with organizational objectives and purposes.
3. The decision is compatible with subordinates' interests.
4. The subordinates are mentally and physically capable of carrying through the decision.

The conditional nature of decisions, being based upon anticipated acceptability to others, has led to considerable emphasis and research on the leadership style of the executive. Presumably, an executive who communicates and knows those decisions which are compatible with employees' interests will be a more effective decision maker than one who does not. If this is so, then such an effective decision maker will presumably also have a style of management that is communicative and consultative—that is, democratic rather than authoritarian. During the 1950s and 1960s a stream of research explored those leadership characteristics and styles which were most effective. This research gave rise to contrasting leadership dimensions, such as authoritarian versus democratic; employee centered versus production centered; task oriented versus socially oriented; participative versus nonparticipative; communicative versus noncommunicative; and so on.[1,2]

The importance of leadership personality and style has not, however, proved to be a dominant determining factor in implementing decisions or influencing behavior. Recent studies suggest that leadership style may be a consequence of employee behavior rather than its cause[1,3] —that is, the situation or interaction of employees with managers may mold the behavior of both. Vroom and Yetton set out to see whether the human situation and relationships might play a role in determining the leader's decision process.[1,4] They constructed a normative model that poses situations, in the form of questions, that may influence leader or subordinate behavior. The questions the leader asks himself are these:

1. *Quality of Decision:* If decision was accepted, would it make a difference which course was adopted?
2. *Leader's information:* Do I have sufficient information to make a high quality decision?
3. *Subordinate's information:* Do subordinates have sufficient additional information to make a high quality decision?
4. *Problem structure:* Do I know exactly what information is needed, who possesses it, and how to collect it?
   a. If not, is the necessary additional information to be found within my entire set of subordinates?
   b. If not, is it feasible to collect the information by augmenting the group to include outsiders before making decisions?
5. *Importance of acceptance:* Is acceptance of decision by subordinates critical to effective implementation?
6. *Prior probability of acceptance:* If I were to make the decision myself, is it certain that it would be accepted by my subordinates?
7. *Trust:* Can subordinates be trusted (delegated) to base solutions on organizational considerations?
8. *Conflict:* Is conflict among subordinates likely as to preferred solutions?

Vroom and Yetton then relate these eight situational variables to six decision procedures:

1. Make decision
2. Make decision after obtaining information
3. Share decision by seeking individual advice and suggestions
4. Share decision by seeking group advice and suggestions
5. Make joint decision with employees with executive as moderator
6. Go back to start to restructure the problem

The study then goes on to identify fourteen main situations that an executive might face making a decision, together with appropriate decision rules to apply. The main determinants of the decision process are (1) whether the executive needs acceptance, and (2) whether he can solve the information problem. A somewhat more simplified set of decision rules than those used by Vroom and Yetton is shown in table 10-1.

The study showed that, in both recalled and standardized decision situations, managers' behavior was influenced more by the situation than by their own personality or previous leadership style. The actual behavior of managers on recalled decisions of their own, compared with normative behavior on standard problems, showed that managers deviated toward participative management—that is, they were neither as authoritarian nor as democratic as decision norms might suggest. The most obvious reason for the difference is that managers may use different decision rules or perceive their actual situations to be more complex than standard problems.

Therefore, a question of perception enters the decision process. People see decision situations differently. Heller, studying the perception of decision situations, found that executives see themselves as more participative than their employees see them. Similarly, employees see themselves making decisions jointly or by delegation more frequently than their superiors do. On a five-point scale, Heller, as did Vroom, studied a series of decisions as perceived by the leader and subordinates, with the results shown in table 10-2.[15]

Table 10-1
A Simplified Set of Decision Rules

Situation	Decision Rule	Style
1. Acceptance probable or unimportant; leader has information	Make decision himself	Authoritarian
2. Acceptance probable or unimportant; employees have information	Make decision himself after getting information	Authoritarian
3. Acceptance unlikely; subordinates not trusted for delegation	Share decision by individual advice	Participative
4. a. Acceptance unlikely; cannot delegate; conflict involved, or		
b. Employees have information and can help define problem	Share decision by group advice	Participative
5. Acceptance unlikely; cannot delegate, and employees can help define problem	Joint decision	Democratic
6. Problem structure not understood by executive; need more information or larger outside group	Joint decision	Democratic

Table 10-2
Decisions as Perceived by Leaders and Subordinates

	Percent as Perceived by:	
Leader or Decision Style	Leader	Subordinates
Own decision, no explanation	15%	14%
Own decision, with explanation	21	19
Own decision, prior consultation	37	25
Joint decision	20	26
Delegated decision	7	16
	100%	100%

Notice how close the perception is for the first two (authoritarian) decision styles. But the executive sees himself as being much more consultative than his employees do, and his employees see themselves involved in a joint or delegated decision much more than the leader does. Heller concludes that influence power sharing in decision making is widely used, but a perceptual gap separates the two groups of management as to degree of decision-making involvement.

Perceptual Gaps in Management

Perceptual gaps among management groups are inversely related to interpersonal competence, and these perceptual gaps obscure a meeting of minds regarding expectations in the decision process. If people perceive the same decision situation differently, they are likely to arrive at different decisions or expectations about decisions. Why persons differ in their perception may be influenced by their own interests, situation, socialization, or competence. We are all aware how different testimony in court can be about the same event. The Japanese play *Rashoman* is classic in literature about how four people, deeply involved, perceived the rape of a Samurai's wife by a bandit in utterly different ways.

How can a decision have the same meaning to many people, if they all perceive it differently through the lens of their own life? And if they all perceive the decision differently, how can they carry out a common purpose, which is what a decision presumes to be? Argyris's answer to this question is that they do not really have a common view of a decision. They see the decision principally, says Argyris, through the prism of the pyramidal values they hold.[16] Pyramidal values are the hierarchical objectives of the organization regarding the task-oriented goals of individuals—that is, the organizational level of an individual (as well as his individual personality) refracts the perception of decision situations.

In a study of innovation and change involving three organizations, 100 decision-making meetings, and 300 cases, Argyris found that in a majority of cases, the pyramidal values of participants predicted behavioral patterns in decision making. The interactions involved executive committee members who desired the research director (executive in this case) to take care of administrative matters for them, with the result that he fulfilled their expectations by making decisions. In consequence, the executive committee was removed from the innovative, conflict, or risk aspects of decisions, and they concerned themselves with operating procedures. This interference in operations made subordinates, in turn, feel dominated. The employees felt the executive committee did not listen to them, resisted change, and interfered unknowingly. However, the executive committee and research director were unaware of these views and disagreements with subordinates. Argyris concluded from his study that supervisors are not aware of interpersonal problems and disagreements and are not able to solve them effectively when they do become aware, due to low interpersonal competence among both managers and subordinates.

This conclusion brings us to the most serious impasse yet encountered in the decision process, because if managers and subordinates are not competent to perceive accurately the situation in which a decision is made, how can the decision have any persuasion and currency among them as a means of concerted action? If people are incompetent, obtuse, or intractable in their perceptive relations, and if accuracy of decisions depends on accurately perceiving situations, then decisions and organizations are not possible. But we know decisions and organizations are possible and do function after a fashion, however poorly. Perhaps what is amiss is not with people and organizational perceptions, but with the completeness of the theory. Perhaps there is something more to the decision process than the perception of situations. Perceptions in human situations are, for the most part, effects. We may see what a person does (effect), but we may not perceive what he feels (cause)—that is, some of the causative elements of the decision are missing from our decision rules.

Nonperceptual Characteristics of Decisions

A person is more than what he says or does. These are only his visible, perceptible attributes. The gap is in our inability to see what he wants, feels, or creates. These are the driving forces that implement decisions. Shaner has likened the management problem to that of physics, in which changes in matter are the effects that are seen, but energy is the cause that is unseen. From this he suggests an environmental, or perhaps situational theory of management,[17] which has been adapted to the schematic illustrated in figure 10-1.

In this schematic, the area of the perceptible includes the definition of problems and goals; the organization of tasks, resources, and tools; and the realization of the goal as an output. These (steps 1, 5, and 9) are all

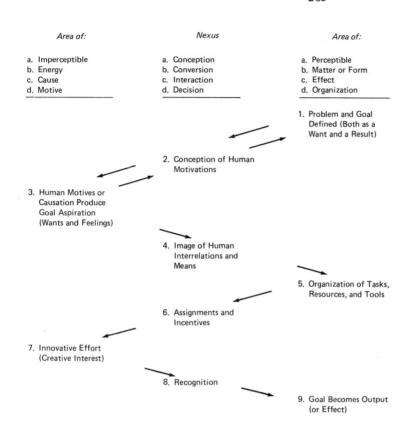

Area of:	Nexus	Area of:
a. Imperceptible	a. Conception	a. Perceptible
b. Energy	b. Conversion	b. Matter or Form
c. Cause	c. Interaction	c. Effect
d. Motive	d. Decision	d. Organization

1. Problem and Goal Defined (Both as a Want and a Result)

2. Conception of Human Motivations

3. Human Motives or Causation Produce Goal Aspiration (Wants and Feelings)

4. Image of Human Interrelations and Means

5. Organization of Tasks, Resources, and Tools

6. Assignments and Incentives

7. Innovative Effort (Creative Interest)

8. Recognition

9. Goal Becomes Output (or Effect)

Figure 10-1. Perceptual and Nonperceptual Steps in the Management Decision Process.

manifestations of a decision that can be observed in the form of executive discussions, data gathering, modeling, planning, organization, investment, personnel actions, production activity, marketing services, and product output. These are the subjects of management texts that become represented as the decision process because they are the most obvious; and the more tangible the effect, such as accounting or modeling, the more highly elaborated and manipulative the skill becomes. But these manifestations are only the tip of the decision iceberg. Beneath are all the inner workings that make decisions and management possible.

The causative forces are what humans feel and want (step 3) that impels them to activity, interaction, organization, creation, production, consumption. But in this impulse, they are relatively inarticulate. True, some of their wants and feelings become known through conversations, market research, interviews, polls, demands, demonstrations, coalitions, and politicking, but these are only conventional wants that are extrapolated from existing goods and services. The important, imaginative satisfactions of human needs come from anticipating and conceptualizing a want that exists but is inexpressible, and therefore imperceptible. Prior to the invention of television, for example, there would have been no way to ascertain the extent of people's wants for visual broadcast reception. They could not know because they had never experienced it. Yet an inventor, Lee De Forest, conceived of a technology to transmit pictures and conceptualized a human need for imagery. How could he know that? Perhaps by his own experience as a human being that imagery is richer in meaning and emotion than the written word or voice broadcast.

The link or nexus between the problem definition and the human motivation is a managerial conception or imaginative act (steps 4 and 6) based partly, perhaps, on data and the perceptible, but partly, also, on insight into the human experience. This insight into the human experience may be through a manager's own sense of need or his sensitivity to the needs of others. Many inventors and entrepreneurs who have this feeling of the imperceptible need do not themselves have an idea of the extent of the need. For example, when William C. Durant was forming General Motors in 1908, Henry Ford was prepared to sell his company for $8,000,000 (when the prior year's profits had been $3,500,000). However, Durant was unable to raise a $2,000,000 loan from the banks, who were antagonistic to the automobile industry, and the plan failed. Two years later, Ford earned $35,000,000 in profit in a single year.[18] No one at the time, not even Ford, had an idea of the size of the need that people had for personal transportation, even though Ford had conceptualized this imperceptible need eight years earlier.

Sometimes executives are unable to recognize a problem or latent need that exists even when a technology and product is at hand to provide a solution. The Xerox process went unrecognized and undeveloped for nearly twenty years after its invention and then turned into the fastest growth product of its era.

The decision function, then, is to conceptualize human needs (step 2) and then create an image of the human relationships (step 4) that will make possible the organization of tasks, resources, tools, and persons. Still, there is more to the imperceptible. The organization will not work unless there is creative interest someplace within it to provide the effort. That creative interest is nurtured by management's proffer of incentives, assignments, and recognition (steps 6 and 8). But the effort only comes into being because some of the persons in the organization have an interest, which responds to the incentives and recognition. That interest is creative and innovative in any organization that is new or facing change. The installation of new technology is innovative. The change in market distribution or products is innovative. The adapting of an accounting system to a computer is innovative. Somewhere there must be a creative interest and innovative person to make these changes.

The creative side of work accomplishment is little understood. People are not articulate about how they create. Creation is an imperceptible art on which an organization depends for its realization and output. Creation does not come from management direction, compulsion, prescription, or command. Creative effort comes because some individual wants to respond to a situation in which the assignment, the means, the incentives, and the recognition enliven his interest to the point where he conceives a way to perform a new task or to change an old one.

The hidden, imperceptible side of a decision (steps 2, 3, 4, 6, 7, and 8) are all the motivations and conceptions linking human effort to manifest results. Management is the link that sets up the circumstances, situation, or psychological set that causes a response or reaction to occur. The executive or decision maker does not act; he imagines—the people act. The decision maker has anticipated in his imagination how they will act. If his image is essentially true, the reactions will occur as he expected. If not, the executive will not realize the output or goal.

The decision maker's image is always blurred, as Lao-tzu said. Henry Ford did not really see the extent of the need for personal transportation, nor de Forest for television, nor President Nixon the feelings about Watergate. But even if the image of the imperceptible is blurred, if it is essentially true, then it has mental power and engenders confidence. If the image is not realistically perceived, as in Nixon's case, the opposite occurs—the loss of mental power and confidence.

Innovation and Art in Management

The imperceptible side of the decision process makes management an art, requiring innovation and creation to conceptualize the problem and its alternative solutions. Management has been heavily beset in recent years with attempts to make it a science, which has tended to obscure the artistic aspect of management. A science is devoid of values, wants, feelings, imagination, creation, and the subjective. Science is concerned with the perceptible, the sensory, the objective, and measurable. The attempt to make management a science has turned it into a study of the tip of the iceberg, with careful measurement of its typology and topography.

The effects of management are now carefully documented and researched. These include the accounting effects, profit, marginal costs, inputs, outputs, products, production flow, technical means, capital budgets, models, manpower allocations, staffing costs, organization structure, interpersonal effects, leadership effects, behavioral effects, organizations as objects, people as objects, and people's actions as objects. The mass of research and data on all these objects represents a massive detailing of the effects of management, much as draftsmen detail topographic maps. But where is the cause? It is under the iceberg, in the perceptual gaps of science, where few investigators are inclined to explore. The imperceptible side of management is avoided because it is unfashionable and unpopular to be unobjective and not to consider the possibility that human organizational and decision behavior may be subjective, nonscientific, nonmeasurable, creative, imaginative, and artistic—an art.

Suppose for a moment, however, that management is an art and that decision making is an imaginative art. How might management and decision making then be described? The decision process would seem to be, first, a conception of what might be, and second, and image of how to be it. It would be, as Carl Jung said, similar to having an image of ourselves and living our own legend. It would be the same as inventing a future. It would be, according to Herbert Simon, equivalent to finding an occasion to make a decision and inventing the design with which to accomplish it.[19]

That executives "find" and "search" for occasions to make decisions means that opportunities for decision making are not obvious. They are not obvious because they are not easily perceptible; they have to be imagined and inferred—that is, the finding of problems is an art, because unmet human needs are latent and not apparent. The decision maker has to feel a need himself, and infer among others a felt need, which he does by apperception and imagination. The definition of problems is a creative art. Similarly, the design of a solution is a creative art. The literature of management commonly describes the planning and decision process as a series of steps (heuristics) along the following lines:

1. *Find and define a problem (unmet need).*
2. Establish objectives that satisfy the problem and are coordinated with prior decisions or plans.
3. Determine the functions (work) to be performed.
4. Gather and analyze information about the work functions.
5. *Identify alternative solutions or courses of action.*
6. Set up criteria to judge alternatives.
7. Decide upon one alternative solution.
8. Formulate plan to implement solution.
9. Design controls.
10. Install and test the system.
11. Evaluate the decision.

In this list of decision steps, numbers 1 and 5 are highly creative activities. We have already seen that finding a problem presumes a conceptualization of imperceptible human feelings and needs. The finding of alternative solutions is, similarly, an imaginative act. Alternatives are often treated in management literature as though they were obvious, a mere listing of the apparent. Alternatives which are that obvious and apparent are not solutions at all, but merely extensions or extrapolations of present practices. The nonsolution approach to decisions is the cause of the truncated, institutional decision discussed in chapter 3, and the systematic character of disorder explored in chapter 2.

What passes for planning and decision alternatives in many cases is the compilation of accounting, economic, and technical information that makes possible trade-off calculations of one set of existing practices versus another. The result is a technoeconomic choice among means, but it is something less than a solution to unmet needs. A solution to unmet needs is creative and involves, besides a technoeconomic means, the conceptualization (or imagination) of the feelings and interests of the people affected by the decision, and the capability and interests of subordinates to implement the decision.[20] If these human reactions are not correctly anticipated, the result will be felt in either diminished market demand or productivity.

The reason that innovation is not more prominently recognized and appreciated as a vital role of management is that it is often mixed with other activities performed by the same person. Joseph Schumpeter was careful to point out that the innovative or entrepreneurial function is not the same as the managerial function, although the two may be performed by the same (or different) person. The manager is an organizer of things known; the entrepreneur is the creator of things yet unseen. The manager works with the organization of production, whereas the entrepreneur innovates, creating new processes. These two activities are not the same, either in practice or in theory.[21] Schumpeter shows further that the innovation and entrepreneurship are not to be confused with ownership or risk. The owner and capitalist is compensated for the competitive cost of money, and for risks related to capital repayment and fluctuating interest rates. Only the entrepreneur and innovation create, or warrant, profit. The entrepreneur is a leader who makes decisions applying new innovations to new human interests. Leadership rather than ownership is what matters. The failure to see this distinction is a common fault of both economic and sociological analysts.[22]

If innovation is the critical element in decision making and leadership, as Schumpeter argues, from whence does it come? Duncan, a Scottish philosopher, rejects the idea that decisions originate in intuition. Intuition has a technical meaning in philosophy as the mental act of grasping the truth of a statement when no evidence beyond the statement itself is required. This is not what happens in decision making, claims Duncan; rather, decision making originates in hard work (experience), interest, and intelligence. But intelligence, according to Duncan, consists of having the memory, reasoning, and imagination to picture what may happen in the future and adjust ourselves to it.[23]

This concept of intelligence is very similar to one deduced by Sir Herbert Read in his analysis of art. Read said we must recognize two distinct kinds of intelligence: one may be called Cartesian logic, since it originated with Descarte's separation of thinking from sensuous dependence upon things; and the other might be called aesthetic intelligence, since it maintains contact with the sensuous world of feeling at every stage of thought.[24] Contact with the sensuous world is an essential part of intelligence, according to the Swiss pedagogue Jean Piaget (in *The Origin of Intelligence in Children*)[25] because it is the means by which the human organism relates to its environment—groping among experiences, avoiding harm, seeking satisfactions, finding purpose and intention. Intention (the origin of intelligence) is the power of evoking images, symbols, and speech. Intention acts upon things, and from things, to set up relationships between the self and others.[26]

Herbert Read therefore concludes that human beings think in pictures and the image always precedes the idea in the development of human consciousness.[27] An art has never attempted to grasp reality as a whole, which is beyond human capacity, but, rather, has been a reflective recognition of that which is significant in human experience. Imagination might be described as a crystallization from the amorphous realm of feelings of those forms or relationships that are significant or symbolic. This crystallization from feeling and experience produces the icon, or image, that precedes the idea. Thus the creative process is seen to be from experience (past images) to feelings, feelings to (new) images, images to ideas, ideas to words, words to models (objective, factual or mathematical), models to alternatives, alternatives to choices, choices to decisions, decisions to organization, and organization to action and implementation.

If we may say in management that products and organizational structures are the equivalent of form in art, then the process of decision making is the design of forms. Form is the very essence of being; and being is that, according to Heidegger, which achieves a limit for itself. Form completes itself by placing itself within limits.[28] Limitation is the means by which management designs itself, limiting its goals, limiting activity to resources, limiting output by inputs, limiting products to requirements (needs), and limiting organizations to work functions. An organization is a set of limits, which in turn defines a set of relationships; and those limits and relationships are its image or form.

In these terms, management can be described in the same way that Conrad Fiedler described architecture: as in every intellectual activity, there is progress from the formless to the formed. Forms owe their existence to needs and wants or to technical ability, and they are moulded according to outside requirements. But the process of creation alters the form until the materials and constructions recede and the form or image of the intellect emerges and develops toward its own identity.[29]

Management therefore takes people's interests, along with materials, and shapes them into a set of organizational relationships in which the original form of the input recedes and becomes a new output moulded to outside requirements and needs. The act of creation is the image of this transformation, which is an innovation that has never been done before. This image comes to the entrepreneur as a new icon, drawn out of his old feelings, images, experiences. The icon precedes the idea, which then becomes words (objectives), models (fact gathering), designs (relationships), alternatives, form (decisions and limits), organization and action.

Without the art of management, the form and organization would never take shape. But a study of the form of organization (that is, the topography of the top of the iceberg) will not reveal how it came to be created. The study of organization as such—its accounting, economics, models, structure, relationships, facts, and objective behavior—will yield only the form and effect that some image maker had previously wrought, and it will tell little about the creative decision by which he wrought it.

If this concept of creativeness in decision making seems elusive, perhaps the advice of successful entrepreneurs will help illuminate it. Conrad Hilton, for example, felt that the greatest accomplishment of his career was his vision of a need for international hotel services with distinctive hotels related to the locale. His idea for carrying this out was to buy the Waldorf Astoria as a symbol of prestige, build the first hotel in Paris (postwar) that had been constructed in thirty-three years, and buy the Statler chain.

Sam Goldwyn, founder of MGM, once explained how he felt a desire by the public for excitement through visual storytelling when he saw his first motion picture. Motion pictures at that time were mainly short subjects. He gave up the glove business, talked a friend (Lasky) out of the tamale business, and convinced Cecil B. DeMille to give up the stage. The three plunged into a full length feature, *Squaw Man,* without having any experience in motion picture production. Their first showing was a disaster because none of them knew the technique of perforating film to match the drive sprocket in a projector. Sam Goldwyn's advice to young managers is to have devotion and enthusiasm for ideas that bring a new dimension or excitement to the public.

David Sarnoff, founder of RCA, said much the same thing. He said a person must immerse himself in the facts and situation he is interested in and stretch his imagination. After having come up with an idea, submitted it to criticism, and received a hundred reasons why it cannot be done, a person has to make the decision to proceed on the basis of what he believes in. That is leadership.[30]

Businessmen sometimes talk of the creative side of decisions as "vision." Hilton, Goldwyn, and Sarnoff were men of vision in their fields. They said their visions came from their immersion in their fields (depth of experience), their interest in their projects, their feeling for new needs of people, and their perserverance in the face of obstacles. If they are right about themselves and how they succeeded as decision makers, then practice (depth of experience) is an essential part of the decision-making art; and the heuristic guide for businessmen and entrepreneurs alike is to create a concept and image of a transformation process that finds and fulfills new human needs.

The Management of Innovation

The previous section has treated the innovative process in decision making from a personalized view of the individual entrepreneur—how he sees it, and how he enters into the creative mode. As organizations have become larger and technology more complex, the innovative process itself has become organized, functionalized, somewhat specialized, and assigned as a management role. Obviously, there are limits on the degree to which innovation can be fractionated, because innovation is an integrative process. That is why top management involvement is essential for the performance of the final integration of the idea.

The management of innovation takes place through a planning process that is usually composed at minimum of the chief executive; the financial, research, and marketing executives; and a planning staff (which may be separate or a portion of the financial, research, or marketing departments). The process takes place through the development of a strategic plan that is descriptive of the alternative, future choices of the company. The alternative future choices of an organization are usually made up of (1) an operating plan that expands or improves the existing products and markets of the company, (2) a development plan that seeks new technologies within the company's capability and applies them to new market needs, (3) a diversification plan that seeks technologies and markets beyond present organizational capability, and (4) a divestment plan that eliminates products (services) whose life cycles are spent.

The operating plan is the heart of the existing business and profits of the company, and thus provides the base for all other expansion. For the most part, operating department heads and their middle management can be relied upon to exploit existing market and product opportunities in a competent organization. Top management attention is needed, therefore, mainly for the development, diversification, and divestment plans. Each of these plans requires a technical, market, and financial assessment. The critical element in the development plan is the technological assessment of new research ideas. In the diversification plan, the critical element is an apperception of new consumer needs. In the divestment plan, the key element is the financial assessment. Thus top management brings together in the strategic plan the key innovative ideas of the company concerning an expansion of the existing business, as well as the finding of new technologies, markets, and the best use of funds.

Ansoff has suggested that the major contributions to the management of innovation are:

1. Maintaining personal contact, through executive and staff time, with the internal organization's interests and abilities, and with the needs of social environments.
2. Allocation of top management resources among the perceived needs and opportunities.

3. Development of objectives and alternatives.
4. Communication and leadership of top management throughout the thought process, but especially in eliciting a strategy formulation from the senior marketing and technical executives.[31]

The management of innovation in a complex organization is a subtle art because organizations tend to socialize individuals into conventional thought, which often suppresses creative ideas. Carefully assessing the feasibility of new ideas (which applies conventional wisdom to creative thoughts), while nurturing imaginative ideas so they can get through the screening process requires creative executives at the top. As David Sarnoff pointed out, there are always a hundred reasons why a new idea cannot work, but there has to be one influential decision maker who has the interest, conviction, and vision to see how it can be made to work.

Notes

1. Editors of Nation's Business, *Lessons in Leadership* (New York: Doubleday, 1965).

2. John McDonald, "How Businessmen Make Decisions," *Fortune* (August 1955), pp. 84-137.

3. Henri Fayol, *General and Industrial Management,* (London: Sir Isaac Pitman & Sons, 1949).

4. Alfred P. Sloan, Jr., "General Motors Corporation Study of Organization," reprinted in Ernest Dale, ed., *Readings in Management* (New York: McGraw-Hill, 1965), pp. 215-219.

5. Chester Barnard, *The Functions of the Executive* (Cambridge, Mass.: Harvard University Press, 1938).

6. Chester Barnard, *Organizations and Management* (Cambridge, Mass.: Harvard University Press, 1948), pp. 112-133.

7. John McDonald, "How Businessmen Make Decisions."

8. Marion B. Folsom, *Executive Decision Making* (New York: McGraw-Hill, 1962).

9. Ibid., p. 116.

10. Paul J. Gordon, "Heuristic Problem Solving," *Business Horizons* (Spring 1962), pp. 43-53.

11. Barnard, *The Functions of an Executive*, pp. 165-166.

12. D. Katz and R.L. Kahn, "Leadership Practices in Relation to Productivity and Morale," in D. Cartwright and A. Zander, eds., *Group Dynamics: Research and Theory* (Evanston, Ill.: Row, Peterson, 1960).

13. Porter, E. Lawler, and J.R. Hackman, *Behavior in Organizations* (New York: McGraw-Hill, 1975), pp. 422-434.

14. Victor H. Vroom and Philip W. Yetton, *Leadership and Decision*

Making (Pittsburgh, Pa.: University of Pittsburgh Press, 1973), pp. 12-13, 32-45, 53, 119-122, and 136-141.

15. Frank A. Heller, *Managerial Decision Making* (London: Van Gorcum/ Tavistock, 1971), p. 11 and pp. 73-74.

16. Chris Argyris, *Organization and Innovation* (Homewood, Ill.: R. Irwin, 1965), pp. 80-87, and 122-125.

17. E.L. Shaner, *Environmental Theory of Management* (Austin, Texas: Saegert Publishing Co., 1961).

18. William C. Durant, "The True Story of General Motors," in Ernest Dale, ed., *Readings in Management* (New York: McGraw-Hill, 1965), pp. 14-19.

19. Herbert A. Simon, "The Decision-Making Process," from *The New Science of Decision Making* (New York: Harper & Row, 1960); also appearing in Edwin Mansfield, ed., *Managerial Economics and Operations Research* (New York: W.W. Norton, 1966), pp. 8-10.

20. Douglas C. Basil, *Managerial Skills for Executive Action* (New York: American Management Association, 1970), pp. 152-170; also, Barnard, *Functions of an Executive,* pp. 165-166.

21. Joseph A. Schumpeter, *Business Cycles* (New York: McGraw-Hill, 1939), pp. 102-109.

22. Ibid.

23. A.R.C. Duncan, "Techniques of Decision Making," in Ernest Dale, ed., *Readings in Management* (New York: McGraw-Hill, 1965), pp. 387-393.

24. Herbert Read, *The Origins of Form in Art* (London: Thames and Hudson, 1965), pp. 152-157.

25. Jean Piaget, *The Origins of Intelligence in Children* (New York: International University Press, 1952).

26. Herbert Read, *Icon and Idea, The Function of Art in the Development of Human Consciousness* (New York: Schocken Books, 1965), pp. 1-18.

27. Ibid., pp. 1-18.

28. Martin Heidegger, *An Introduction to Metaphysics,* trans. Ralph Manheim (New Haven, Ct.: Yale University Press, 1959), p. 60.

29. Conrad Fiedler, *On the Nature and History of Architecture*, privately printed by Victor Hammer, Lexington, Kentucky, 1954, pp. 12-13.

30. *Lessons in Leadership*, pp. 7-10, 72-74, and 93-94.

31. H. Igor Ansoff, *Business Strategy* (Baltimore, Md.: Penguin Books, 1969), pp. 34-39.

11 Social Choice Methods

Social choices are decisions resolving issues in a political context among groups of people with differing interests. Social choice methods are applicable in corporations and voluntary social institutions as well as government, particularly at the level of the governing board, where there are fundamental issues of basic direction and who shall govern occur. These are group decisions resolved by bargaining and compromise, which are the essence of the political context in private or public decisions.

In the past chapter we saw how the individual entrepreneur, or the planning process in a complex organization, made decisions by having a conception or perception of unmet human needs that could be solved by an emerging technique. The innovative decision in such cases is an image of a transformation process by which a new technique will meet a new need; and these sets of new relationships bring form to a new organizational structure.

Now we wish to ask ourselves what happens when there is no entrepreneur or planning process capable of creating the new need-solution concept? Obviously, the human needs go unmet in the private sector, with one of two consequences: (1) the needs are latent, waiting for the innovative inventor to discover them, as, for example, happened with wireless communications or communication satellites; (2) or, if recognized by the consumer, citizen, or user, they become sources of frustration, alienation, or unrest. These feelings of unrest are legion: inflation, present medical care, housing costs out of reach of ordinary people, high food prices, deteriorating environment, air pollution, crime, war, unemployment, discrimination and more (see chapter 2). These recognized needs become the focus of political action and thrust themselves before the organized public as issues. They become issues as some interest groups, or coalition of interest parties, organize themselves to force decision makers in private or public institutions to recognize their demand or need. Thus Ralph Nader forced automobile manufacturers to respond to consumers' demand for automotive safety, almost single-handedly at first, but later with the help of an organized interest group that he himself formed. Similarly, John Gardener by his personal initiative, and later the organization of Common Cause as an interest group, were largely instrumental in forcing the reform of election campaign financing into legislation, which later became the legal foundation for prosecuting the Watergate violations. In a sense, Nader and Gardener can be looked upon as social innovators on public issues, in the same way that Hilton, Goldwyn, and Sarnoff were innovators to meet private needs. Nader and

Gardener had visions or images of a set of needs and relationships, in safety and election reform, that satisfied an incipient public need.

Social choice methods of decision making are intended, then, to advance the social innovations that serve the public purpose—that is, they are perceptions of problems that reflect a commonality of individual needs, and the solution is a social or technical invention that attempts to solve the problem and satisfy the need. For the most part, these inventions are social rather than technical, a social invention being a new set of incentives, penalties, or services arranged through governmental actions. Technical inventions in government are related mainly to defense, space, and industrial regulation through standards.

The social choice methods are decision processes in the same sense as in the private sector. They are all of the class (in the behavioral model of Vroom and Yetton; chapter 10) defined as decision procedure 6—go back to start and restructure the problem. Vroom's decision rule on this procedure was to augment the groups of individuals consulted and get more information—that is, social issues are a class of unstructured problems (or needs) that are pressing to be solved. When the executive or decision maker does not know the structure of the problem, he must go back to the people who feel the need, identify and structure the problem and nature of the need, and then gather data upon its extent, costs, and alternative solutions. The social choice methods, then, are basically addressed at the means for structuring problems and solutions among conflicting social interests.

Equilibrium Tendencies in Social Interactions

Social choice is a means of decision making in the public sector, when there are conflicting interests. The conflicting interests represent human needs that are differently perceived by various groups of people and may come into being in a variety of ways. These differences of perception may have their origins in (1) individual personality, experiences, and values; (2) group interactions and the socialization of individuals' attitudes; (3) the level of information available to the individual or group; (4) the attitudes and prevailing policy of the public at large; and (5) the structure of government decision-making methods.[1]

Individual experiences and perceptions give rise to feelings and an attitudinal preference for either stability and security or change in specific ways that would enhance the individual's ability to satisfy his wants. Individuals, with a variety of such preferences, will tend to associate with other people, or groups, of reasonably like mind, not only for reassurance and validation of their own ideas, but also for potential group action that is more effective than individual action.

However, within the group of reasonably like-minded people itself, there are also differences of view; and the individual tends to become socialized by the group to accept something less than his own unique desires, but rather a viewpoint that represents sufficient consensus within the group to hold it together as an affinity association. The group socializes the individual by acceptance, interpersonal communication, recognition, rewards, and penalties, which reinforce group thinking and suppress unique thinking.

Individual and group attitudes will be shaped by the amount of information available to them, which is often meager. The attitude toward national defense or crime, for example, is more likely to represent recent individual experiences than intensive knowledge of the state of preparedness, grievances of aggressors, or the economics of remedial action. The function of the group, in part, is to augment the information and knowledge available among its members; but social choices and conflicts do not wait upon data accumulation, which will always be incomplete and uncertain in any case.

Conflicts begin to occur primarily when two groups holding differing views clash over some issue, such as rezoning a residential area into commercial development; or when one interest group demands a change in an existing policy of the public at large—for example, when elderly citizens seek increases in monthly Social Security benefits due to inflation. In the latter case, the action of the interest group (the elderly) is shaped by the public policy of Social Security, and by the decision structure of government to seek redress through congressional legislation.

In the process of its conflicting interactions, a group often will learn more information, change its attitude, and change its demands. For example, a lobby for the elderly may learn that its demands for increasing Social Security payments are affected by more information regarding (1) the effect of inflation on taxpayers and other groups as well as itself; (2) the degree of inflation, present and prospective; (3) the monetary and fiscal causes of inflation; (4) those remedial steps which have been taken to control inflation; (5) the stringency of resources in the federal budget; (6) the competing claims for federal expenditures in defense; energy, education, poverty, and health; (7) the relative power and views of competing interests; (8) the practical voting strength of the group; (9) extent of sympathetic congressional delegations; (10) the costs to the group in time, money, and information gathering to press its claim; (11) who the key decision makers are on the issue and what attitudes they hold; and much more.

All these influences and information have an impact on the interest group, moderating its demands, again informing its members, again socializing its expectations, and rethinking a basis for settlement. This reassessment is the basis for gravitating toward an equilibrium. The equilibrium is a judgment (or decision) of how much added gain can be achieved with how much added effort (cost or sacrifice).

At the same time, other competing interest groups will also have been exposed to the same abrasions and reeducation in the conflict. They, too, will make reassessments as to how much gain for how much effort is worthwhile. The conflicting groups separately but interactively will arrive at some compromise or equilibrium position that sufficiently satisfies their differing interests to call the conflict to a halt for the time being. That halt becomes a kind of joint equilibrium, in which each group comes to rest because it feels it has marginally gained as much as it can with the effort, resources, and political pressure it has available. In this sense, and by this process, social choice occurs through an interaction among conflicting social interest groups, and the interaction tends toward an equilibrium or social compromise.

Social Choices in a Political Context

Social choices are made in a political context at the margin of the status quo. A political context is one in which competing interest groups bargain under structured rules of conflict for influence over decisions of governance. The political context is composed of the accepted rules for bargaining, compromise, and agreement. Those who accept the rules for governance seek evolutionary change within the political system; and those who do not accept the rules of the governing decision structure seek revolutionary change.

By definition, then, all evolutionary policy change is marginal; that is, made up of small changes, revisions, improvements, and amendments to the existing governing process. The existing governing process, together with existing laws and practices, is the status quo, or the existing state of things. Evolutionary policy accepts the existing state as given and seeks to make improvements on it as necessitated by pressure groups with new demands and needs.

By working from the existing state toward improvements, all proposed changes are marginal, or changes in the boundaries of the system. For example, a marginal change in the Social Security law would add an incremental benefit for recipients, possibly with an incremental tax on wages to support it. Or, the boundaries of the Social Security system might be altered by including farm workers who formerly were excluded.

The marginal approach to political revision has to commend it (beside the innate conservatism of people who desire security) two practical advantages: (1) it does not reopen, or reopens minimally, the stressful conflicts among interest parties; and (2) it economizes and aborts the information selection problem.

The justification for not reopening the conflict among interest groups is that such strife is divisive to the society, and once fundamental issues are resolved, presumably the assessment of conflicting interests have been resolved. For example, according to an incremental view, there would be no need to reopen the whole issue of Social Security, whether it represents an insurance principle, whether the trust fund is an income-producing resource or a sink for deficits, whether retirement benefits are a right, or who should be included or excluded. All those issues were argued once, years ago, and put to rest. That no one is complaining about or reopening these fundamental issues underlying the system suggests that the system must be satisfactory to most—that is, the old conflicts were resolved. The conflicting interest groups came to a satisfactory equilibrium or compromise. The only issues that remain are marginal—how much more benefits at any point in time and how much more taxes. These questions, by accepting the status quo (of social security), do not reopen the fundamental conflicts, or only reopen them minimally; and, hence, compromises can be made on the margins of how much more and when. Thus marginalism in politics constrains the reopening of conflicts, keeps Pandora's box closed, and deals with only marginal new demands.

Marginalism also economizes on the information-gathering and selection problem by focusing only on new net benefits versus new net costs. By truncating the decision to increments, information analysis of the whole problem is avoided. It is not necessary, for example, under this view to reexamine the entire scope of Social Security: Can it be financed? Is it coordinated with private retirement plans? Does it do justice to the recipients? How does it affect or is it affected by full employment, employability, job discrimination, and employment opportunities? That is, everything is related to everything else in the social process; and marginalism reduces all these awkward questions and information requirements to the immediate issue of minimal revision to quiet the pressure groups.

Incremental and Extensional Nature of Alternatives

Policy alternatives under review for social choice are generally few, incremental, disjointed, and extensional. The desire to minimize conflict, information requirements, analysis, time, cost, and effort in policy decisions—to preserve social stability and equilibrium—has the corollary of limiting the decision to few alternatives, or even to one that is an extension of past practice.

The first limitation in alternatives originates in those interest groups who make demands. They are likely, as we have seen, to have limited information and to be reacting to recent, typical experiences. The alternative is then seen as an obvious remedy to that experience. Hence, the elderly suffer loss of purchasing power of their Social Security income during inflation, and the obvious remedy is to increase the income. Or, the recent experience has been an increase in burglaries, and the remedy is seen as having more police walk the beat.

The simplistic nature of the demand for remedy elicits a simple political response; and the alternatives may be restricted to yes or no to the demands, or to a few related alternatives. To obtain more information or propose solutions, the policymakers or analysts who act on the decision are motivated to explore as few consequences of the alternatives as will satisfy the constituents, because the more options they open up, the more difficult it will be to get a consensus or compromise.

The political process of negotiating consensus has the effect of continually narrowing the issues, the alternatives, and the analysis of consequences—that is, the decision mechanism works elminating all but the least undesirable choice, which usually will be the one that departs least from the status quo.

This process of elimination will be considered by all of the interest groups concerned in a fragmented series of evaluations. A policy issue, such as Social Security or national security, will be considered by the bureaucracies concerned, legislative committees, budget analysts, the executive, political parties, state or local caucuses, trade associations, labor organizations, universities, news analysts, and the many private pressure and interest groups. Each of these groups will consider the issue separately and disjointedly, and will start with differing preferences and levels of information. Their evaluations will have differing degrees of thoroughness and expertise. Hence, they will arrive at different results that are disjointed or unrelated to other people's considerations. This process has been called "disjointed incrementalism" by Lindbloom and Braybrooke.[2]

Lindbloom argues that the process of disjointed incrementalism makes rational economic decisions impractical in the political context. The reason is that these fragmented, disjointed evaluations of issues by pluralistic interest groups are all made on differing bases of values that cannot be rationalized into a set of priorities or objectives. Indeed, he argues that the rational ideal of decision making in social policy is impractical because it is not adapted to:

1.   Man's bounded rationality or limited problem-solving capability
2.   Inadequacy of information
3.   Costliness of analysis
4.   Failures in constructing a workable evaluative method
5.   Intermixture of fact and value in decision making
6.   Need for strategic sequences of learning or bargaining modes
7.   Interdependence among problems and solutions

The process of adaptation through disjointed incrementalism avoids these difficulties by restricting the scope of the problem to few alternatives on the margin with minimal information, and by letting the interest groups disjointedly evaluate the narrow choices until a compromise emerges by the process of elimination.

The difficulty with such a choice process, as Lindbloom recognizes, is the problem of neglected consequences[3]—that is, the simplification of policy evaluation is achieved by omission, and the omissions may cause harmful failures. Two kinds of adverse effects occur: (1) unanticipated failures due to the narrowness of the analysis, and (2) roughly anticipated failures that were ignored as being secondary to the problem.

Environmental failures are examples of the first case. The second case is illustrated by disjointed policy that concentrates on national security at the expense of inflation and rising taxes. Lindbloom argues that these neglected consequences become corrected in subsequent decisions that focus serially on environmental improvement, inflation, and tax reduction. The serial, remedial, and reconstructive features of incremental improvement of policy, first one field and then another, thus are conducive (Lindbloom claims) to a comprehensive remedy of the neglected consequences in the long run.

The self-correction of disjointed incrementalism has proved to be more of a hope than a reality. Inflation, rising taxes, and deteriorating environment have persisted over decades and are still with us. One reason that neglected consequences receive only superficial remedy is pointed out by Galbraith—the uneven distribution of economic and political power.[4] The inequality results from monopolies and oligopolies or imperfect competition, which creates large organizations with large resources, planning apparatuses, and information bases. These large organizations have both the financial and informational resources to unduly influence policy in their own interest. Power is the ability of a group or organization to impose private purposes on the public. Thus, the military-industrial complex has had the power to impose its purposes on the public more effectively than have either the low-taxation or antiwar groups. Similarly, the large corporations have more effective resources for imposing a policy of economic expansionism on public policy than do consumers for imposing a policy of price stability and low taxes. Indeed, the inequality of political power persistently biases public policymaking by disjointed incrementalism to settle on one interest group's policies, not to remedy the neglected consequences. It is this bias of policy settlement that creates the systematic nature of disorder discussed in chapter 2.

Negatively Perceived Goals

Individuals have a multiplicity of goals and values that are fluid and changing as the impact of current events affects the feelings and reactions of persons experiencing change. In this flux, the ordering of priorities is exceedingly difficult for individuals for several reasons. First, experiments have shown that the cognitive strain on the human mind from continuous, comprehensive scanning of events and reactions is much more difficult than selective focusing on few choices.[5] Second, individuals react more strongly to recent events than to past events, which leads to matching expectations to recent experiences and settling for some satisfactory level experience as to what is possible.[6] This "satisfying" behavior is an acceptance of what appears good enough for a single goal among multiple values that are in flux due to changing events.

The combination of these behavioral characteristics (that is, focused rather than comprehensive scanning, impact of recent events, flux of events, fluidity among multiple values, and satisfying recent experience) yield a stronger emphasis within the individual on negatively perceived events than on a positive set of preconceived goals. In a political context, the result is that citizens respond more vigorously to adverse events than to ideal platforms. They exert more pressure to cure unemployment than they do to create a stable economic system.

The negative perception of adverse events by citizens imposes upon the decision structure of government a concern for remedial actions rather than orderly design of an adaptive society. The decision process becomes one of crisis government rather than the systematic evaluation of social choices. Social choice thus is a form of decision making that responds to negatively perceived events more forcibly than to preconceived goals.

While normal behavior among individuals does respond actively to recent events, individuals also have an approximate image of themselves and how they see themselves living.[7] Such images of the self presume multiple value schemes. One attempt to elicit such images and value schemes is through scenario writing in systems analysis, which attempts to tell a story of alternative futures. The scenarios become a studied means by which specialists reduce the cognitive strain upon individuals by providing them with a simplified way to do comprehensive scanning of alternative futures and alternative choices. The question then becomes, which of these scenarios most closely approximates an individual's image of living his own legend? Or how would one modify it?

The scenario and systems approach to policy problems had a brief trial in the period 1960-1968, first with the application of systems analysis to defense problems and then, by a directive from President Johnson, to all federal agencies. Systems analysis ran into many of the difficulties cited by Lindbloom for any rational decision process, most specifically the ambiguity of ordering social values and the information problem. The result was that systems analysis did not become an influential factor in decision making and, in fact, was largely ignored by legislators. The rejection of systems analysis in this period is often taken as a failure of the method. But an alternate argument is equally possible; that is, the method was feasible enough for legislators to see that its success would jeopardize their power to influence their own reelection. In other words, systems analysis failed because legislators wanted it to fail; and, in fact, disjointed incrementalism is the means and incentive for ensuring reelection and manipulating political power.

Satisfying Self-interests of the Policymakers

Social policy tends to reflect the self-interest of policymakers because citizens do not have a clear awareness of their self-interest. To an elected official, the political process of disjointed incrementalism means that all issues are taken up separately, partially, and serially, and are resolved with minimal adjustment to existing practice. Or in voting terms, minimum, serial changes alienate the fewes voters at any point in time. In practical politics, this means fragmenting the opposition and giving the elected official the highest probability of reelection. The process also represents the incumbent as a compromiser of conflict, a peacemaker among contesting views; and, thus, he is partially absolved of responsibility, because he can claim that the political forces or interests caused decisions that some of his constituents may feel were adverse. Incrementalism and fragmentation diffuse responsibility, enabling the elected official to avoid responsibility for the past and avow better hopes for the future.

With such powerful incentives to the elected official inherent in serial, incremental politics, the idea of comprehensive and positive evaluation of policy priorities is repugnant. A comprehensive evaluation of positive policy stances aggregates the opposition, by rallying those who may oppose any one plank of a comprehensive platform. Returning now to a rational comprehensive mode of policy evaluation, such as proposed by systems analysis, we can see that the posing of scenarios that gave constituencies alternative choices among ranked orders of objectives would be a decision model that a politician, under the present system, would want to avoid because it would jeopardize his reelection.

This is not to say, however, that the voter does not need or want a series of scenarios giving him some option to live his own legend. Indeed, research indicates that constituencies are currently without a concept of their own self-interests, and thus they have a need to crystalize the options that are possible for them to achieve. The role of leadership is to generate visions of what might be so that citizens may choose among them; but the present process of fragmented, incremental politics does not elicit such leadership, and advances incentives that work against its emergence. The result is that elected officials as policymakers act to satisfy their own self-interests, of which reelection and raising the related campaign financing rank high. Research into policymaking by Bauer has shown that policymakers use strategies, decision rules, and styles of role playing in advancing their own interest to compensate for their limited informational and computational abilities, and that most citizens are not clearly aware of their own self-interests.[8] Small businessmen, for example, calculate their own self-interest meagerly. They have established a standard of reinforcing and defending the status quo of their present firms while wishing for something a little better, rather than perhaps envisioning an economy where the capital flows to small business would cause them to burgeon with growth. With constituents having such a meager concept of their self-interest, an elected official can readily substitute surrogate goals that are closer to his own. Thus in the absence of a mechanism in the decision process to give the citizen a vision of his range of choices, the choices become those of the elected decision maker.

Role Structure and Bargaining

Not only does the ordinary citizen have a poor conception of his own self-interest, but he also has an ineffectual level of knowledge about the political process. Citizens have a general belief in a democratic creed or process, and the majority have believed that the American government conforms to that democratic norm. However, citizens have only a general idea of the rules, roles, and procedures by which the government really functions.

Role structure and rules of bargaining are major determinants of policy outcomes. The rules, roles, and procedure of government are known intimately by the political hierarchy that is elected to office by the rules of the game. This political hierarchy is committed to the governmental process because it is its base of power; it acquires rights and decision authority by means of its members' elected role. Its elected role, in turn, is government by constitutional provision, legislative authorizations, and parliamentary rules of procedure. These authorizations collectively are the "rules of the game" by which the political hierarchy exercises decisions if it is to exercise power at all. Its interest in staying in office and power commits it to play by the rules of the game, even in the face of policy differences with others, including rivals.

Dahl points out that policy disagreements are settled by colleagues and professionals who are part of the political stratum and hierarchy. These officials themselves do not command undivided support, and their power to settle disagreements depends on using the rules of the game. As a result, professionals use established bargaining and parliamentary rules to resolve issue conflicts, and they accept the decision as binding until it can be changed again through regular procedures, which is their code of democratic legitimism.[9]

If a strong leadership group believes that it cannot revise policy through the regular internal procedure, it may appeal outside of the political hierarchy to the citizenry, either to reopen the issue or change the rules. These appeals become increasingly emotional and irrational, until the citizenry must react. Citizen reaction may reflect mere partisan loyalty, clues about their interests, or their withdrawal into apathy.

The ordinary citizen's attitudes are irrelevant to policymaking, except when those in the political stratum acting in their own self-interest, appeal to the public; and even then, the public attitudes are filtered through the political stratum and become known only through the subjective evaluation by the professionals seeking election.

The role of the citizen in the governmental decision process is essentially passive, unless the professional finds it desirable to appeal to him. The role of the professional is to resolve issues by established bargaining procedures, adhere to decisions at least until they can be appealed to the political hierarchy or the public, and to transform citizen attitudes into a subjective assessment of personal and public purpose.

A decision process that adheres to these roles and rules does not guarantee that the public purpose is an optimum resolution of either individual interests or public welfare. The two most notable areas of slippage are found in the absence of a mechanism by which the individual can gain a greater conception of his own self-interest vis-à-vis politicians' self-interests, and the need for an adequate voice to express that individual interest without it becoming transformed by the subjective needs of the policymaker.

Transaction Models

Since the decision process is within a political hierarchy and governed by a set of decision rules (that is, bargaining and parliamentary rules), policy is formed by a series of transactions in which issue content is exchanged for votes within the political stratum. The first formulation of an issue into a policy proposal (for example, a new health care program) is conceived as close to the ideal form as its framers believe feasible. However, the proposal may appear to other politicians as being impractical because of being overly costly or beyond the capability of the health professions, perceived as infringing on private prerogatives, or extreme in light of other priorities. The framers of the proposal will then (if they do not have enough votes) have to enter into transactions with their near-supporters, offering to moderate the issue content by reducing costs, services, infringements, or its priority in exchange for supporting votes. The effect of this bargaining and compromise is to change the proposal, moderate the issue, and reduce the differences among conflicting views. The policy process may then be said to have several distinctive features:[10]

1. Policy is formed by a transaction model in which the role players exert continuous influence on each other, especially concerning the priority of treatment that shall be given to competing issues.

2. The process is conflictive in that competing issues and interest parties assume adversary positions on issues and against each other in the voting posture.

3. The bargaining over issue content to obtain a winning majority of votes tends to moderate issues, reduce demands, and bring contrary views closer together. In this sense, the demand reduction aspects of bargaining bring about near resolution of conflict, at least for the time being.

4. The process is distributive in allocating priorities among issues; and since these issues normally carry with them rights, authority, and income, the decision process distributes authority and income. Indeed, income and authority distribution are two of the principal functions of government, as we saw in chapter 7.

Leverage in Transactions

Leverage is a principle instrument for entering the transaction process. Leverage is the introduction of new information into the policy decision process; and the ultimate import of that new information depends on its bearing on the ultimate voting balance for the issue. The most obvious form of leverage is that which can deliver a specific number of votes; but other information is important as well, such as attitudes, compromise areas, revisions of issue content, data on costs or benefits, policy stances of various coalitions, attitudes and determination of political leaders, organizational structure of participants, resources of various groups, etc. All this information has a bearing upon the final outcome.

Gergen has identified three main dimensions along which these leverage influences may be classified: (1) issue relevance, (2) organizational resources, and (3) personal efficacy of the respective leaders or political actors.[11] Issue relevance is the degree of self-interest in the policy that engenders commitment. The greater the relevance of the issue to a person, the stronger is likely to be his attempt to exert leverage. Also, an issue's relevance is concomitant with the degree of its priority compared with other issues and the firmness of its proponents in bargaining to limit compromise.

Organizational resources are the organizational backing that various groups place behind the issue in terms of finances, staffing, publicity, initiatives, campaigning, and control.

Leader efficacy is the political ability to conceptualize and to communicate an issue in ways that will develop widening rings of constituency and voter support. Research has attempted to identify leadership personality traits that lead to personal efficacy in politics; but recent findings suggest that political effectiveness depends upon the situation. Differing situations call for differing strategies and leader behavior. In this respect, political behavior is situational in the same sense as it is in business organizations (chapter 10)—that is, personal efficacy in political policymaking depends upon effective communication, consistent public purposes, and acceptance based upon constituents' interests and capability.

These three aspects of leverage may be used three-dimensionally to assess the positional strength of contesting groups—that is, the strongest decision position would be represented by high issue relevance, large organizational resources, and great leader efficacy. By locating the positional strength of contesting groups in such a three-dimensional model, one would have an idea of the bargaining strength of the parties and the nature of the outcome. In other words, leverage analysis is a means of estimating political compromises and results.

Equally important from the viewpoint of practical politics is that the leverage concept provides indicators of where and how to interject information and influence into the policymaking process. These crucial points in the decision process might be called leverage points. The leverage points are the places where new information may be used to influence the strength of issue relevance, the allocation of organizational resources, or the attitudes or efficacy of key political actors.

A strategy for entering the transaction process to influence the outcome of a policy decision would be to inject information at the leverage points to strengthen the issue relevance among constituents, mobilize maximum organizational resources, and form a coalition among the effective political leaders.

Coalitions

Coalitions help resolve policy by strengthening leverage and bargaining sufficiently to create a majority voting structure out of the smallest winning coalition. Coalitions are made up of groups of people, who may differ within narrow range on an issue, but who agree sufficiently on the division of benefits and rewards among themselves to form an ad hoc voting bloc on a specific issue. The key to understanding coalitions is to see that they are engaged in "games of division." Since the government is engaged in the functions of redistributing authority and income, the games of division are about the allocations of authority and income. Two possible states of rewards may exist in such divisions: the rewards and benefits may or may not be large enough to satisfy competitive but compromising groups with regard to the share of authority or income that they will each receive under a policy proposal. If the rewards are too small, the groups will tend to lose interest, or the issue relevance will decline to the point of inactivity in the policy process. If the rewards are large enough, Fouraker has shown that the winning coalition will be the smallest winning coalition, and the members of the winning coalition will be those who have the minimum aspirations.[12]

The stake to be divided by the policy decision thus will have to be large enough to meet the minimum aspirations of a minimum number of groups who can make up a winning vote, because that is the marginal point at which a compromise agreement can be reached in a conflictive environment. The smaller the stake, the narrower the issue may be to split rewards among small numbers and still have adequate benefits to make the issue worthwhile or relevant to the constituents. Thus private bills in a legislature, or special interest legislation (such as an issue involving coal miners versus coal operators), can have smaller winning coalitions than general purpose legislation. In broad general legislation, such as national security, Social Security, or health care, the minimum winning coalition must encompass very diverse coalition groups; and thus the stake must be very large to spread the rewards, even thinly, among many parties. This leads to a corollary of the principle of minimum winning coalitions; that is, the diversity on the issue and the size of the minimum winning coalition is proportionate to the stake, or reward to be split.

Issue Relevance

The assessment of policy outcomes is probabilistic before the crucial vote, due to the flux and uncertainty of participants' true feelings on an issue. Still, an estimate of feelings and policy outcomes can be made by assessing the issue relevant to the voting constituency involved, along with the positional strength of the principal political actors.

The positional strength of a political leader, as we have previously seen, is the sum of his own personal efficacy in conceptualizing and communicating priority issues, plus the organizational resources he has with which to build support by campaign outreach. In many cases, the organizational resources are the most important element in determining outcomes, especially when the issue affects a narrow constituency base, or when issue relevancy is weak. In those two cases, large organizational resources can propagandize the small constituency or outvoice a large constituency that has an apathetic or weak interest in the issue. This, of course, is the strategy by which lobbyists are effective in having special interest legislation or policy decisions made in their favor.

When the issues are more general and crucial to the entire public, the personal efficacy and positional strength of a leader, in addition to organizational resources, are essential to secure a desired decision. The leader's positional strength will be determined by such factors as his reputation and the exent to which his previous authority by consent is recognized; his communication skill; his ability to conceptualize an appeal; the number of coalitions he leads or influences; his compromise and bargaining skill; and his organizational resources. Leaders differ on the extent to which they have these qualities or the capacity to exercise them in different situations. As an example, we might consider the basis of the positional strength and personal efficacy of recent presidents. All of us may differ on the assessment of recent presidents, but they provide a useful illustration because they generally are well known. President Johnson was regarded as a master of compromise in small group dealings when he was majority leader in Congress. And as the President, he secured passage of a large portion of his legislative proposals. President Kennedy, in contrast, was able to secure passage of only a small portion of his proposed legislation, but he engendered great public enthusiasm, especially among the young, by his ability to conceptualize and communicate issues. In table 11-1, the attributes of positional strength of recent presidents are (subjectively) assessed, by using an S to identify stronger attributes, and a W to designate apparently weaker ones. Readers may wish to revise the exercise based upon their own perceptions.

Any evaluator is likely to perceive leaders and presidents differently; but each evaluator is likely to be consistent in assessments, and thus demonstrate a pattern of leadership that influences policy outcomes. In table 11-1, for example, all recent presidents have had strong organizational resources as a means to office and power, but all except Kennedy have also been rather weak on conceptualization and communication. Kennedy's strength lay in his ability to appeal to the public at large, and he is thought of as a charismatic leader. Yet he was unable, during his short presidency, to build an effective coalition and bargaining position to implement his program. Presidents Johnson and Nixon are

Table 11-1
Attributes of Positional Strength

	Presidents				
Attributes	Eisenhower	Kennedy	Johnson	Nixon	Ford
Prior reputation	S	W	S−	S−	W
Communication	W	S	W	W	W
Conceptualization	W	S	W	W	W
Coalitions	S−	W	S	S	W
Bargaining	W	W	S	S	S−
Organizational resources	S	S	S	S	S−

most alike in their positional strength, which is typical of the practical, professional politician. What they lacked in public appeal, they made up for by exhibiting strength within the political hierarchy by commanding strong coalition and bargaining positions, along with their organizational resources. Presidents Johnson and Nixon are practical illustrations of the Dahl hypothesis that policy decisions are made by rules of the game within the political stratum, and citizen attitudes are largely irrelevant to policymaking, unless politicians appeal to them. President Kennedy did make such appeal, but was unable to effectuate it in legislation or execution.

Presidents Eisenhower and Ford are anomolies in the political system, because their positional strength is not typical of either the practical politician nor the charismatic leader. President Eisenhower came into office largely on the basis of his prior reputation as a military statesman who forged a winning coalition in World War II; and in office he continued to have strength in organizational resources and spanning broad coalitions. However, he seldom exercised his strength by bargaining to implement programs or conceptualizing appeals to the public. President Ford, coming in as the first appointed president, had some organizational resources and bargaining strength from his prior experience in Congress, but he had the task of forging a power base either by making appeals to the citizens by overcoming his tendency toward prosaic conceptualization of issue relevance, or through coalitional support among broad segments of conservative elements in society.

The point of this illustration is not to try definitively to characterize recent presidents, because doing so is subjective and varies by perspective; rather, it is to show that orderly assessment of leaders' positional strength, by a consistent set of evaluators, can indicate future policy outcomes. Such assessments of positional strength are one element of field policy studies. The procedures for field policy assessment are described by Gergen.[13] Briefly, they consist of the following ratings by evaluators:

1. Identify issue contents and compromisable subcontents.
2. Identify constituencies and actors in the issue.
3. Rate all nominees (constituent groups and actors) concerning their stance on the issues.
4. Rank positional strength and organizational resources of each major actor or leader.
5. Rate the issue relevance to all parties.
6. Rank the intensity of feeling by participant groups on subissues.
7. Evaluate the personal efficacy in coalition and bargaining strength of each major leader on each major subissue.

(The last step will suggest the compromises that may secure a minimum winning coalition.)

While all of these evaluations are judgmental, they will organize the essential conditions under which policy decisions are made. The policy outcome will normally be determined by the issue relevance and the leaders' positional strengths.

Voting Structure

The previous section has emphasized the positional strength of leaders as a main component of policy outcome; but the final choice is determined more by issue relevance than any other single factor. Issue relevance determines the size of the vote that frequently influences its composition.

The voting pattern on a specific issue is composed of the voting structure (who is authorized to vote) and the voting participation (who chooses to vote). Voting structures are established by law as part of the authority-allocation process. Thus, law, bylaws, resolutions, or a constitution determine the voting membership composition of such groups as citizens, Congress, the Supreme Court, Executive Branch, Cabinet, congressional committees, administrative commissions, corporate boards of directors, stockholders, and governing boards of voluntary institutions. The voting structure is therefore formally established as an eligibility list.

The participants who vote among the eligible members are determined by their degree of interest in the issue, which we have called issue relevance. Voting participation is frequently very low. The citizenry voting in a general election is often of the order of one-half to two-thirds of the voters, thus indicating that a significant minority regard the issues as irrelevant. The absentee and nonvoting members of legislatures may also run high (nearly one-half) on routine business, and approach 90 percent on issues of great relevance. Governing boards of voluntary social institutions frequently have difficulty getting a quorum to conduct business. And the participation is only somewhat better in labor organizations and corporate boards or annual meetings.

The basic core of participating voters is generally made up of those committed to the institution, who vote for the continuance or extension of existing policy. Thus, an in-group of the political, corporate, or social establishment is normally in attendance with a quorum and a majority to sustain present management decisions and practices. The normal voting behavior of this group is to support the status quo.

The nonparticipating members become voters only when issues are of intense personal interest. When issue relevance is high, these occasional participants enter the voting structure, for which they are eligible, normally to make a change or revision in policy. Therefore, the higher the participation rate among eligible votes, in most cases, the more likely is the possibility of policy changes.

The appeal to nonactive voters is usually made by a political leader who is seeking to overturn a policy, change the voting and transactional structure, oust leaders, or seek new policy innovation. These are perturbing changes to the political stratum of the in-group, and the changes would be opposed and defeated under the regular, internal decision rules of the professionals. The challenging leader must then enlarge the voting participation to augment votes for revision or change. He does this at his peril, because by doing so he has alienated his peers who control the internal decision process. The challenging leader must, to survive, either develop a campaign to win a majority among the nonactive votes to oust the in-group, or at least to amass a formidable minority carrying enough votes to force its way into the in-group as a new coalition.

The formation of a new majority, or a formidable minority coalition, requires a leader having a considerable conceptualization ability and communicative skill, as well as a substantial organizational resource; and an issue with a high degree of relevance to many voters. The conceptual, communicative, and resource conditions are the means to create a sense of vision and an awareness of self-interest among voters on an issue. And issue relevance is all-important in final voting behavior, because it determines whether the voting turn-out will bring in enough new votes (among those eligible) to achieve revision.

Seen in this light, the politics of revision are always more difficult than the politics of the status quo. The conservative element can always continue the status quo through its control of the internal decision process among the professional politicians. The change element can only achieve control by augmenting the voting participation and changing its composition by having a high degree of issue relevance. This characteristic of voting behavior is another element leading to crisis government.

When a voting pattern does emerge conducive to change, the change is likely to be minimal, for the reasons already discussed. The vote will be at the margin, allocating the least new authority, resources, or income that will satisfy the minimum aspirations of a minimum coalition able to form a majority vote. These marginal allocations will already have been arrived at by compromise among the leadership coalition through bargaining in a transaction model, which trades off priority issue content for a split in the reward among the coalition.

Stated in this manner, political bargaining may seem crass; but in fact it is a form of conflict resolution, and it is almost a mirror image analog of what happens in private markets. We saw in chapter 10 that private enterprise decisions are behavioral and empirical, in which choices are made at the margin to split a reward (profit-wages-prices) among interest parties who compete and bargain on the basis of their self-interest and wants. The major difference between public and private decision making is not in the process or crassness involved, but in the currency used. The currency of private decision making is money traded off for services (wants), while the currency in the public sector is votes traded off for wants. Both are traded by a transaction model that seeks to balance the currency with the wants. The air of precision in private decision is only a reflection of the fact that money is exchanged more frequently in the market than are votes in the public forum. Since the political feedback system is slow and infrequent, the political decision maker has to anticipate citizen feelings over longer periods with less exactitude. The uncertainty of citizen feelings, in the absence of rapid feedback control, enables the political policy-maker to interpret voter interest in the interim, frequently through the filter of his own self-interest. The private decision maker also interprets stockholder, employee, and customer wants in the light of his own self-interest. This illustrates another difference in the two-decision process. Both policymakers filter other peoples' aspirations through the parameters of their own self-interest: the private policymaker is expected to do so, the public policymaker is not—the public policymaker is supposed to act for the public purpose rather than his own.

Notes

1. Harry Eckstein, *Pressure Group Politics* (London: G. Allen, 1960), chapter 1.
2. David Braybrooke and Charles E. Lindbloom, *A Strategy of Decision* (New York: Free Press, 1963), chapters 3 and 5, esp. p. 105.
3. Ibid., pp. 124-127.
4. John K. Galbraith, *Economics of the Public Purpose* (New York: Signet, 1973), chapter 10.
5. J.S. Bruner, J.J. Goodnow, and G.A. Austin, *A Study of Thinking* (New York: John Wiley, 1956), chapters 4 and 5.
6. Herbert Simon, *Models of Man* (New York: John Wiley, 1957), pp. 204-205. Also, "Theories of Decision Making in Economic and Behavioral Science," *American Economic Review* XLIX, no. 3 (June 1959):253-283.
7. Carl Jung, *Man and His Symbols* (Garden City, N.Y.: Doubleday, 1964).
8. R. Bauer, I. Pool, and L. Dexter, *American Business and Public Policy* (New York: Atherton Press, 1963), p. 129.

9. Robert A. Dahl, *Who Governs?* (New Haven, Ct.: Yale University Press, 1961), pp. 315-324, esp. p. 321.

10. Raymond A. Bauer and Kenneth J. Gergen, *The Study of Policy Formation* (New York: Free Press, 1968), pp. 173-175.

11. Ibid., pp. 181-190.

12. Lawrence E. Fouraker, "Level of Aspiration and Group Decision Making," in Messick and Brayfield, eds., *Decision and Choice: Contributions of Sidney Siegel* (New York: McGraw-Hill, 1964).

13. Bauer and Gergen, *The Study of Policy Formation*, chapters 5 and 6.

12 Systematic Decision Models

Systematic decision models seek to integrate the various decision-making approaches, from the rational economic models through the empirical, behavioral, and social choice methods—that is, to integrate the essentials of all the ways of examining decisions described in chapters 9, 10, and 11. The attempt to encompass so wide and diverse a range of methods is clearly very ambitious; and the results can hardly be expected to be completely successful. Nevertheless, systematic decision methods are useful to consider to achieve a more holistic view of the management process.

The impetus behind using systematic decision models originated with the applications of computers to management problems in the postwar period. Mathematical methods and computer technology had been successfully applied to such wartime problems as submarine warfare and aircraft targeting. Further operations research progress was made with regard to postwar aerospace problems of calculating ballistic missile trajectories and establishing space navigational guidance. Operations research came on stream for industrial applications about the same time in inventory control models, production control, waiting-line problems, and most especially in optimizing a mix of variables through linear programming. Several of these models, particularly those involving random search or linear programming, would be very difficult to accomplish without a computer because of the large number of calculations required.

The body of literature that most clearly reflects these systematic decision methods, then, is found in the fields of systems analysis, operations research, computer technology, and mathematical modeling. More recently, the application of these techniques has led to additional bodies of literature in management science, decisions sciences, and policy analysis. A survey of this large literature is beyond the scope of this chapter; and instead an attempt will be made to discuss how systematic methods go about organizing assumptions, data, and variables into a model. For the most part they proceed by a scientific method from observation to hypothesis of causal relationships, and then to measurement of the observations (or variables), their formulation, and their testing.

Since scientific methods begin with observation, difficulty is experienced from the very start because much of the decision process is imperceptible. We noted in chapter 10 that only three out of nine steps in the decision process described there were observable. The more subjective parts of the decision process have to be inferred from some behavioral manifestation—for example, whether the decision maker is trying to optimize profits, avoid losses, reduce a threat, or garner a winning coalition of votes. For the most part, the observer is required to take the decision maker at his word to describe his behavior; and thus most systematic methods start with various verbal models of the decision, and then proceed to program or quantify the word model. We therefore begin with the question of how these verbal models come into being, and then proceed to discuss how they are structured into a more formal (often mathematical) statement.

Scenarios, Missions, Protocols, and Delphi Technique

Decision making is anticipatory in that it deals with future events and expectations. Human expectations are subjective, based upon feelings and value judgments that are not open to direct observation. Yet they are the starting point for the decision process, because they provide the motive and response patterns by which individuals and organizations function. The cumulative expectations among individuals or organizations form sets of needs; and hence some form of needs analysis is the first basic step in the decision process.

The two most common forms of needs analysis are statistical or participative. The statistical analysis of needs presumes some historical pattern of behavior that has been observed in the light of a concept or theory, which can then be measured by data over time. For example, the idea of a poverty level as a measure of need is based upon historical subsistence patterns over time, an economic theory about consumption, and data on the number of persons below a minimum consumption level. Similarly, the educational needs of a population are based on historical levels of educational attainment in relation to jobs and citizenship requirements, a theory of education, and data on the demographic distribution of educational levels.

The second common form of needs anlaysis is participant observation, which is characterized as open-ended market research in business, or as field study techniques in the social sciences. In these approaches, the participant observer enters a field situation, such as an organization or interview sequence among individuals, without a hypothesis about their expectations or needs. The observer instead enters into a wide-ranging or open-ended discussion about hopes, problems, and expectations, and at the same time observes keenly the situational setting of the individual or organization together with the behavioral patterns that emerge. These discussions and observations are carefully recorded in detail during or after the interview, sometimes on a tape recorder, but most frequently in the form of very complete interview notes of the conversations and transactions that comprise the observation. These detailed notes of transactions are sometimes termed "protocols," which is the literal meaning of the word. The compilation of a large set of field notes or protocols, therefore, provides a data base of a sample of people's needs and expectations.

The difficulty, of course, is to analyze the protocols objectively, since they are compiled as open-ended subjective expressions. The field notes are usually analyzed by two or more trained social scientists who read through the entire compilation of field notes to discern common patterns, actions, expectations, or transactions that emerge repeatedly. These common transactions are identified with a common term and then scored quantitatively as to frequency. The result is a quantitative set of individual responses forming hypotheses about the needs and expectations of those persons. These hypotheses can be further tested on a larger scale by more structured forms of interviews or observations, which are often cast into the form of a questionnaire or survey instrument.

Once some sense of need or expectation has been determined, either by these survey methods or by the intuitive estimate of a leader, the realization of expectations may be composed into scenarios. Scenarios are word descriptions or stories of how future events may be handled to fulfill the expectations of a group of individuals. Scenarios may take the form of political platforms, programs, scripts, or stories portraying the unfolding of expected events. In war gaming, the scenario is the unfolding of a military threat together with the tactical alternatives for trying to counter the threat. In political gaming, the scenario is the description of a critical problem (such as the energy crisis) together with the alternative programs for coping with it. In individual lives, the scenario is the story of how a person meets an individual crisis (boy meets girl) and resolves it. Thus scenarios are the images of expectations realized, the self-fulfilling prophecy, or, in Jungian terms, the living of one's own legend.

The scenario is vital to the decision process because it identifies the direction of activity that must be realized to meet the expectation—that is, the scenario has in it purposes to be accomplished, and these purposes are missions. Mission analysis is the examination of scenarios and expectations to determine what work must be performed, what objectives are implied, and what needs to be done. The scenario of the energy crisis, for example, implies objectives concerning substitute fuels to replace the diminishing supplies of petroleum and natural gas. Thus mission analysis identifies the objectives that need to be realized in coal, solar, geothermal, and nuclear energy production to replace petroleum. These objectives become the "missions" of the energy program.

The "missions" of a program usually require a means or technology to accomplish them. Thus the mission to bring geothermal energy into existence as a feasible supply requires new technologies for geologic exploration for hot water reservoirs, new means and materials to handle corrosion from geothermal fluids, and new energy conversion methods to utilize the lower temperatures of geothermal fluids compared with existing fuels. The next decision question then is, can these new technologies be developed? The two main methods of dealing with this question are technology assessment or a delphi technique.

Technology assessment is basically an extrapolation of the existing state of the art to see what innovations in methods and materials are necessary for adaptation to a new requirement, such as producing energy from low-temperature, corrosive geothermal fluids rather than from fossil fuels. Technology assessment identifies research and development needs, probabilities of achievement, together with the strengths, weaknesses, costs, and trade-offs of each approach. The result of this technical analysis is a preferred alternative for technical development, presumably the most probable of success or the least costly.

Sometimes the technological state of the art is sufficiently unknown so that extrapolation from the existing state of the art is unlikely. The space program presented such problems, because there was not sufficient technological precedent for extrapolation from existing practice. The stationary space communication satellite, for example, involved two functions for which there was no experience: (1) the station-keeping function of maintaining the satellite in stationary orbit at a fixed point over earth; and (2) the design of a long-endurance electronic repeater that would beam signals back to the earth over long distances using little power.

The delphi technique is one means with which to deal with these more speculative technological problems. The delphi technique assembles a group of scientists and experts in a particular field and asks interactively among them two basic types of questions: (1) are there any scientific laws that preclude this technology from being realized, and (2) if not, what are the experiments that would most probably satisfy the requirement? The successive dialogue among experts on such innovative issues tends to focus a scientific consensus of opinion on the most likely alternatives for research. Note that these judgments are also from the subjective realm; they are probabilities based upon informed opinion.

In summary, then, the decision process starts with the objective organization of subjective opinion, first by needs analysis to determine expectations among the ultimate users, second by scenario and mission analysis to explicate the unfolding of events to realize those expectations, and third by technology assessments from experts to estimate those experiments which are technically possible.

With this much subjective input to go on, we are now ready to examine the more objective activities of the decision process. However, we must always be conscious that, no matter how elegant, refined, or expensive the decision model may ultimately become, the results in terms of human achievement are no better than the subjective needs analysis that went into the decision in the first place. If the expectations were wrongly stated, the solution will be wrong, no matter how magnificent the technological or management achievement. That is why there is a saying in the high technology field: Beware of elegant solutions for which there is no problem. The only safeguard against solving nonproblems is to check back reiteratively with the client or users as designs, performance, and costs become known to see whether the latter indeed meet the former's expectations.

Performance Requirements and Decision Variables

The purpose of going through a rather elaborate approach to the determination of needs and expectations was to establish objectives and goals for management purposes. There are other ways to establish objectives, of course, such as having the chief executive officer announce them, or asking people within a producing organization. However, these ways are not sufficient or appropriate in themselves, if one is seeking to manage a healthy organization that is responsive to human needs. Healthy organizations adapt and grow over time because they serve and respond to human wants and expectations. Therefore, the process of goal or objective determination is vitally involved with the users or clients if management is to serve the purpose of doing for individuals those things which they would do for themselves as long as they had the knowledge, resources, and techniques—which is after all the purpose of organizations and management.

Assume then that our needs analysis, mission determination, and technology assessment have given us definable objectives of what users or consumers want. The next step is to convert these objectives into performance goals and specifications. The specific statement of performance requirements is the means of identifying decision variables and (ultimately) establishing management control of an organization. For example, a user (in this case the government) wants a communication satellite. The minimum performance specifications, we determined after investigation, are that the satellite must be able to operate 12 channels of communication at 500 watts of power over 48 months while not varying more than 2 degrees in orbit. Such a performance specification becomes the object of a design study to determine whether one can indeed place the satellite into a stationary orbit and correct its orbit within a variation of less than two degrees, and at the same time operate twelve communication channels at the required power output for forty-eight months. The design studies showed, in historical retrospect, that hydrogen peroxide tanks could provide sufficient thrust over the life requirements to correct the orbit within the variation specified, and that a newly invented high-power microwave tube could provide the necessary power over a forty-eight-month period, with solar cells supplying the power source. The next performance goal, was to determine what all this research and development would cost. Hence the next step was making a cost analysis of the proposed engineering development program to be submitted for the government's approval before proceeding.

A more frequent form of performance specification in commercial development is the inclusion of a cost parameter as part of the performance specifications. In geothermal energy development of a water-dominated reservoir, for example, the performance specification might be that the geothermal energy source must be capable of producing fifty megawatts of electric power over thirty years, with reinjection and corrosion control, at a bus-bar price of thirty to thirty-five mills per kilowatt hour and a 16 percent return on investment after taxes. In this specification, the bus-bar price is a competitive cost specification determined by electric energy conversion from competing fuel sources, such as petroleum at $12 per barrel, coal, or nuclear power. The return on investment is the return needed to secure risk funds in the capital markets. The power plant size specified is a minimum usable plant. The thirty years is a necessary operating life over which the electric utility can depreciate or amortize its investment. The reinjection and corrosion control specification is necessary to prevent land subsidence at the surface and to assure that the geothermal fluid can be handled both in steel pipe and in the reservoir.

The performance specification typically contain (1) an output requirement, which may be expressed in volume, speed, configuration, or quantity; (2) a life-time or endurance requirement—that is, how long must it last?; (3) a cost requirement, often determined by examining competitive alternatives; and (4) an investment requirement, usually determined by using the going risk rate in the capital market. These performance specifications also become the decision variables for management. Management adopts a go or no-go decision depending on whether the decision variables can be met. The structure of the decision is generally, in cost-effectiveness terminology, a fixed effectiveness model with minimized cost; that is, in the geothermal example, the physical performance goals become fixed standards that must be met (and thus are termed fixed effectiveness). These standards are the ability to generate fifty megawatts of power for thirty years with no subsidence and minimal corrosion. The principal measures that determine whether these performance standards are achievable are the geothermal well-head temperature, heat flow over time, well drawn-down, and the mineral content of the fluid with its corrosive and precipitate characteristics. Given appropriate measures of these characteristics, a fixed effectiveness of performance calculation can be made—that is, fifty megawatts of power for thirty years with no subsidence and manageable corrosion. Thus the decision is a fixed effectiveness decision with respect to achieving these physical variables.

The second part of the decision model is: what will be this performance cost and the rate of return? This part of the decision is determined by using a cost minimization model—that is, the cost must be some minimum below the competitive cost of other fuels. For example, the power cost must be less than thirty-five mills per kilowatt-hour (kwh), which we assume can be achieved by using petroleum, coal, or nuclear power. The lower the cost below thirty-five mills per kwh, the better the geothermal power alternative is from a decision viewpoint (because the lower the cost, the higher the rate of return, or the more competitive the price). If the geothermal power could be developed at twelve to fifteen mills per kwh, it could compete with petroleum down to the old domestic price of $4.50 per barrel. Or, at $12 per barrel, geothermal energy at a twelve to fifteen mill cost could generate a rate of return on investment well beyond the 16 percent target needed to obtain risk funds from the capital market. Thus cost minimization can also be looked upon as a profit optimization model as well.

In sum, the performance specifications become the decision variables management uses to decide whether to proceed. This decision is generally based on a fixed-performance (effectiveness) cost minimization model. Moreover, the performance specifications and the cost targets become, as we later see, the organizational goals management then uses to control the project or enterprise.

Systems Analysis

Systems analysis is an integrative and inductive thought process that seeks to relate a user need or performance specification to the whole environment and the component activity within a producing or delivery organization. Systems analysis may be looked upon in a theoretical sense as concentrating the energy reserves sufficiently to make an organism function, or in a practical sense as reducing uncertainty, risk, or the probabilities of failure.

The theoretical construction of system theory comes in part from biological systems, in which the more complex an organism is the more capability it has to store reserves of energy with which to counteract the laws of entropy.[1] Entropy is that phenomenon of the second law of thermodynamics by which energy use always degrades from high energy forms (more concentrated) to lower energy forms (more random and disperse). Thus a piece of coal is a concentrated form of hydrocarbon heat energy that, once burned, is dispersed into a lower energy state of gas and ash that cannot be reconstituted back into coal. Entropy in the physical world is a one-way conversion, toward entropic death, ashes and red stars. Biological species, however, have the capacity to reverse (temporarily) this one-way conversion toward entropic death by storing up energy in their cells. Thus a horse is an improbable animal from the viewpoint of physics, because the law of gravity indicates his heavier part or backside should point downward toward the ground. Yet the horse stands upright in defiance of his center of gravity, because it has combusted food, in the form of carbon heat energy found in grass, to store in its muscle cells to create sufficient power to overcome the law of gravity. It can muscularly control not only its uprightness but also its running speed—that is, the horse has a balance of stored energy that enables it to achieve a state of equifinality, or a balanced energy offset to entropy.

What has this theory about biological systems, horses, and entropy have to do with management? System theory provides management with a perspective called systems analysis, which commends a manager to examine, before making decisions, where he and his decision stands with respect to his environment. An environment is made up of all external (to the system) networks of organisms and organizations (which are complex social organisms). All such interacting organisms and organizations subsist on common energy sources, whether that source be food or fuel, and whether that energy be stored in human bodies, capital equipment, money, other nations, or biological species. In other words, management is the art of economizing and utilizing scarce resources to meet human needs. The ultimate resource is the energy locked up in the food/energy chain, past or present, in fossil fuels, uranium, or crops. The ultimate management decision concerns the use of this ultimate energy resource to optimize human needs within the balance of nature. This may seem to be a larger question than most managers care to ask themselves, or indeed need to ask themselves if they just intend to simply make money. Yet even for the narrow-minded money-maker, the systems approach is essential as a step toward understanding competition, if nothing else.

The value of systems analysis as a decision tool is that it assumes that everything is connected with everything else, and every decision has an opportunity cost that trades off, or sacrifices, one benefit to obtain another. That means that every decision has competitive and alternative interactions. Thus what are all the interactions in the environment that this decision or action may affect? To begin answering this question, the interactions may be defined as (1) the environment, (2) the thing (our system or action) that we propose to accomplish, and (3) the components of our system.

The environment includes all the physical, social, and ecological interactions around us, each of which is itself part of a larger system or network of events. These networks at their highest organizational level make up nations, the food chain, and energy cycles. At the competitive level (at which the manager wishes to examine them), the environment is made up of consumers; competitive consumer wants; competitive enterprises; competing uses of capital, material, or energy; social organizations; governments; legal rights; weather; crops; pollution; and threats.

The enumeration of threats is a propitious place to commence a systems analysis. If we are building a sailboat for ocean cruising, the threat is the force of the winds; the high-wave seas; anchorage, or the lack thereof; harbor obstacles; ocean size; and lack of food, water, or supplies at sea. Each of these threats define a performance specification for the sailboat—respectively, sail and mast strength, beam and freeboard, maneuverability, collision strength, navigational capability, and storage capacity. These performance characteristics, taken together with length and time of cruise, will determine the boat size and configuration. Thus the environment imposes conditions and constraints upon the decision maker that become part of the performance specification, and may be called threats or merely the requirements for survival.

There are other environmental conditions or threats: that supplies will not be available, that competitors can deliver the service more efficiently or cheaply, that consumers will change their minds or demand, that a flood will destroy a key part of the enterprise, that a key employee of the organization will quit, that pollution (ours or others) will destroy an environmental quality such as water on which we depend, that government laws or regulations will restrain us, that someone will sue us for infringing a legal right, that nations will destroy our efforts by war, or that we will die before the enterprise is launched.

These threats, and more, are the survival conditions faced by a decision maker; and the existence of the threats creates uncertainty. The uncertainty is not resolvable, because no one can know which of the threats will occur. Yet systems analysis asks that the decision maker at least try to anticipate the major threats, estimate the probability of their affecting his enterprise, and examine alternative ways of reducing the risk or uncertainty.

We come to the second and more practical aspect of systems analysis, which is the examination of risk, uncertainty, probabilities, and alternative costs for risk avoidance. The depth of perception brought to this risk-avoidance analysis will prove to be one of the key elements in the survival and profitability of the project. (Notice one other thing that has occurred by assuming this holistic examination of the whole system and its environment—we have switched from deduction to induction, from analytical thinking to synthesis. This may well be the most important contribution of the systems approach.) For example, it was deductive, analytical, and scientific to observe human needs and convert them to performance requirements and decision variables. This analytical approach enabled us to hypothesize a human want and how (technologically) to fulfill it. Having arrived at the what and how of the decision by analytical and reductionistic thinking, we now, by a systems approach, ask a much larger question—Why does this decision or action have a place in the scheme of things, in the network of competitive demands, in the food and energy chains? Is there actually a problem? Will this concept or enterprise survive? Can it meet the survival threats that in the end defeat most things?

To deal with these questions of environmental conditions, we must think inductively about how our action will affect all related interactions, and what are the probabilities of the outcome? These are large questions upon which philosophies are founded and enterprises succeed or founder. But they are vital to the decision maker, because they enlarge the performance specifications from mere analytical thinking to encompass those environmental conditions that will determine survival, probabilities, and risk, which is what the decision maker is ultimately paid to decide.

Criteria

A decision maker is basically concerned about developing a strategy for the maintenance (survival) of himself or his institution, together with establishing a probability of growth in profit, sales, output, employment, technology, clients, knowledge, or some other key variable of his endeavor. These internal organizational objectives are encompassed in criteria, which reflect the internal needs of the organization as well as the external performance requirement derived from analytic and synthetic methods previously discussed. Criteria are needed to sum the essential components of a decision, because the task of the decision maker is to compare alternative choices using a common standard, which is the essence of the decision.

Criteria are thus the standards by which alternative plans are evaluated: they are the sum of the analytical and synthetic performance characteristics with which a decision maker can fashion a strategy for survival and hopefully growth. The remaining steps in a systematic decision process after criteria are determined (and the balance of this chapter) are concerned with the estimation of operational results of alternative plans. The laying out of these alternatives is the process of implementation planning. The decision maker must then choose among the alternative plans. The choice is based on which plan most nearly fits the criteria.

We can consider decision criteria by again examining our example of geothermal energy development, which is a relatively new technology. The first geothermal power plants in the United States have been installed within the past decade at The Geysers in California (northeast of San Francisco) in an area where dry-steam reservoirs are tapped by oil-drilling technology and converted to electricity in flash-steam power plants. A second set of geothermal wells is being developed in Imperial County, California, by drilling into fracture zones of geological faults to tap hot water reservoirs ($400\text{-}500°F$) that have varying amounts of dissolved minerals, sometimes quite corrosive. Additional exploration for geothermal development is being conducted in Nevada, Idaho, Montana, Utah, and Hawaii, where the reservoirs generally contain purer water, nearer to the surface, but of medium temperature ($300\text{-}400°F$). In the next half-century, perhaps 5-10 percent of the total electric energy of the United States will come from geothermal power as a substitute for fossil fuels, located mainly in Western states near recent volcanic activity or fault zones.

The decision thus is to decide where to explore and invest in geothermal energy. Some trade-offs are clearly involved, because the cost of a power plant increases inversely with temperature, while the cost of a well increases directly with depth and corrosiveness. Thus for well costs alone, an Idaho site might be preferable for reasons of shallow wells and pure water, but power plant costs would be high due to low temperatures. An Imperial County, California, site would provide higher temperatures and lower power plant costs than the Idaho wells, but the wells would be more costly because they would have to be drilled deeper and would contain more corrosive fluids. Moreover, finding a producing geothermal well any place represents the same kind of gamble as finding oil. The odds are estimated to be sixteen to one; thus an exploration company in a new area must be prepared to drill sixteen or more holes at a $0.5-1.0 million each to find one producing well. For openers, then, exploration is at least a $10-15 million gamble.

The survival criteria of the decision maker in this case is to survive the sixteen-to-one odds against him, and then proceed with a viable alternative plan to satisfy consumer energy needs. Survival strategy against high, adverse odds may take two main forms: (1) to possess large enough capital (perhaps $50 million or more) to diversify the risks and play the average odds, or (2) to try to reduce the odds by drilling in partially explored fields where more knowledge of geological structure is obtainable.

With this much background, we can summarize the decision criteria of a geothermal developer:

A. Internal survival criteria
1. Control adverse exploration odds by using large capital or superior knowledge (have $50 million or extensive geologic information for a field to equal or beat the sixteen-to-one odds).
2. Generate sufficient funds or revenue to maintain a technical organization capable of exploration and development (for example, a minimum of a ten-person organization costing $600,000 per year).
3. Develop alternative operating plans that at least break even at the risk rate necessary to obtain funds from the capital markets (for example, 16 percent after taxes).

B. External analytic performance specifications
4. Provide electric power to meet consumer needs at a comparative price (thirty-five mills per kwh or less).
5. Provide a usable scale of power output (fifty megawatts or more for thirty years).

C. External environmental performance specifications
6. Avoid damage to the existing environment (in Imperial County this means minimizing land use and adverse effects on its rich agricultural base).
7. Minimize water quantity and quality impacts to be compatible with alternate uses (in Imperial County this means using agricultural drainage water rather than fresh irrigation water for power plant cooling towers).
8. Abate air pollution (in The Geysers, this means reducing sulfur dioxide emissions to less than three ppm).
9. Prevent subsidence, which would destroy alternative uses such as irrigated agricultural fields (this requires reinjection of geothermal fluids back into the reservoirs, which may have the effect of precipitating deposition that will plug the reservoirs).
10. Avoid inducing seismic activity (this means not lubricating fault zones or cooling the reservoir by reinjection to an extent where earthquake damage is induced).
11. Avoid blowouts or provide liability indemnification (a blowout is an uncontrollable eruption of hot geothermal fluids, possibly corrosive, from a well—it must either be quickly controlled, or the surrounding damage indemnified).

12. Conduct the development within the land leasing rights, permit system, and state and local regulations that are applicable.

These twelve criteria constitute the decision parameters for geothermal development. Any alternative plan or technology must meet all twelve criteria or the decision is no-go—that is, without meeting the twelve criteria, the organization cannot survive. If several alternative plans at least minimally meet the twelve criteria, then the choice among alternatives will be restricted to that one which maximizes criterion 3 or 2—that is, profit or organizational capability. With definite criteria in mind, the decision maker's next step is to develop and evaluate alternative implementation plans to see which one best meets the criteria. The development and evaluation of alternative plans is the subject of the balance of this chapter.

Function Determination

Function determination is a systems analysis of the work to be performed in delivering a mission to its customers; and the alternative technologies for performing the functions define the work design or tasks that the delivery organization must commit itself to manage. A decision is first of all a commitment; and it is more than an investment commitment of capital or money. The commitment is to manage people and work, in all their ramified detail, to deliver a service to a user. The money commitment is relatively the more simple, because it appears to have a summary elegance and simplicity to it—that is, return on investment. Besides, the decision often relates to other people's money. But the work commitment is real, because it involves the work of the executive and all the people in the organization. The work commitment entails personal effort, motivation, conflict, and unexpected adversities. The job of the manager is to manage the toil, to minimize it, and to achieve the end result. To do that, the manager needs to anticipate and know as much as he can in advance about the work tasks and commitments. The work tasks and the people performing them are what he is really managing. The manager tries to anticipate this work design and commitment by anticipating it with a plan.

The first step in creating the plan is to determine the functions to be performed. Function here means a work function, in the same sense as in engineering. The work function of a particular lever is to raise a 100-pound weight a distance of 1 foot with a force of 20 pounds. This defines a task that can be designed. The work function states the output, the technical means, and the input. The output is 100-foot pounds of lift. The means is a lever with a five-to-one ratio to the fulcrum. The input is twenty pounds of force applied over a distance of five feet. If done by hand, the human task is to apply twenty pounds of muscular pressure for a five-foot span, which means the person will press and bend nearly to ground level. This is not a terribly difficult task to do once. But it is strenuous if done repeatedly and would encounter some endurance limit for the average person. The manager needs to know the endurance limit (and motivation) to staff a work function requiring, for example, 100-foot pounds of lift at a rate of 60 times per hour. Or, if the task is a mental one, such as programming a computer, the manager needs to know the intelligence capability and rate of the operator.

Work design ultimately leads to the definition of specific mental and physical tasks. However, work design starts by considering the desired output from the sum of many tasks, or the total function that must be accomplished to deliver a service or mission. The way to think about function determination is to define the output first and then describe the main work activities to be performed, starting with a verb. For example, the mission and output of a geothermal energy plant is to produce electric power. The main work functions needed to produce the electric power are:

1. Explore the subsurface geophysical structure to locate a geothermal reservoir.
2. Drill or penetrate the earth to tap the hot geothermal steam or fluids.
3. Transmit the geothermal heat to a power plant through well casings and transmission pipelines.
4. Separate the fluid and vapor into usable heat components.
5. Exchange the heat, if necessary, by using an expansive secondary working fluid.
6. Convert the working fluid into rotary motion (for example, by a turbine, piston, etc.).
7. Convert the kinetic energy of motion into electrical energy (for example, by a generator).
8. Transform the electric energy into appropriate voltage for transmission.
9. Transmit the voltage to the user.

These nine major work functions cover the work to be performed in delivering electric energy from a geothermal resource. Each of the nine functions can be further broken down into detailed tasks and activities that must be assigned and performed to manage and complete the project. For example, the geological exploration will include core sampling, chemical analysis of core material, heat gradient measurement, electric resistivity measurement, gravity measurement, seismic and sonic measures, mapping, etc.

In attempting to make a function determination, one should be careful not to prejudge the technology or means, because doing so will limit innovation. An example of such an error or prejudgment is contained in the preceding function determination. Functions 5, 6, and 7 implicitly presume the existing state of the art in electrical power generation; that is, the heat will be converted into electricity through a flash-steam or binary cycle process, which turns a turbine. A less restrictive, and hence more innovative, form of function determination would be to strike functions 5 through 7 and substitute a phrase such as, "Convert heat into electrical energy." In this function statement, the means of conversion are left open; and some new, innovative form of conversion, such as the total flow or the helix screw processes might be used.

As another and perhaps more familiar example, we can determine the functions to be performed by any vehicle. The mission or purpose of a vehicle is to transport objects through physical space at velocities faster than human walking. The functions to be performed are:

1. Move the vehicle with a power source.
2. Regulate the speed.
3. Navigate the vehicle.
4. Brake or stop the vehicle.
5. Communicate to or from the vehicle as needed for navigation.
6. Route the vehicle.
7. Store the cargo.
8. Store the vehicle.

These eight work functions can be used to design any vehicle from a horse-drawn cart or automobile to a spacecraft. The differences are in the technology of means. Depending on the power source selected in function 1, the rest of the design will vary. Select a horse as the power source, then speed regulation is by rein, navigation by a human rein holder, stopping by a shoe brake, communication by road signs, routing by dirt roads, cargo storage in a passenger seat and dray box, and vehicle storage in a barn. Change the power source to an internal combustion engine and the speed increases. The design to meet the eight functions at higher performance speeds change somewhat to speed regulation by an accelerator or cruise control, navigation by steering wheel, stopping by hydraulic braking system, communication by road sign and radio, routing by paved expressways, cargo storage in passenger compartments, and vehicle storage in a garage.

We now look at a rocket propulsion motor as the power source. Assume a thrust that can propel the vehicle beyond the orbital speed of the earth and we have a space vehicle. The eight work functions are: move the vehicle by use of a rocket engine; regulate the speed by control of the burning rate and thrust; navigate by varying thrust direction with automatic, computerized controls operated by astronauts, ground control, or celestial navigation instruments; stop the vehicle by an atmospheric reentry and ocean recovery system; communicate with the vehicle by radio; route the vehicle by computer-programmed space trajectories; store the cargo in space capsules; and store the vehicle on launching pads secured with gantry towers.

These illustrations suggest that function determination is the single most important stage of management planning and control, after mission and performance specification. A function determination, correctly made, outlines the total workload to be managed without constraining technology or innovation.

Task Determination

Task determination is technology specific and presumes that the trade-offs among alternative means have been evaluated to determine the most cost-effective techniques. The broad work functions are broken down into detailed human tasks, depending upon the technology used. To arrive at the detailed task level, the functions need to be further specified into subsystems, components, equipment, materials, and human activity. This work breakdown structure may be conveniently thought of in terms of indentures or subactivities contributing to the work function. For example, the vehicle is an automobile to be moved by an internal combustion power source. The indentures or work breakdown might therefore be:

1. Function—move vehicle by internal combustion power train
  1.1 Subsystem—engine assembly
    1.11 Component—engine block
      1.111 Component material—cast iron
        1.1111 Equipment—casting and boring machines
          1.11111 Task—human activity of casting the block
          1.11112 Task—boring the block

The tasks in the work breakdown structure are not as cut and dried as the illustration may appear, because the arrival at task specification presumes a substantial amount of engineering design. For example, the nature of the exact tasks illustrated here will be determined by how large the car is; whether it has four, six, or eight cylinders; whether it is gasoline or diesel fueled; whether it has a regular bore or stratified-charge engine, etc. In other words, engineering evaluations will have been made of the possible trade-offs among alternative techniques before the task can be specified. A trade-off is the examination or choice of one design or technology over another based on either cost or performance. Suppose that at very small cost (1 percent increase) an automobile designer could achieve, with a stratified-charge engine, 5 percent added mileage with a 20 percent reduction in emissions. Then the trade-off of increased mileage or decreased emissions versus cost would be favorable; and the manager would tend to decide upon the stratified-charge engine. This trade-off decision would determine the specification of boring to be done under human task 1.11112, and indicates that a significant level of engineering analysis and design precedes the assignment of human tasks in the work breakdown structure.

Networks, Decision Trees, and Schedules

Networks, decision trees, and schedules are the management means to organize and control the sequence of tasks to deliver an output meeting time and cost objectives. A network is the arrangement of probable events in a sequence that will deliver the desired outputs. An example of a network of events for assembling an internal combustion engine might be shown in simple form as shown in figure 12-1. These events in building and assembling an engine can be assigned time estimates for their accomplishment, thereby producing a control schedule by which the work can be managed. The time may vary somewhat, depending on the human skill or nature of materials used, and these variations can be expressed as high or low estimates of the time required. Time is also equivalent to cost, in terms of labor and equipment costs. The variations in time estimates can then be summed into cumulative cost estimates for all the tasks, with a high and low cost and time schedules, which will be the control parameters within which budgets and output can be monitored.

In the example of the automobile engine shown in figure 12-1, the degree of certainty of building the engine is high, subject to minor variations in time and cost, because automobile engines have been built for seventy years and the technical knowledge is well settled. When the technical art is not well known, higher degrees of uncertainty exist whether the task or event will occur at all. When the probability of outcome is uncertain, networks can be used to construct decision trees by assigning probabilities to the events together with investment costs. Figure 12-2 shows a high-risk venture, such as exploring for geothermal resources, with hypothetical probabilities and costs. Assume that the exploration enterprise has $12 million, no more, and anticipates the likely events shown in figure 12-2.

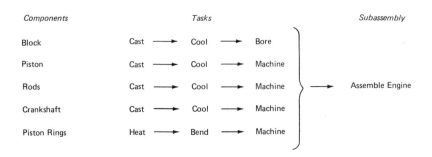

Figure 12-1. Network for Assembling an Internal Combustion Engine.

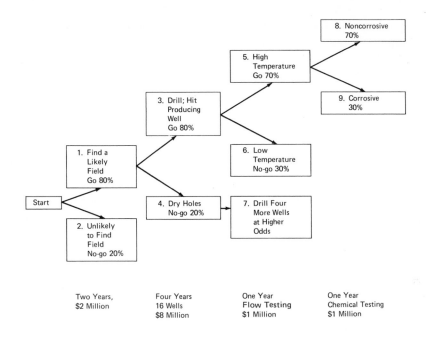

Figure 12-2. Decision Tree Showing Probabilities and Costs for a High-Risk Venture.

The venture starts exploring for geothermal resources by conducting field geology surveys, and the probability of its finding a likely field after two years of effort at a cost of $2 million is 80 percent. If no likely field is found, presumably the decision is to cut the losses at $2 million and quit.

The probability of hitting a producing well in a likely field after four years of work, by drilling sixteen wells at a cost of $500,000 each, is 80 percent. If no producing well is found, the decision may be no-go with a loss of $10 million, or alternatively to go for broke by drilling four more wells in a field where the odds are apparently worse than sixteen to one. The no-go venture at this point does not have enough money left to try to explore and drill in a new field.

For the go venture with a producing well at the end of six years and $10 million, the decision is to go on to test the temperature and volume of the well by measuring the flow of the well over time, at a cost of $1 million over a one-year period. The probability of having a high-temperature well is 70 percent.

Assume the venture has a high-temperature well; it then tests the chemical reaction in the recovery and reinjection system at a cost of another $1 million and another year. The probabilities of the well being a noncorrosive usable fluid are 70 percent.

The venture has now spent all of its funds, $12 million in eight years. The probability that it has a saleable and usable geothermal heat source is 31 percent (that is, the product of all the probabilities: $0.80 \times 0.80 \times 0.70 \times 0.70$). Although the decision tree does not seem highly adverse at first glance, since the odds at each stage appear to be fairly favorable, the integration of the odds into an overall probability of success at 0.31 certainly makes it a high risk venture that few investors would care to take. In other words, the decision tree indicates that this is not an attractive venture for most investors. Indeed, from a management standpoint, the decision tree is an unsatisfactory one in the sense that too much front money (that is, $10 million) has to be committed before any realistic estimate of the overall risk is obtainable. A more satisfactory decision tree might be constructed by putting more funds (perhaps $3 million) into more geologic measures, and drilling indicative bore holes to improve knowledge and probabilities before committing to an $8 million deep-drilling program.

Cost Analysis and Control

Cost analysis can establish cost control over the work flow of a project by using networks, decision trees, and schedules where the probabilities of performance have been narrowed to acceptable risks. Cost analysis of a system consists of pricing out the tasks to be accomplished in a network of events leading to a deliverable output or service. Previous sections have shown how the work functions of a system were converted into tasks, sequences, schedules, and networks defining the process, or work flow, needed to create the desired output. The tasks themselves are made up of human effort (labor time and cost), which is used to transform materials (material costs)—often with the use of equipment (capital costs)—into a service that fulfills the performance specification of the mission. Cost analysis thus accumulates the labor, material, and capital costs into a cost estimate of the output.

The purpose of cost analysis is fourfold: (1) to break down costs into their components to test their reasonableness for competitive bidding or pricing, (2) to accumulate costs into an aggregate investment to test against fund availability or limitations, (3) to compare aggregate costs to the value of the output to determine return-on-investment or benefit-cost ratios, and (4) to establish budgetary goals to measure performance and control costs. A simple example can be illustrated by the cost analysis of a set of tasks related to geothermal development from the decision tree shown in figure 12-2. Assume that we wish to break down the tasks and establish cost control over the $12 million of estimated expenditures needed to attempt the discovery of a new geothermal field. The tasks are shown in table 12-1.

This task list now shows time estimates and cost estimates for exploring a new geothermal field. The total cost is $2,000,000 and the time required, if all

Table 12-1
Breakdown of Tasks Related to Geothermal Development

Tasks	Schedule	Cost
1. Surface geologic survey	5 months	$ 175,000
2. Mapping	2 months	75,000
3. Borehole drilling	6 months	150,000
4. Chemical analysis of borehole samples	2 months	75,000
5. Gravity survey	6 months	200,000
6. Magnetic survey	3 months	150,000
7. Explosive soundings	7 months	200,000
8. Seismic array measures	9 months	150,000
9. Electric resistivity measures (after 3)	4 months	125,000
10. Test well drilling	12 months	700,000
	56 months	$2,000,000

tasks are done sequentially, is fifty-six months. Suppose management feels that nearly five years is too long, and work should be completed in about two years. Then the tasks may be planned to be done in parallel or concurrently. Task 1 needs to be completed before any other work starts, but then tasks 2 through 9 could conceivably be carried on concurrently. Upon their completion, task 10 could begin. Thus the longest sequential tasks among these concurrent activities (1, 3, 9, and 10) become the "critical path," totaling twenty-seven months, and the other tasks are scheduled in with some "slack time." The network of the schedule would resemble figure 12-3, in which the numbers identify the tasks, the solid line is the critical path, and dotted lines represent slack.

This network provides a schedule of time and costs that enables management to monitor and control the performance of the project. Management knows that it must keep tasks 1, 3, 9, and 10 on schedule or the project cannot be completed in twenty-seven months. Management also knows that there are eight months of slack time in task 2, which means it does not need to be monitored carefully; but task 8 must be monitored almost as closely as the critical path, because there is only one month of slack time in its schedule.

Moreover, management also has budgetary control over the schedule by dividing, or allocating, the cost per task over months in the schedule. Thus a monthly expenditure rate for each task can be monitored to see that the task or project is not overspent. A simplified calculation for this network indicates that the cash flow requirement will be $35,000 per month while task 1 is under way, will rise to $125,000 per month when tasks 2-9 are concurrently in operation, and will drop back to about $60,000 per month while the drilling program (task 10) is operable.

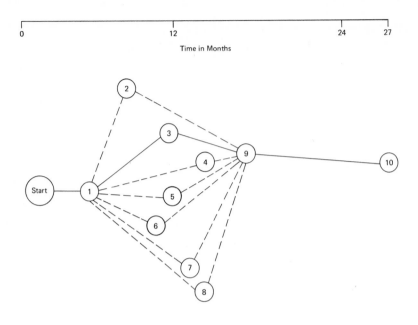

0   12   24   27

Time in Months

Figure 12-3. Network of the Exploration Example.

Program Organization and Management

The task list, network, schedules, and cost analysis can next be used to design the program and management organization together with manning tables of personnel needs—that is, organization design originates in an analysis of the work flow.

Suppose, for example, we are executives of an oil company engaged in petroleum exploration, production, refining, and distribution, and we decide to enter the field of geothermal energy exploration. The network illustrated in figure 12-3 becomes the plan with which we create a project organization, using existing functional departments, to perform the geothermal exploration. The design is called a "matrix organization," which means that the geothermal project buys the time and expertise of existing departments, through subcontracts or work orders, to perform its tasks for it. Thus the geothermal project management cuts across normal organizational lines, forming a matrix of tasks. In the organizational chart shown in figure 12-4, the normal functional departments of the oil company are shown across horizontal axis, the project organization is shown vertically, and the task numbers from the network in table 12-1 show the work that is performed in the function department on as ordered by the project manager.

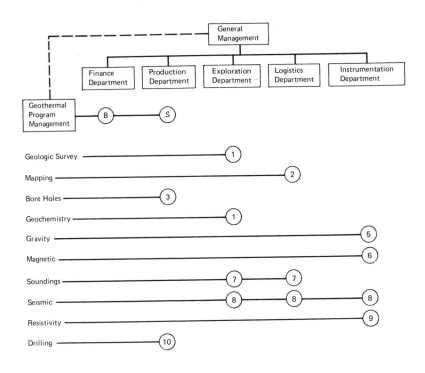

Figure 12-4. Illustrative Program Organization.

Figure 12-4 illustrates that the geothermal program manager buys services from functional departments. He buys budgetary control services from the finance department; scheduling, bore-hole, and test-well drilling services from the production department; geologic surveys, geochemistry, sounding, and seismic services from the exploration department; mapping and field equipment from the logistics department; and measurement services for gravity, magnetic, and electric resistivity measures from the instrumentation department.

Each of the tasks in the network becomes a work order to the functional department, which can be expressed as an organizational and manning table, with a schedule and budget. A work order from the geothermal program manager to the exploration department to perform the seismic array survey, with support from the logistics and instrumentation departments, is illustrated in figure 12-5.

The work authorization, with its cost anlaysis, provides the basis for establishing manpower requirements, equipment and materials requirements, and the subcontracts from the exploration department to the logistics and instrumentation departments. The several departments also have the basis for formulating their own schedules and budgets to control their part of the work.

From: Geothermal Program Manager

To: Director, Exploration Department

Subject: Work authorization for seismic array survey

You are requested and authorized to perform a seismic array survey in the ten-square-mile area known as parcels 27 through 40 of the book of maps on page 68 of Exploration County with the purpose of providing seven continuous months of seismic array measurements to measure the extent and location of tectonic plate or microseismic earth movements. The measures should show the time, duration, and magnitude of all microearthquake activity at sample points in the area, which can be extrapolated onto a seismic map showing fault lines throughout the study area. The authorized budgets and time schedules. together with manning tables, are shown below.

Time schedule: Begin January 1, complete September 30, nine months

Total budget authorization: $150,000

Cost analysis and manning table:

Exploration Department

1 Geologist	9 man months	$ 35,000
1 Geophysicist	3 man months	10,000
1 Electronic engineer	2 man months	6,000
1 Lab assistant	9 man months	9,000
Materials and travel expense		10,000
		$ 70,000

Logistics Department

3 Field survey trucks	9 months	5,000
6 Field crewman	54 man months	50,000
Supplies and materials		10,000
		$ 65,000

Instrumentation Department

3 sets seismic array equipment	9 months	15,000
	Grand Total	$150,000

Figure 12-5. Sample Work Order.

Information Systems

A company-wide management information and control reporting system can be designed by accumulating the budgets, schedules, and manning tables for each cost center, program, and department. The manning tables, budgets, and schedules are the basic information inputs to a management data base. They describe all the work flow to be accomplished—when, by whom, and at what cost. Hence they form the basis for a management control loop by comparing actual performance with scheduled performance, and then showing the exceptions or off-schedule tasks to management for remedial action.

The management information system thus is created by accumulating all the work orders by cost center. The sum of all the work orders issued by the geothermal program manager result in the accumulated budgets, schedules, and manning tables shown in earlier sections. The sum of all the work orders received by the exploration department from program managers, plus any basic workload budget of its own, become the control budgets, schedules, and manning tables of that department. Hence, every cost center has series of tasks assigned to it that are reportable in costs, schedules, and manning requirements. The information system accumulates a larger data base than management can or cares to monitor, because as long as the work flow is being performed on time and within budget, management can rely on its delegation of authority to section heads to perform the work. Management is interested in the slippages or exceptions, and thus the information system is designed for exception reporting.

The data in the information base is used to compare actual performance with scheduled performance. If actual performance falls behind the plan, management is alerted to the exception by the information reporting system; and then management may intervene to reestablish control over operations. The first intervention by management is likely to be an inquiry to the section head of the control center falling behind in performance asking for an explanation of the reasons or causes for lagging. The explanations may be various, such as lack of sufficient personnel or equipment, supplier failures, equipment failures, greater complexity to the task than anticipated, or questionable competence of the manager of the cost center. Suppose for example in task 8 in the previous section, the instrumentation department does not have enough seismic array sets to send three out into the field on schedule for the geothermal exploration. Then the management intervention is simply to obtain more equipment on time or change the schedule. Suppose the geologic structure of the study area is much more complicated than anticipated; then the management intervention is to bring in more geologists and field crews or change the schedule. Suppose the head of the exploration department is a poor manager and does not seem to be able to give clear assignments and schedules to competent people. Then the management intervention may be to train the director of the department to be a better manager, or to get another manager.

In any case, the heart of management control is in being alerted by the information system to the exceptions where actual performance is falling behind plan; and the heart of the information system is the input of work orders that show budgets, schedules, tasks, and manning requirements, so that planned performance can be identified in the first place to compare with the actual performance.

Quantitative Models

Quantitative models can be constructed to optimize costs, schedules, manning, returns, and results if the output is measurable. The information system provides the basis for constructing quantitative models of the work flow in an operation. The inputs to the quantitative model are usually the same as those required for an information system; that is, the cost and schedule of the inputs—staff, labor, material, management, land, and capital.

Models also require an output that can be measured. Operations most susceptible to modeling are those which have a physical unit of output, such as numbers of autmobiles or tons of coal. Service industries, such as hospitals, may seek a workload measure similar to the number of hospital-days' care, but this has no qualitative evaluation concerning the quality of the days' care or whether the therapy was successful. The qualitative measure may need to be established separately by internal quality control, or by quality surveys made after the fact.

Given a measurable output, the model seeks to optimize the inputs to yield the most effective or efficient combination of resources to achieve the result. Modeling thus seeks to help management balance resource requirements, minimize costs, or maximize returns. The means for constructing such models may be explored more intensively in the literature of operations research. The discussion here is intended to show the linkage in management terms among tasks, networks, budgets, information systems, modeling, and management control. In this sense, modeling is a tool for accumulating management information systems data into a control measurement—that is, the extent to which the operation has achieved a balanced use of resources, minimum costs, or maximum returns. Or alternatively, quantitative models are one form of evaluation and control of operations.

Evaluation

Evaluation of program performance provides the feedback in a control loop that enables management to correct operations and keep them directed toward management goals. Management is a goal-oriented art that seeks to direct operations toward its goals. Systematic decisions methods are organized means for directing those operations by using control and feedback techniques. This chapter began with mission analysis, performance specifications, systems analysis, and criteria—all of which were means for planning goals down to the task and working levels of an organization. The evaluation process thus is conducted to see whether these planned goals have been achieved. The information system and quantitative models discussed earlier illustrate how information feedback on tasks, networks, schedules, budgets, and cost centers may establish *internal* control, either in the form of keeping actual performance in line with planned performance, or by a resource optimization model. Internal control, however important, is only part of the management job, because management undertook its goals (in the mission analysis) to serve an *external* need of some user group, either customers or citizens. Therefore, a crucial part of the evaluation process is whether user needs are, in fact, being served.

The simplest test of whether user needs are being met is found in the performance of commercial products in the market—that is, does the customer keep buying them? Most business executives pay keen attention to data on market share and repeat buyers, because these are evaluative tests of success in meeting user needs.

The evaluation process in business is therefore frequently in the form of market analysis. The most common forms of such evaluation are sales statistics analysis of market share and buyer loyalty, or consumer attitude surveys reflecting the users' evaluation of the product or service vis-à-vis other products or services in the market. The evaluation process in government services takes the form of needs analysis and attitude surveys, because there is no direct market test. These evaluations are thus more deductive—that is, they deduce need and satisfactions from demographic data, incomes, social indicators, human requirement levels (for example, of consumption or health care), attitude surveys, and voter returns. The evaluation results thus complete the management control loop, which may be illustrated graphically to encompass all of the sections of this chapter (figure 12-6).

The System and the Inexplicable

The system of management explicates the goals and activities that management will control, but everything else in the environment that is unmanaged becomes the potential for unexpected and inexplicable events that are the source of change. Management is a closed loop system of governing selected events, as the previous section and figure 12-6 have illustrated. The art of management is to concentrate resources on a few selected goals and activities. To do anything else would dissipate scarce resources. By the very act of concentrating attention on selected events, all other events outside the internal organizational system—that is, in the environment—are left unattended. Management thus succeeds by

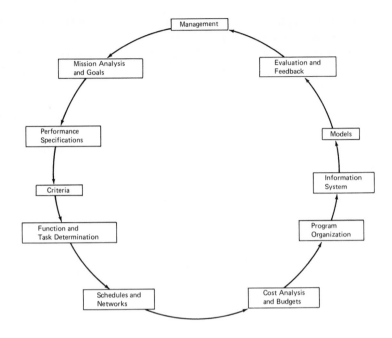

Figure 12-6. Systematic Management Control Process.

controlling selected activity; and all other activities in the environment that have linkages back to the organization are potential sources of change and surprise.

Think of an organization and its activities as a system; then all else is the environment. The system of automobile manufacturing is to organize people and materials to produce cars; and all else is the environment. A car is relatively useless by itself, unless there are roads, filling stations, garages, highway patrols, accident insurance, hospitals, parking, gasoline, and oxygen. The automobile manufacturer does not manage all these social, physical, and ecological events; the manufacturer only manages the production lines for cars. Who manages the rest? Oil companies, legislators, construction engineers, doctors, insurance executives, police officers, mechanics, and OPEC manage some of the elements, and some remain unmanaged. Oxygen and the atmosphere are unmanaged by human beings, and they function by their own laws as part of the natural ecological system of which the whole earth is a part. The ecosystem impinges on the automobile executive's system by introducing some surprises These surprises come as unexpected events through unknown linkages between the combustions of fuel in an internal combustion engine, which require oxygen, and the atmospheric chemistry that is triggered by sunlight—that is, automotive engine emissions include hydrocarbons, carbon monoxide, nitrogen oxides, and aldehydes, among many other compounds. The hydrocarbons and nitrogen oxides, by photochemical reaction under sunlight, form pollutants deleterious to plants and humans by releasing a singlet of oxygen that oxidizes plant and human tissue. Thus the unknown linkages in the environment (prior to the 1950s) brought about a change in automotive manufacturing, whereby automobile executives now had to incorporate air pollution control equipment in car designs. The elusive singlet of oxygen had been unmanaged in the environment, and suddenly its linkage to human health demanded that the automobile executive manage it and include air pollution in the automotive system concept.

Change thus is the transformation of the inexplicable and unknown in the environment into the explicable and known by some unexpected and untoward impact on the system being managed. Change is surprise, usually an unfavorable impact on performance, which requires management to modify its activities and alter its organizational system.

The events and phenomena surrounding an organization may be divided into the managed and the unmanaged. The managed activities are those goals and tasks that management selects to perform; and these may be directed and controlled by the systematic decision methods covered in this chapter. All other activities in the environment or the organization are among the unmanaged; and many of these environmental events have linkages back to the organization, either known or unknown. Change therefore is an impingement of unexpected environmental events upon an organization's performance in such a way that management must take action to correct or counter the surprise event.

Note

1. Bertanlanffy, L.V., *General Systems Theory* (New York: George Braziller, 1968).

13 The Management of Change

The concept of the unmanaged is virtually unrecognized and unknown in management literature; yet it is the most important dynamic in the process of change. The unmanaged consists of all those portions of an organization's environment to which management does not pay attention and, in some cases, does not understand. An organization, as we saw in the last chapter, selects a limited number of goals and activities on which to focus its attention and limited resources. The selection of these activities creates an organizational system and process; and everything else beyond the selected system becomes the organization's environment. The events occurring in the system's social, physical, or ecological environment are often treated as being beyond management's control or purview. All of these unattended linkages with the social, physical, and ecological environment thus are the unmanaged; and it is from the unmanaged that surprises and changes come.

The major sources of change coming from the socionatural environment are various forms of (1) weather and natural catastrophe, (2) ecological linkages, (3) technological innovation, (4) aggression, and (5) new ideas or social inventions. Storms, drought, or earthquakes can unexpectedly devastate large regions. Only large societies with stored up reserves of capital or food can rehabilitate the losses. Societies in the past, such as those at Chichen Itza or Angkor Vat, have succumbed to weather or natural catastrophe.

Ecological linkages, which are surprisingly complex, may recycle hazards that were previously unknown to man. For example, the singlet of oxygen has emerged as a health hazard by its recycling into the human respiratory system from automobile emissions after undergoing atmospheric photochemical reactions. Similarly, about 80 percent of human cancers today are attributed to chemical pollutants disposed of into the environment. These ecological linkages are difficult to trace, but nonetheless represent grave health risks.

Technological innovations frequently bring serious new threats, militarily or competitively. Among recent new military threats in the past generation have been the atomic bomb, missiles, spy satellites, laser-beam weapons, and fusion radiation bombs. Among industrial innovations changing competitive balances have been microcircuitry, computers, numerically controlled tools, carbide cutting tools, microwave transmission, the innumerable synthetic carbon compounds, biological transplants, gene cloning, and DNA.

Concerning aggression, every epoch has its wars, but perhaps the conquest of Peru by Pizarro is among the most dramatic examples of a society closed in on itself to the exclusion of its environment. The Incas had developed a remarkably intricate social management system spreading from Columbia to Chile. The essence of the management concept was the building of military roads and supply stations, the conscription of logistical support labor, the relocation of dissidents, the establishment of crop quotas, the allocation of workers to agricultural acreage, and the maintenance of a running census of all land, crop outputs, population, and labor use. Perhaps no other large society, before or since, has established such meticulous control down to the individual task level of the social process. Yet this same carefully managed society succumbed to Pizzaro's 177 troops when it had 50,000 troops confronting him in the field. Atahuallpa's concentration of management attention was on controlling the internal population, and defeating his brother in a civil war over succession. His 50,000 troops were resting at Caxamalca after successfully defeating his brother. Pizarro was part of the external environment, the unmanaged, the insignificant, to which little management concern was given. Atahuallpa could have stopped Pizarro's perilous ascent up the narrow mountain trails of the Andes at any time with a few men and boulders. But once he was allowed to become ensconced and hidden in the village of Caxamalca, Pizarro treacherously invited Atahuallpa as his dinner guest and then ambushed the Inca and his bodyguard. Suprise, deceit, horses, and muskets killed the bodyguard, and eventually massacred the leaderless troops on the surrounding plains. The Inca society was meticulously managed internally, but unknown and unexpected aggression from its environment, in the form of a handful of conquistadors, destroyed the whole society within a few years.

New ideas and social inventions present the most subtle, and sometimes imperceptible, form of change. New ideas, of course, emerge from individuals within the cultural environment. Social inventions frequently occur as legislation, such as Social Security, no-fault insurance, accelerated depreciation, or corporate institutions. The modern business corporation is slightly over a century old as a social invention. Its size and success has been encouraged by the nonprogressive income tax, accelerated depreciation, federally funded research contracts, expensing of research, tax treatment of capital gains, and other tax shelter devices. Under these stimuli, the multinational corporations now rival many sovereign governments in economic power. Social inventions also originate within organizations, such as the creation of organized research laboratories, "think tanks," matrix organizations, systems analysis, franchising, discount merchandising, conglomerates, etc. Individuals may create new ideas and concepts causing cultural change, such as communes, no-fault divorce, group marriage, dual breadwinners, civil rights, women's rights, dropping out, environmentalism, consumerism, or the substitution of a leisure culture for the Puritan work ethic. These new ideas and values cause goal displacement, substituting new goals for old ones. This process of goal displacement and substitution is a critical factor contributing to change.

Environmental Variables as Independent Parameters

Environmental variables originating in the cultural or natural ecology are the independent parameters of social change. Social change may be looked upon as perturbations in the existing social organization, an unexpected event that throws the system off course like the winds buffeting an aircraft. Managers of a social organization have certain forces or variables in hand, such as goals, resources, personnel, schedules, and all the directed events described in the last chapter. These are the dependent variables—that is, they depend upon management, the system process, or outside forces. The independent variables are the outside forces that are neither part of the internal process nor of direct management control. The independent variables are the change forces of which we have been speaking: natural catastrophe, ecological linkages, technological innovation, aggression, or new ideas.

The usefulness of identifying the independent variables is to bring them within the cognizance of management. Management may still not be able to control them, but at least managers can keep their "weather eye" looking out for change. Management thus can try to track and anticipate some forms of change, through indicators or measures that suggest the imminence of change. We do this now, of course, in selected areas, by means of military intelligence reports, weather reports, hurricane watches, seismic measurements, economic indicators, and social indicators. But one area where the change forces or independent variables are not watched systematically is the realm of new ideas and social inventions. This is partly true, perhaps, because (1) the evaluation of new ideas is very difficult, and (2) we have an aversion to social inventions, which makes us prone to avoid or ignore them because of their upsetting effect on the social order. The argument put forward here is that, because social inventions are upsetting to the social order, they bear watching and surveillance. Moreover, their surveillance can be made systematic by a concept of the evolution of social change, which is discussed in the next twelve sections.

Structural Design of Institutions in Their Environment

The structural design of institutions depends on (1) goal and technical assumptions about its survival on which the social process is built, and (2) on the environmental change forces that impact it. The structural design of institutions takes its shape from the way institutions came into being and the way they survive. The United States came into being as a colony of England with a set of semidemocratic assumptions, a colonial sea trade, and an agricultural economy. The United States has survived by expanding its mercantile and agricultural base, adding an industrial sector, establishing its military independence, and strengthening the authority of its democratic institutions. Every one of these survival parameters (dependent variables) has had enormous ramifications.

Take agriculture alone. Agriculture in the United States is composed of a collection of monoculture regions: the corn belt, the cotton belt, wheat, soybeans, potatoes, livestock, fruits, and vegetables. The major crops making up U.S. agriculture number about thirty selected foods and fibers on which we subsist. These are intensively cultivated using huge fields, equipment, and water sources that change the entire natural ecology of the region, sometimes with adverse effects (for example, the Oklahoman dust bowl during the thirties). The American Indians in the West utilized several score of plants as food and fiber (which we do not use) as gatherers without changing the natural ecology. Beyond these, the edible potential of natural plants is in the hundreds, including many weeds we try to get rid of such as dandelion and sorrel. Yet the entire institutional structure of our society is geared in part to those thirty-odd crops. Land ownership practice awards title in fee simple to the cultivator of crops, whereas the Indians held land in common. Major cities are located in supply and transportation corridors to serve agriculture. Economic institutions such as grain exchanges and farm price supports are invented to make agriculture feasible. Political institutions, such as representative government and a senate representing a land area, are governance concepts based upon agricultural needs.

The gamut of institutional parameters dictated by a military establishment or a massive industrial sector are even more influential design factors in the structure of our institutions. The needs of the industrial sector have determined the institutional design of the modern corporation, as discussed earlier. The military establishment has dictated the structure of the highly technological military-industrial complex.

Finally, the strengthening of the authority of democratic institutions to manage this complex process has made political institutions more pluralistic and representative, frought with coalitions, a republic in concept—and less democratic in the sense of individual citizen choices after the manner of Athens or the New England town meeting.

In short, the United States came into being under a set of English institutional assumptions. Then it learned, or chose, or was forced to survive by centralizing those institutions into a massive economic power base—agricultural, industrial, military, and political—which is what we have today. This structural design of our institutions has had important benefits, mainly security and rising living standards. The institutional design has also had some unhappy side effects, mainly abuses of power and frustration of individual development. These side effects have been a source of unrest—Watergate, congressional misconduct, corporate bribes, student protest, drop-outs, crime, and drugs by a few, and withdrawal from the work ethic to leisure by many. The disaffection and unrest have brought along new ideas and new values, which are the seeds of social change.

Atrophy in Institutions

Institutions come into being under legislation or custom, which gives them a resource base and hence a life of their own. Institutions also confer privilege, power, and wealth on their leaders and hierarchy, which they wish to preserve. Corporations do not die like human beings; they go on ad infinitum unless competition affects them. Political institutions are even more immune to change. The Constitution has not been rewritten for two hundred years, although Jefferson thought it should be rewritten every generation. Congress is immune to change, even in the face of its corrupt practices; and its internal ethics committee has been unable to revise its structure or practices—just as the Watergate prosecutor was unable to investigate the presidency until he became an independent agent.

Institutions thus have a need to maintain themselves as organizations very much as they are; otherwise their members lose their privilege. In the absence of sunset laws, which only recently have been considered and have yet to be implemented effectively, institutions have indefinite (hence infinite) grants of authority and resources that they cannot or will not relinquish, because of the internal needs of their organizational members. That authority grants to institutions are interminable makes the organization unchanging; and unchanging organizations in the face of changing individual needs eventually causes institutions to atrophy and become displaced. Atrophy in institutions become a reinforcing factor in change, as the needs for organizational maintenance frustrates the responsiveness of institutions to new needs of individuals.

Evolutionary Stages of Management

The United States appears to be on the brink of social change, just as it was in the 1930s. The counterculture of the 1960s has perhaps gone underground, but the thrust of many of its ideas persist, such as environmentalism, consumerism, civil rights, women's rights, free sexuality, casual dress, hair styles, leisurism, political apathy, and less interest in work. These new ideas have brought new politicians who think small instead of big. Small is beautiful and more environmental. Politics becomes more incremental; business grows slower. Society is waiting for Godot, and so the plot thickens. Dramatic plots thicken by foreclosing options until the hero has only heroic choices left. Societies that foreclose options and have no means for heroic choices also find the social plot thickening into an evolutionary cycle.

Management and institutions go through evolutionary cycles, which stem from the ferment and new ideas emerging as counterploys to unresponsive and atrophying institutions. Social evolution may be related to the availability of options that create a taxonomy of structural changes. The taxonomy of social evolution may be conceived in terms of needs, missions, authority, functions, tasks, allegiance, and process. Each of these structural elements have evolutionary counterparts in social development. These relationships are shown in table 13-1.

Social Unrest and Innovation

Social unrest and innovation begin as a fermentation of new ideas stemming from individual needs that have gone unmet by existing institutions, and result in a weakening of authority. The first signs of social unrest are the weakening of authority of existing institutions. In the United States, the "generation gap" is a sign of weakening authority of the family and of the ability of parents to provide guidance for their children. The children feel that parental guidance is "out of date" and not in keeping with new individual needs. Parents guide their children by old customs and institutions, which the children are unwilling to accept. Thus the institution of marriage is changing, and with it attitudes toward sexuality, divorce, abortion, women's rights, dual breadwinners, and new parental roles. The authority of government is weakening, as seen in political apathy, distrust of government, annoyance with taxation and overregulation, as well as crime and violence. The authority of business is weakening, as seen in people's disbelief in the energy crisis as well as distrust of oil companies, industry efforts toward pollution control, and pricing practices of business regarding inflation. Indeed, a conspiratorial theory of business is held by many consumers who feel that most economic ills (such as energy shortages, pollution,

Table 13-1
Structural Evolution of Societies

Structure	Evolutionary Period
Individual needs	Fermentation and unrest (disorder)
Mission	Opportunity-creation-social invention
Authority	Adaptive period
Functions	Formulation period
Tasks	Developmental period
Allegiance	Ideation and ideology emerges (order)
Process	Socialization period (order that may become unadaptive regimentation)
Alienation	New needs go unmet; unrest, disorder, and recycling of social evolution begin again

and inflation) are manipulations of business. Hence citizens are more prone to want business more heavily controlled, without thought to the rising costs and slowdowns that regulation may bring.

In short, disaffection by individuals over their inability to govern their own lives has caused them to question the authority of existing institutions and to cast about for ideas to change the institutions, or at least to live their own lives as little molested by institutions as possible. These denials of authority give rise to countervailing ideas, ploys, plots, and sometimes revolutionary activity. The new attitudes toward marriage are countervailing ideas. No-fault divorce, abortion, and the pill are ploys used by women in their struggle to free themselves from a fixed institutional role—indeed, women's rights is a movement seeking to establish for women a new institutional role and authority over their own jobs, bodies, and property. Revolutions have not yet emerged except in a few cases, such as the Symbionese Liberation Army, the black riots, student riots, and terrorist activity.

All of these activities are, in fact, alternative management schemes for society. They are countermanagement thrusts at the establishment to create new forms of management and new leaders. Seen as management schemes for changing society, rather than as threats to the established order, these countervailing ideas are part of a concept of change management. They are ideas of needs to be taken into cognizance as potential sources of change by existing organizations and social processes. However, we have already seen that existing institutions are relatively unchangeable, due to the privilege conferred upon its members that they are unwilling to relinquish. Hence some organizations atrophy and tend to become displaced.

Institutional Displacement

Social unrest is a threat to the established order and an opportunity for new institutions. Dissatisfaction can be converted into new wants and new satisfactions, and that conversion is a management problem. Thus unrest and disaffection are opportunities for creation and invention of new management organizations. Those who seize these opportunities to define new missions and to create new social inventions are change managers.

There are many different types of change managers, depending upon the degree of their allegiance to the established order. All change managers are willing to alter the established order and create new institutions. Those change managers who wish to create new missions and services within the authorities of the existing social processes may be called evolutionary change managers. Those who seek to establish competitive organizations by usurping some of the authority of existing institutions may be termed counterploy change managers. Those who wish to overthrow existing institutions and seize their authority for themselves are revolutionary change managers.

Revolutionary change managers are generally suspect by most citizens, except in dire distress, because they are perceived as merely substituting new masters for old, and possibly inferior ones. Unfortunately, the stigma upon revolutionaries is also projected on other change managers as well. This is unfortunate, in that change is inevitable; and indeed the evolutionary and usurper change managers are trying to relate change to the established system. They are entrepreneurial, imaginative people trying to design new managerial structures that will work within, or at least along side, the existing order. Thus they are agents of adaptive change, trying to introduce new missions, services, and institutions to meet changing human needs.

The resistance to change managers of any kind, whether by those who profess ideological allegiance to the established order, or by those defending institutions to maintain their privileges, requires most change managers to resort to overkill to be heard. Thus women's rights, which is a version of constitutional equal rights assured by the Fourteenth Amendment, has to overcome the idea of male chauvinism with excessive publicity and propaganda and try to pass the Equal Rights Amendment to be recognized. Or in another sphere, the United States, to put down Japanese aggression, used atomic weapons upon Hiroshima, an overkill upon a nation already militarily defeated.

The prevalence of overkill in change management has the effect, in many cases, of displacing old institutions with new ones. The United States displaced the old governmental institutions of Japan with new ones, just as the Union carpetbaggers displaced the institutions of the Old South with new ones. In less dramatic fashion, supermarkets have displaced Mom-and-Pop stores, Arab tycoons have displaced Texas tycoons, conservative fund managers have displaced go-go venture managers, and socialization of medical payments is displacing private-paid practice—that is, institutional displacement occurs when change managers design an alternate institutional structure, meeting new missions and new needs, in the face of old institutions that are nonresponsive and losing their authority by atrophy or nonuse.

Adaptive Stage of Management

The adaptive stage of management occurs when others, seeing the success of a social invention, imitate the success and, in the process, test the authority structure of the existing social process across the board. Once institutional displacement begins, an adaptive stage of management occurs in which the new institutions and new missions are adapted and applied broadly across all of their likely social uses. For example, the concept of self-service food supermarkets originated early in the century as a competitive institution to the corner grocer. Supermarkets had the competitive advantage of lower prices, broader ranges of merchandise, and personal selection. Not only did supermarkets displace the independent grocer, but broad-range discount stores appeared in most other specific merchandise fields (including drugs, appliances, clothing, electronics, and auto parts), and in general merchandising threatening venerable department stores. Now the food supermarkets have become so competitive among themselves that the profit on food has all but disappeared, causing these stores to broaden their merchandise range further to seek higher profit-margin items among convenience or luxury items commonly sold in other discounting fields.

A successful social invention thus is tried, tested, and applied across society for all of its possible uses. The same adaptive change occurs in other fields, in legal inventions, government institutions, technological discoveries, and ideas. The legal concept of no-fault automobile insurance is being adapted gradually state by state, and the no-fault concept is being applied to divorce. The government institution of social security for retirement benefits is being applied as social security for medical benefits, unemployment benefits, benefits for handicapped, children, single mothers, and low-income families. The discovery of silicon diodes in electronics was adapted as transistors and microcircuits successively in military weapons, computers, communications, machine controls, television, radio, and hand calculators. The mathematical idea of linear programming has been applied successively to military problems, computers, inventory, transportation, production, and business problems.

In most of these adaptive changes, two important effects occur: (1) a transfer of authority, and (2) a transfer of resources. In the supermarket example, the new institution of food chain stores acquired the decision authority and the resources formerly held by the independent grocers. Perhaps the most massive institutional displacement historically has been the adaptive succession of United States institutions over those of the Old World. The availability of land in the New World caused adventurers, immigrants, pioneers, and the oppressed to seek new resources and new life styles for which they had to adapt old forms—like the English village system, to the New England town, to a republican form of governance. In the adaptive process every authority was tested, from the tea tax to the British Crown, the Continental Congress, the Constitution, the Confederacy, the Union, the Western sheriff, the proprietory form of management, the antitrust laws, the election financing laws, etc. Whenever authority gave way, power and authority were usurped and old institutions withered. When new organizations succeeded to power and settled conflicts, as with the constitutional government and Western sheriff, new institutions began. The institution-building phase of the adaptive period occurs as authority conflicts are settled and become imbedded in law, property rights, or decision-making privileges.

Formulation of Processes

The formulation period follows the settlement of authority, as the decision maker uses his recently acquired authority to delegate functions and assignments to others who work to carry out the new mission. The formulation period is one in which the tasks and functions of the new social invention are assigned and organized in the manner described in the previous chapter. Through such formulation, the organizational structure of the new institution becomes defined in terms of responsibilities and authorities, and the process flow is created by the network of task assignments. Thus Cortez's conquistadors, by being allocated land and mineral rights for their exploration in Mexico, became the bureaucracy of New Spain. Similarly, the U.S. railroads, by their land sales as well as by constructing and operating their transportation lines, became the principal economic powers of the West. More recently, the labor unions, in challenging the authority of management over wages and working conditions, have formulated a new authority base over the collective bargaining process.

Development of Functions and Institutions

The development of functions and institutions evolves as alternative technical means are explored to improve effectiveness. After the initial formulation period, the development period continues through the exploration of improved technical means of performing tasks. Tasks can be performed in a variety of ways depending on the technology available. For example, once the railroads were established, the wood-fired locomotive was replaced by the coal-fired one, which was in turn replaced by an oil-fired one, and again was replaced by diesel engines. As a result, tasks change and disputes occur concerning essential levels of labor and crew size. Basically, however, the development period is one in which technological experimentation occurs to find easier, cheaper, or more effective ways to perform organizational tasks.

Ideation

Ideation or rationalization of established institutions comes with their success to solidify their foundations and to create the symbolic basis for allegiance. By this stage, social evolution is well advanced. The new mission is broadly perceived by all; authority and task distributions are settled. The social process is working. The society has adapted to the new mission and survived; wealth and pride increase. The thinkers now give thought to explaining and rationalizing the social invention by ideas, descriptions, theories, histories, philosophies, sciences, legends, rights, freedoms, symbols, heroes—and all the panoply of cultural self-esteem. These ideas become the ideology and symbols commanding attention, loyalty, allegiance, patriotism, social drill, and sacrifice.

Socialization

The emergence of ideology becomes the means for conditioning the youth and newcomers to accept their lot so that the existing social process may function smoothly. The lot of the newcomers and youth is an allotment of routine tasks, because authority and wealth has already been distributed. There is little left for youth but to accept the leftovers or challenge existing authority. Socialization is a conditioning of youth, by high ideology and symbols, to accept the social process as it is and to quiet any dissatisfactions or challenges, which they may feel, for the sake of stability and security for all.

Means-Ends Displacement

The displacement of ends by means accompanies socialization as individuals accept what they can get instead of what they want. The socioideological drill conditions individuals, especially youth, to accept the social process as it is and to try to find a niche within it, despite the crowding at the top where authority, wealth, and income are largely claimed and ensconced in legal rights. But the social process, which youth are expected to accept, is a means of doing things, not an end in itself. The ends are what individuals (including youth) want for their own development and maturation. To the extent individuals accept the social means and forego their own wants and fulfillment, a mean-ends displacement takes place. Numerous writers, and especially Jacques Ellul,[1] have noted that in our era technological needs frequently supersede human needs. Individuals are fitted into machine-like jobs, instead of jobs being fitted to people. In the United States, where capital formation has become the means of survival, technological research and capital development are maintained at high levels, even though large portions of the population remain unemployed or excluded from the labor force. The preferred policy treatment of technique over individuals is an example of means-end displacement.

Order and Disorder

Means-end displacement leads to alienation of individuals from the social process, which in turn moves the society from order toward disorder. As individuals fail to find a satisfying place for themselves in the social process as it is, either through underemployment or lack of opportunity to fill their interests, allegiance to the existing order diminishes. Eventually apathy and then dissent replace allegiance. Social unrest begins a new cycle as dissatisfied individuals seek new ways to live, new services, new work, and new life styles. If the society is flexible enough to open itself to change, the change and renewal cycle begins again, with new ideas and institutions replacing the old. If the society is inflexible, especially closing avenues to authority and resources to the challengers, then social unrest may be expected. The dissidents seek confrontation, disorder, and violence as a means of changing the system, since more moderate avenues to change seem closed to them. The emergence of student and race riots during the past decade, together with rising street crimes, violence by youth, and terrorism by the dispossessed, suggest that the United States is on the brink of institutional and social changes that need to be facilitated peaceably, or else they may erupt with increasing violence.

Change as Orderly Renewal

Orderly renewal of the social process requires the facilitation of change by reallocating resources and authority to meet emerging human needs. To avoid violent and revolutionary change, a society must have change mechanisms in working order to facilitate the reallocation of resources and authority so that dissatisfactions can be turned into new missions, institutions, and satisfactions. Resource reallocation is a particularly intransigent problem, because resources confer authority. However, resources also become locked up in existing institutions that refuse to relinquish them. The means for locking up resources are legal rights, constitutional rights, legislation, property rights, barriers to entry, monopolization, patents, licenses, regulations, franchises, contracts, restraint of trade, administered pricing, credit practices, influence, lobbying, power politics, and strong-arm methods. Against these formidable restraints on resource allocation, the orderly change mechanisms are few—mainly competitive markets and constitutional change.

Competitive markets have been difficult to maintain in the United States, despite antitrust laws, because corporations with large internal cash flows and wide horizontal market power have come to dominate the marketplace. And amending the Constitution, to say nothing of revising it, has proved so difficult that constitutional change is glacial in its pace. Thomas Jefferson, of course, believed that the Constitution should be rewritten with each generation, but this flexible change mechanism has not been realized. As a result, the United States has very limited means of change and renewal, which is part of the problem of recent stress and dissent.

The main attempts at change are by legislation, but these changes are minimal and incremental, because Congress represents existing institutions and itself as insulated from change by the Constitution. Unless the composition and power of Congress can be altered, which has not been done in the history of the Republic, elections merely bring new faces to represent the same existing institutions. The immutability of congressional authority can lead to abuse and irresponsibility, as evidenced by recent scandals of improper conduct by congressmen, and by the persistence of such maladies as inflation. Inflation is symptomatic of fiscal mismanagement in government, and Congress has the sole fiscal authority to levy taxes or appropriate funds. It is hard to see how Congress has escaped responsibility for inflation, since no other institution has authority over fiscal policy. Yet inflation has been a chronic problem in the United States for a century, without an outcry against the irresponsible institution that created it. The only likely explanation appears to be that responsibility is so diffusely spread among the many members of Congress that there is no responsibility at all. Change in the constitutional authority of Congress can only come about by an amendment initiated by Congress itself, which is improbable, or by state legislatures, which is also unlikely because they are heavily dependent on the receipt of federal funds.

In summary, the change mechanisms of the U.S. society are weak, compared with the power and legal rights of existing institutions. The main change forces are the limited competition of the marketplace, minimal revisions in the authority of existing institutions by legislation, and the infrequent amending of the Constitution. The orderly renewal of the social process in the United States thus is slow and difficult, which has its counterpart in conflict, unrest, and diminishing allegiance to law and order.

Management of Renewal

The management of renewal is a highly entrepreneurial or leadership art, consisting of exploiting all of the alternatives to shift resources and authority to bring about change to meet new human needs and missions. Given the available levers or mechanisms of change, the management of change consists of amassing new resources by means of the market, legislation, or constitutional amendment. Entrepreneurs manage change by means of the market by entering a new field not currently dominated by large corporations, either by using a new technical or market idea. Such entrepreneurs have difficulty at first accumulating resources, except by relying on their own funds, because credit and equity funds are not usually available to them in the capital markets. Yet persistent entrepreneurs do succeed in new markets by arduous work and the slow accumulation of their own internal cash flow. The relative difficulty of this entrepreneurial change process is reflected in the slow growth rate in the economy generally.

Since change by constitutional amendment is largely unavailable to the citizen, the other main form of managing social renewal is by means of a legislative change. Change by legislation involves leadership in the formation of a new coalition or power bloc that has either votes or money. Such power blocs can be forged by citizens with dogged persistence and charisma. Cesar Chavez has over twenty years managed to form an agricultural labor bloc (by forming an effective organization and using the tactics of peaceful confrontation) that has recently been granted collective bargaining rights and authority by legislation. The recognition of the industrial labor movement earlier had similarly taken forty years (from 1890 to 1930) of leadership effort in organizing a coalition into the AFL and the CIO. Consumerism, civil rights, and women's rights are also examples of the use of leadership in accomplishing change through voluntary organization and legislation.

A second and more common form of legislative change is by means of money and lobbying. This avenue is open mainly to existing institutions with large resources, such as the liquor, auto, highway, oil, utility, and firearm lobbies. These lobbies usually represent institutions with large resources seeking to consolidate and reinforce their authority and rights. As such, they are frequently barriers to change, rather than managers of change and renewal.

The management of renewal is the amassing of acceptance, either in the marketplace or in the political arena, to shift resources and authority to new endeavors.

Terminal Decisions

Terminal decisions occur in the social process when the accumulated authority and resources of existing institutions preclude new initiatives by change managers. Terminal decisions occur usually during times of unrest and change, when existing institutions seemingly close off all options open to change managers, leaving them with nothing to lose and no alternative but to oppose the existing order. Thus the tea tax imposed upon the American colonies was a terminal decision made by the British Parliament that seemed to foreclose all options to the colonies for their own participation in self-governance or representation. Similarly, inflation, unemployment, and the loss of control over its balance of payments by the Weimar Republic in Germany lead to the Nazi insurgence. The trigger, or terminal decision, was the exigent necessity of foreign exchange controls over exports and imports, without stopping the flow of materials to industry. This created the unlikely coalition between industry, a strong man, and the dissident dispossessed. Another example in history of a terminal decision is the issuance of the Diocletian edicts establishing price control over the Roman Empire, which dried up the flow of goods, led to taxation in kind (goods), and brought into being Medieval feudalism, which made it possible to pay the taxes in kind.

Terminal decisions have a way of being innocuous in appearance but momentous in effect. They appear innocuous because they are rather insignificant extensions of the existing authority of institutions, pushed one notch too far. The tea tax was, to Parliament, an insignificant extension of its broad authority of the British Empire. The German exchange controls, or the Diocletian edicts, were small extensions of existing authority to meet temporary exigencies of the times.

If terminal decisions are seemingly insignificant and innocuous in the present, how can a society tell in advance that they are monumental and in fact terminal? If societies knew how to detect terminal decisions, they would not disappear as regularly as nations do in the sweep of history. The only way a society can tell the significance of its decisions is by listening and being sensitive to its dissidents and change managers. If Parliament had been listening to Samuel and John Adams, that brace of firebrands from Boston, they would have sensed the terminal significance of the tea tax. If the Weimar leaders had been sensitive to Hitler's raving, they could have dealt with foreign exchange control before there was a crisis. If the Emperor Diocletian had been listening to the barbarian troops populating his Roman legions, he would have known that the regional authority of Roman prefects and praetorians was too weak to control both prices and the local economy.

Terminal decisions are detectible only through a sense of humility about the tenuous authority of existing institutions, together with a concept of the taxonomy of change. Since humility is not easily nor widely acquired, and since a theory of change management has not been recognized in literature or leadership, the social process continues to cycle through its evolution from innovation to allegiance to dissent, from order to disorder. It is hoped a study and practice of change management can bring about more orderly, internal renewal within the social process without resorting to violent dissent, but to do so requires that the change mechanisms be kept in working order. The change mechanisms are the means for shifting resources and authority to meet new human needs. These change mechanisms in the United States are currently weak, being limited mainly to a few open markets and to incremental legislation. Meanwhile, the legal, property, and institutional rights of existing organizations are powerfully entrenched. The United States may be approaching a turning point at which it either refurbishes its change and renewal mechanisms, or slips into terminal decisions unaware.

Note

1. Ellul, Jacques. *La Technique* (Paris: A. Colin, 1954).

14 Alternative Missions, Scenarios, and Institutional Designs

The fixity of institutions precipitates their end, as we saw in the last chapter. Institutions become fixed, immutable, and unresponsive when they dig in their authority and lock up their resources to maintain themselves substantially as they are. They do this partly because the incentives of wealth and position built into the organization impel the managers to keep what they have. Besides being greedy, which is powerful enough, institutions also are myopic. Institutions do not think; individuals do. Moreover, individuals find institutions hostile to novel ideas, because the institutional decision process is a group activity. Group thinking among managers results in a conservative averaging of ideas. Average ideas do not create change; innovative ideas do. Thus organizations have difficulty arriving at innovative decisions.

How can innovative ideas be introduced into the normally plodding and self-maintaining course of institutional decision making? This may be a question to which there is no answer. If there were a clear or obvious answer, some societies should have learned to renew themselves rather than succumb to displacement as regularly as they have in history. Even among U.S. business corporations, only about two-thirds of the 100 largest corporations remain in that group from one decade to the next, and only about one-third persist among the 100 largest for over two decades. Hence, the displacement rate is high among all institutions; only the time span varies. A few corporations have remained among the hundred largest for fifty years. A few nations have survived for centuries—the Roman Empire for eight, Greece for four, England and Spain for three, the United States so far for two, and Germany for one.

If there is any solution to the self-renewal process among institutions and societies, it probably consists of two vital elements: (1) keeping the change mechanisms working for resource and authority reallocation, and (2) developing a surveillance methodology within institutions for examining alternative courses of action. The first vital element—that is, keeping change mechanisms working—was the subject of the last chapter. This chapter concerns itself with a surveillance methodology for examining alternatives.

Alternate Mission Analysis

Alternate mission analysis is a management inquiry that provides incentives for examining alternate choices by which the institution can shift its resources and

277

authority to meet new sets of individual needs. Perhaps the most important principle in change management within an institution is that some group has to be given the charge, the incentive, and pay for initiating and implementing innovative ideas. The corporate research laboratory in business, and the think tank in government, are attempts to provide innovative alternatives to decision makers. These research laboratories and think tanks have been reasonably effective in thinking up innovative alternatives, and some of the methodology of this chapter is drawn from their successful experience. The research laboratory and think tanks have been rather unsuccessful, however, in seeing their innovations implemented.

The problem of such laboratories has been that implementation beyond the thinking stage requires large resource allocation, and institutional executives have not been certain enough of the success of a new idea to substitute it for their existing mode of survival—that is, institutional managers have a bias toward extrapolating new decisions from old ones, or to perpetuate their existing activity. This bias creates an inertia to stay with existing products and product lines (or services) to the exclusion of truly different service areas in which new human needs may be more urgent. Institutional managers cannot be blamed for this, given equal incentives in both areas, because the existing service area is more known and certain, whereas the innovative one has higher degrees of uncertainty and risk.

One alternative to deal with this risk differential is to permit higher rates of return for new product or service areas than for old ones. This compensatory risk incentive scheme could be provided by taxation—that is, older product lines could bear a higher income tax rate than new ones. Hence the potential rate of return on investment would be higher in new product/service areas that meet new needs than in old ones. Consider an example of the effect of such a compensatory risk scheme as applied to the automotive industry. General Motors and Ford are among the exceptions to the principle that most corporations survive among the 100 largest for only a decade or two, having survived among this group for fifty years. The automobile industry once had about five hundred manufacturers, which were displaced and cut down to several dozen by 1920. The formation of General Motors by a merger of several larger manufacturers then cut the number down to a dozen. Over the decades competition has further reduced the number to two large, one major, and one small automobile manufacturer. So the rule of competitive displacement applies to most of the automobile industry except General Motors and Ford—thus far. Why not to them? Two organizational factors are possible explanations for their durability. First, General Motors, and later Ford, were among the pioneers in decentralization and divisionalization, which moved management incentives and decisions closer to the needs of people. Second, both developed powerful dealer organizations early in their history, giving them horizontal market power to maintain themselves despite competitive threats. Decentralization thus is a change mechanism, and market power is an organizational maintenance mechanism. The two mechanisms together have kept General Motors and Ford in a dominant market position and growing as fast as the economy.

However, the prognosis for the automobile industry in its present form is not entirely favorable. Consumers want cars and like their convenience, but new wants and competitions are emerging—that is, the automobile is faced with problems of abating air pollution, urban and traffic congestions, and a drying up of gasoline as a fuel source within about thirty years. Air pollution abatement is increasing the costs of automobiles. Urban congestion, due partly to automobiles, is making people less satisfied with city life as it is. The finite world supply of petroleum presages competitive demands for energy among heating, cooling, electrical, manufacturing, and transportation users, when alternate energy sources are more costly. Moreover, automobiles require a mobile fuel, such as petroleum, and there are currently no feasible, alternate energy sources in present technology.

Despite these bleak prospects in the long run, the automobile industry has been slow to consider alternative products or services seriously, mainly because the rate of return on investment is more certain on existing automobile products than on a new innovation. But suppose the compensatory risk tax was introduced, whereby the profit on the existing internal combustion engine automobile was taxed at a progressively higher rate each year, but the profit on new forms of personal transportation was taxed at a much smaller rate than at present (or not at all). Then the tax differential between the old and the new products would compensate for the difference in risk and uncertainty. The automobile manufacturers would have a strong incentive to seek new innovations and alternatives for the sake of their own profit growth and organizational survival. The compensatory risk tax would be a kind of "sunset law" applied to business, informing management that it will be penalized for staying with old products and services and it will be rewarded for shifting to new ones. This policy would be the reverse of present policy, which tells business management that it will be penalized for innovation and rewarded for not changing products.

The point of this illustration is that there needs to be a positive incentive and reward for new services to meet new human needs. Perhaps there are better solutions than a compensatory risk tax; if so, they should be considered. Assume for the moment that society has found a means of providing positive incentives for change, rather than penalizing innovation, then we should ask how innovations can be searched out and evaluated systematically?

Alternative mission analysis is a means for exploring a range of new innovations and evaluating them against some common decision criteria to see how well they meet new human wants. In our automobile example alternative missions can accomplish the human need for individual independence via rapid movement of a person's body. An automobile meets this need, but so in varying degrees do elevators, airplanes, helicopters, subways, moving sidewalks, escalators, space craft, and telephones. The alternate mission analysis asks how a human need for rapid personal movement can be accomplished with prospective fuels, technology, and environmental wants—not limited to an internal combustion engine automobile? The alternative mission analysis may include new power sources, such as the hydrogen engine; redesigned cities, with more horizontal and less vertical movement; light-weight, personal, electric vehicles that travel along a pneumatic or monorail main corridor; substituting personal, visual communications for transportation—that is, working and shopping at home; or improving the fuel efficiency of petroleum-fueled cars. The automobile companies are currently pursuing seriously only the last alternative, due to its greater familiarity, certainty, and incentives. The other alternatives would put the automobile companies into the energy business, architectural design, mass transit, or communications. This proposition would only appear to be odd if we thought of the automobile companies as being determined by the technology that the engineers happened to select eighty years ago. Past engineering choices are what make an automobile company, and this is what is myopic. The companies are engaged in the mission of rapid personal movement; and if this is their mission, then all the alternative scenarios are plausible.

Alternate mission analysis thus is a method for looking at all the alternate ways of performing a mission (that is, of meeting a human need), regardless of the current technology or the existing system. This method opens new options to decision makers' thinking and, given fitting incentives, is a potential way of systematizing the implementation of innovations.

Reduction of Missions to Scenarios

Previous chapters have made clear that a scenario is a word picture of how some desired course of action may be developed—that is, the self-fulfilling prophecy, or living our own legend. A mission analysis needs to be converted into a scenario so that the word picture makes clear what the choices or benefits are and how the solution might unfold. Earlier chapters have also given some examples of scenarios. What is new about this chapter and section is that it provides a perspective on the breadth of scenarios.

Scenarios, as they have originated in research organizations or think tanks, have predominantly centered on threat or competitive analysis, or technological alternatives. For the moment we will assume that we know how to do these kinds of scenario writing, since they have been discussed earlier. What else needs to be included in scenarios?

A principal new ingredient of scenarios that needs to be considered to expand the range of innovative alternatives is an analysis of institutional incentives and rights. Institutional incentives and rights, respectively, are the motive force behind and the barriers to change. Moreover, the two are intertwined, because incentives become rights, and rights become incentives. It is the newness, or renewal, of incentives that causes innovation, change, and social renewal to occur. Moreover, these incentives and rights are what cause the implementation of new ideas to occur. Thus the scenarios must include a story of how incentives and rights unfold or are rearranged; otherwise nothing will happen in the way of implementation. Indeed, the present practice of research organizations and think tanks, of confining their scenarios to threat and technological analysis, is the cause of their innovations' sterility and failure to be implemented. There is no reason, without an incentive scenario, why innovation should be implemented. Thus there is no reason why the automobile companies should do anything other than improve the fuel efficiency of their present cars, unless one introduces an incentive scenario such as the compensatory risk tax, which forces them to become not merely an automobile-technology company, but a rapid personal transportation service company.

Thus, there is a confusion between product (technology) and service (human needs) at the heart of the change and renewal process. Managers become confused when people want their technology and product, which creates inertia against change, whereas in fact people want a service that meets their needs and are relatively unaware of (or indifferent to) the technology. The incentive-oriented scenario is a means of breaking the bondage between manager and technology and of making him think in terms of users, needs, and services—that is, the incentive scenario moves the manager from unresponsiveness toward change and renewal.

The difficulty with incentive scenario writing is that incentives are economy-wide, whereas technology scenarios can be more narrowly confined to be company-wide. Thus the technology of an automotive engine, whether Otto cycle, Rankin cycle, Sterling cycle, or hydrogen, can be explored and decided internally within a company. Incentives such as property rights, profit rates, and tax shelters are society-wide. As such, they are beyond the normal decision scope of a company executive; and for this reason, they are frequently ignored as something the business executive can do little about.

However, the principle of this book is that public and private management decisions are closely intertwined and that nothing from the environment (which may come as a surprise) is to be ignored if it impacts a manager's institution. This means that some dependent parameters can be decided internally and directly, and that some external, independent parameters have to be recognized, analyzed, and influenced indirectly. The incentive scenario is one means of analyzing and influencing an external, independent variable. To fail to make this analysis could result in a terminal decision. If the world petroleum supply is indeed limited to about a thirty-year supply at current consumption rates, then the automobile companies have made a terminal decision by confining their scenario to improving fuel economy, without opening their mission and scenario analysis to all forms of rapid personal transportation regardless of current technologies or incentives—that is, the incentive scenario is what opens new technologies and choices.

Assume that incentive scenarios are the "Open Sesame" of new ideas. Nevertheless, the difficulty with incentive scenarios is that they encompass the whole of society. Thus they are difficult to conceive of and write about. One way to conceive of the whole structure of social incentives is to combine policy analysis with what has been termed macrohistorical analysis. Policy analysis, in this sense, is an evaluation of a key array of policy issues on which the decisions and incentives of the whole society turn. Macrohistory is historical (albeit somewhat subjective) evaluation of the major tendency of these key issues in the social evolution. An example of such a policy analysis was given in chapter 2, where a set of policy issues, determining a social configuration was presented. A review of that policy set at this point should indicate that, as we shift from one extreme to the other on the choice spectrum for each issue, the incentives in society shift, and so do institutional configurations and consequences—that is, the incentive portions of alternative scenarios can be written by taking a policy framework, such as that presented in chapter 2, and choosing differing incentives and rights along the spectrum scales. Such an exercise is used in the next section to illustrate alternative assessment and choices processes.

Alternative Assessment and Choice Process

Because incentives are the motive force in the social process, the first set of choices among alternative scenarios, in seeking innovative and orderly renewal, is to assess the alternative designs of the society itself by looking at the incentives and locus of choice across a comprehensive set of policy issues. The incentives and locus of choice across a comprehensive set of policy issues define how a society is constituted, or what its constitution in fact is. Thus the Constitution of the United States begins to define the incentives and locus of choice, which is why the availability of revision or amendment to the Constitution is one of three major working mechanisms for renewal in the American society. (The other two, from the last chapter, are legislation, which subdefines the Constitution, and competitive markets, which allocate resources to human wants.) We start our analysis with the constitution of authority in the United States government on a set of thirteen key policy issues, as defined in the Constitution, legislation, and the workings of the marketplace. This analysis takes the set of policy issues previously discussed in chapter 2 and compares early America with contemporary America across the policy issues. Early America is taken to be the agrarian United States during the period from 1790 to 1870, before the creation of the corporate trusts. The comparison of the two Americas is shown in table 14-1.

Early America had policies tending toward a balanced budget and neutral

Table 14-1
Comparisons of Early America with Contemporary America on Thirteen Policy Issues

Means of Management	Early America		Contemporary America	
	Choice	Consequence	Choice	Consequence
Monetary-fiscal policy	Balanced	Equilibrium (government neutral)	Expansive (unbalanced)	Chronic inflation
Income distribution	Slightly skewed	Fairly equitable	Skewed to the high side	Rich-poor extremes
Capital flows	Open markets	Competitive	Institutionally channeled	Concentrated
Competition	Open	Decentralized economy	Oligopolistic	Centralized economy
Price policy	Free	Competitive	Administered	Inflexible prices
Employment	Labor intensive	Service oriented	Labor extensive	Capital intensive economy
Living standards	Internalize costs	More amenities, less government	Externalize cost	Fewer amenities, more government
Educational accessibility	Fairly wide	Adaptable individuals	Wide access but narrowly trained	Specialized individuals
Technological accessibility	Wide	Less concentrated	Fairly narrow	More concentrated
Barriers to entry	Lowered	Equitable incomes	Raised	Incomes skewed to high side
Voting	Wide issue	Direct democracy	Narrow issue	Oligarchy
Internal order	Participative	Restless conflict resolution	Somewhat coercive	Tending toward police or governmental order
International order	Participative	International bargaining	Somewhat coercive	Tending toward wars and military power politics

monetary policy, because the government was small. Income distributions were fairly normal, because individuals had open access to land and resources. As a result of resource access, capital flows were competitive in open markets. Since capital flows were competitive, business was competitive and open, and was made up mainly of small businesses with decentralized decision making. Competitive businesses have free, competitive market prices. The free prices for both capital and labor made for a high employment (or labor intensive) economy oriented toward providing human services. With high employment and a competitively growing economy, living standards rose and most of the social costs of society were internalized or absorbed in the price structure. The result was less government and more amenities—that is, the economy was relatively self-sufficient and self-regulating. Education was general and rather widely available, with the result that individuals learned adaptively between school and jobs. Technology was widely accessible, leading to a decentralized and less concentrated economy. There were few barriers to entry into business or a profession, since education, resources, and technology were broadly available, with the result that incomes were fairly equally or equitably distributed. Voting was mainly at the local government level on a wide range of issues, or by town hall meetings, which enabled people to participate directly in democracy. Because voting was wide and barriers few, people resolved conflicts participatively without resort to government intervention. The nation tended to its own affairs internationally and resolved most of its conflicts participatively and by bargaining, rather than by war.

In the intervening years since 1870, contemporary America has reversed most of the policy choices that made for the greatness of the United States in its early years. Now the monetary-fiscal policy is expansive and unbalanced, with the result that the citizenry suffers from chronic inflation and erosion of purchasing power. Incomes are skewed to the high side, with rich-poor extremes. The rich generally benefit from institutionally channeled funds that keep capital flows off the open market and result in large, concentrated business corporations. The large corporations dominate markets and administer prices to limit competition; consequently, the economic structure is oligopolistic—that is, competition among the few. Prices are inflexible, going up with inflation but not down with recession. Business makes heavy capital investments to economize on labor, resulting in an economy that is capital intensive but has high and chronic unemployment. The high unemployment requires government to ameliorate the condition of the poor through welfare programs, which are external to the costs in the private economy. Government has become large (about one-fourth of the economy), and most of its expenditures are for income redistribution to aid the disadvantaged on a minimal basis with few amenities. Educational access is wide, but education is narrowly specialized by field, making people less adaptable to changes in employment conditions. Technology is concentrated by reason of patents, licenses, and high research expenditures within large corporations.

Barriers to entry are raised in many businesses and professions by the concentration of capital and technology. Voting on the national level is generally a narrow choice between two candidates whose policies differ minimally on issues; consequently, direct democracy has given way to an oligarchy of those elected through large campaign contributions. Internal order has diminished, as there are less opportunities open to individuals. This lessening of opportunity and of resource access leads to more conflict and strife, including crime. The result is more need for government policing and regulation. The international order is also affected by the "haves" versus the "have-nots," and military power and power politics are required to protect the "haves" in the United States. The consequence has been frequent wars, with the United States having more years at war between 1939 and 1972 than at peace.

If these comparisons of the two Americas are oversharply drawn; every person may modify them as he wishes. But however, modified, a sharp contrast will still remain between the incentives of the two Americas, mainly because early America had free resources in land and minerals to give to anyone willing to work them, and the result was a constantly renewing of change and competition. That renewal of change by competition is what is missing today, as capital and resources are bottled up and channeled within existing institutions.

In summary, the incentive portion of the alternative scenarios of the two Americas are found in the income, capital, competition, price, education, technology, and voting policies of the society. Change any of these incentives, and the social structure changes, as well as the opportunities for renewal. Contemporary America has locked in these incentives to existing institutions, so that individuals have relatively little of the ability to govern their own lives that they did in early America.

Tentative Institutional Designs

New institutional designs may be exercised or created by changing incentives that reallocate resources and decision-making authority. Institutions may be redesigned by changing the incentive system or the authority distribution within the social process. As institutions are redesigned, the entire structure of society changes (as we saw in the previous section by comparing early America with contemporary America). The incentives and authority in early America were highly decentralized to the individual level. The incentives and authority in contemporary America are highly centralized in large institutions, such as the federal government and multinational corporations. The events that caused this change were largely related to the creation of corporate chartering in the 1860s and to a preferential corporate income tax structure since 1913. The centralization of authority in contemporary America could be reversed under the same legislation that created corporate America, thus returning to individual citizens the authority over their own lives.

The playing out of various scenarios, based upon different combinations of the thirteen policies discussed in the previous section, is beyond the scope of this book. However, those interested in seeing how such an exercise in social redesign might unfold are encouraged to read the book *Alternative U.S. Futures.*[1] In this book, the same set of thirteen policies are combined in various ways to show how the United States might develop in the future. The U.S. society is very similar in many respects to Roman society; and hence one scenario is called the "Roman Replay," in which the United States follows, in its own way, along an evolutionary path similar to the Roman Empire. Similarly, historic precedents are used to write a "Greek Replay," a "Medieval Replay," as well as an "Original American Plan." In all the scenarios, the main alterations in the social design of institutions occurs through changes in the tax laws or voting rights. Tax laws change incentives. Voting rights change the constitutional delegation of authority. The point is that simple revisions in tax laws and voting rights can significantly redesign and renew the American society; and each citizen should learn the skills of redesign that would enable him to live the kind of life he wants.

Renewals and Redistributions of Authority

The means by which formal consent to authority comes into being and creates allegiance, or subsequently converts allegiance into dissent by being non-responsive to changes in needs, was sufficiently discussed in chapter 1. Now we wish to examine primarily the means of maintaining order. Society exists to maintain order for individuals. If it cannot maintain order, society serves little purpose. The maintenance of order implies orderly renewal. The means of renewal, we have seen, are the shifting of incentives to accomplish new missions and purposes desired by individuals for their development. Institutions tend to inhibit this change, because organizations maintain themselves as they currently are to secure positions and rewards for their members. How, then, does a society continually shift incentives toward individuals against the wishes and inertia of institutions?

The simplest means of shifting incentives, resources, and authority is through the free functioning of a capital market, where all have free and equal access to the flow of funds generated by the economy. This free access would mean that all corporate funds should go into the open market for bid by all, and not be sequestered as now by such tax shelters as depreciation allowances, nonprogressive corporate income taxes, capital gains, or depletion allowances. If resources are to be freely allocated to their best use in keeping with new needs, then all the capital funds must flow to the market for bids by those who have the highest consumer demand for their utilization. This reallocation of capital through the market has the advantage of being impersonal, fair, and efficient, whereas the present means of reallocating capital through tax legislation is preferential and subject to purchase by the highest paying lobbyists.

The second major means of shifting authority and resources amicably is by giving citizens a larger voting role in setting revenues and appropriations by referenda. Congressmen have a conflict of interest in their fiscal role (see chapter 3), in that they use their fiscal power to get themselves reelected. Citizens have no such conflict of interest relative to fiscal policy. Their interest is the optimum allocation of their own and government resources—which is to say, in the public interest. Citizen referenda vote on fiscal policy would establish more responsibility over the budgets and monetary management than is currently possible with the conflict of interest among congressmen, because taxpayers know that they themselves finally pay the bills. They also know what bills they are willing to pay.

Thus the redistribution of authority and resources could be conducted by means of an orderly and amicable system of relying on free capital markets and budgetary fiscal referenda as a means for renewal. The other alternative, of course, is to continue the present inflexibility by letting capital markets remain oligopolistic and allowing the government's fiscal nonresponsibility to persist. Then the avenue to change is through apathy, dissent, crime, violence, and eventually revolution.

Authority Assumptions

Authority is assumed by those who have the motive, opportunity, and the means; and the assumption of authority occurs as an orderly renewal if society provides the resource means for new entrepreneurs to meet new needs. The assumption of management authority depends on having motive, opportunity, and means. Crime also involves motive, opportunity, and means. Perhaps this similarity is one reason why the borderline between legal and illegal assumption of authority (or rights) is blurred. Those who are unable to use legal means to assume property rights sometimes resort to illegal means. Management and crime thus are two sides of the same phenomenon, where strong leaders do whatever they think is necessary to meet a set of individual human needs. Management does it legally—that is, by the existing rules. Crime does it illegally—that is, by its own rules.

The duty of an orderly society is to provide as many avenues as possible for individuals to carry out their wishes by social rules, rather than their own. This means that an orderly society must constantly be opening new avenues for adventure and entrepreneurship, rather than closing down the scope of opportunity. The interest of institutions, in contrast, is to close down the scope of entrepreneurship and opportunity to restrict competition to the few instead of the many. Thus the social process, to be renewable, must counteract the oligopolistic tendencies of its institutions and constantly seek to decentralize more and more authority and resources to individuals. This not only deters aggressive individuals from crime, it also has the purpose of turning entrepreneurial leadership to the new needs of individuals. The recent criminal activity in the United States among its street people, corporate executives, and elected officials is an indication that the avenues of opportunity are not sufficiently open. Resources are not broadly enough accessible, and neither is technology, education, markets, or capital. When society narrows the avenues of accessibility to the resources and authority required for individual fulfillment, then allegiances wane, dissent rises, and crime increases. The orderly renewal of society thus is a process of continually reallocating authority and resources to new faces, ideas, individuals, entrepreneurs, and human needs.

Capital Flows and Allocations

Capital flows and allocations, above all else in the social process, need to be kept free and open as a means of redistributing authority to satisfy changing human needs. Since the American economy is a capitalistic system, the free flow of capital is the crux of a changing and adaptable economy. The Golden Age of the United States was early America, when capital resources were essentially free to anyone for the taking who was willing to put his labor into their development. The growth of the economy was due largely to individuals converting their labor into capital by applying their efforts to the use of a free resource, such as a homestead or a mining claim. In short, the ample, free resources of the nation were its means of developing itself and achieving greatness. Having experienced the exhilaration of growth and development through free resource allocation, we recently have reversed our policy and confined resources to institutional channels where they can be sequestered, locked in, and used to make the economy oligopolistic. The means of freeing the economy again to be used in the interest of individuals is to free capital markets. This can be done by tax legislation to remove tax shelters so that corporations are taxed on the same basis as individuals.

Reinforcing the Innovative Process

Reinforcing the innovative process is accomplished by using incentives that act as a stimulus to ideas and allow capital accumulations that can be used to fulfill new human needs. Incentives start the entrepreneurial process, and incentives reinforce it. The freeing of capital markets to go to the highest entrepreneurial bidder who wishes to fill new human needs is one means of starting the innovative process. To keep the innovative process going once started, the incentives must continue, largely in the form of allowing the accumulation of reinvestment capital—that is, new entrepreneurs with new ideas are capital poor. They not only need to have free access to capital markets, which they do not now have, they also need to accumulate capital to build their businesses.

The present means for allowing business corporations to accumulate capital for reinvestment is through accelerated depreciation; a flat, nonprogressive income tax; liberal expense allowances; and preferential treatment of capital gains. These tax shelters have the effect of permitting capital accumulation in perpetuity regardless of the merits of the product, service, or institution. The current tax shelters could be revised by substituting tax-free capital accumulation during the early years of a product line, which is subsequently raised to progressively higher rates as time passes. There may be better incentive alternatives than this suggestion; but the point is that the innovative process needs continual reinforcement if the social process is to be renewed.

Incentives and the Vesting of Rights

The reinforcement of incentives causes them to become vested as rights that resist revocation, and thus atrophy is always a present danger. As law and custom make new incentives (or subsidies) available for innovation and then reinforce them by allowing the accumulation of capital flows to encourage development, the recipients become accustomed to the subsidy and regard it as a right. They expect its continuance long after the innovation is developed. The purpose of the subsidy is forgotten, but the security and status of the income flow are powerful incentives to hang on to the subsidy by all possible economic, legal, and political means. Hence the recipients of old incentives and subsidies become entrenched in their institutional arrangements, resist change, and thus atrophy begins.

The many subsidies currently allowed to business corporations are old incentives for innovations long since developed. These subsidies are, again, the preferential tax treatment of corporate income, capital gains, depletion, depreciation, research, interest, debt, and expense accounts. They once may have stimulated innovation and development during the industrialization and growth phase of American economic history; and in selected cases, new entrepreneurs, who once broke into the closed capital markets, still use these incentives to good advantage for innovative development of new products and services. But for the most part, the old incentives and subsidies have now become a deterrent to innovations, growth, and development, because too many old institutions use the subsidies as rights to lock up their resources in institutional channels, while they continue on their old ways without innovation or responsiveness to new human needs. The evidence for this atrophy in institutions, and for the sequestering of incentives as rights, is the declining growth rate of the American economy in recent years, together with high unemployment and persistent inflation—that is, the American economy is suffering from low growth rates due to low rates of innovation by old institutions that are using old incentives to lock up resources within institutional channels as their rights. The old institutions are lacking in ideas and responsiveness to new human needs, but they resist the reallocation of resources by hanging on to their old subsidies by all economic, legal, and political means. Sometimes illegal means are used, such as illegal corporate campaign contributions and international bribery.

Thus, incentives and their reinforcement are essential to foster new innovations, but they involve an ever-present danger that the incentives will merely become old subsidies regarded as rights, allowing institutions to atrophy, innovation to languish, and economic growth to lag.

Preservation of an Open Social System

The preservation of an open, renewable society depends on two conditions: (1) that new individuals with new ideas have access to resources, and (2) that old institutions relinquish their resources to innovative individuals. The first conditions is probably more easily accepted than the second. Most of us like to see innovation and growth, but most of us also resist giving up any resource claims that we have. Yet the economic facts are that resources are limited, and they must be reallocated to those who will put them to the best possible use if the society is to be able to renew itself and change.

One way to make the reallocation process work again is to remove institutional barriers by placing the reallocation function back into the hands of individual decision makers again, which is to say back into free-flowing capital markets. This renewal by reallocation might be accomplished, for example, by placing sunset laws on product lines and institutions, so that they do not outlive their usefulness. If product lines and institutions were allowed to die after a reasonable life span, as individuals die, their resources would become unlocked and reallocatable to individuals of a new generation with new ideas to meet changing human needs.

There remains the problem, of course, that individuals age and need some security against aging, so that when their own innovations and contributions are finished they may continue to benefit from them in income during their lifetimes. This form of income security can be provided by retirement benefits, together with individual decisions by the older people who have accumulated resources to reinvest in younger people with new ideas—that is, the elderly who have acquired resources by their work and innovation can secure a life income for themselves by reinvesting in new enterprises and entrepreneurs through the capital markets. Such a proposal is not greatly different than what happens now, except that it proposes that all resources would be reinvested by individuals, and none would be reinvested by institutions. If institutions were required to pay out all earnings and capital gains to their stockholders, and were proscribed from reinvesting any themselves under sunset or termination laws for corporations (and governments), the entire pool of resources would become reallocable continually by individuals through capital markets, to the benefit of both the senior citizen investor and the junior citizen innovator. Moreover, the society would have a renewal mechanism through continuous reallocation of resources that would make it an open society—that is, open to new individuals and new ideas.

Openness as a Means of Change and Renewal

We have seen that societies tend to seek order by giving timeless allocations of authority and resources to institutions through incentives and subsidies. But the subsidy, once given, becomes an institutional right resistant to change, and then the atrophy of institutions leads to unresponsiveness, dissent, and disorder. Hence, what starts as a social device for order becomes the instrument of disorder.

The primary purpose of society is to provide for order and meet new needs of individuals. Thus the reason for being of society is founded in its adaptability and the maintenance of order through renewal and change. Renewal and change require the renewal of ideas and innovations to fit the times, and this in turn entails change in the allocation of resources and authority. The continual reallocation of resources and authority is an essential process of an open society. An open society precludes the entrenchment of institutional barriers to entry and nurtures the emergence of individual entrepreneurship with new ideas and enterprises so that the society may renew itself and grow. Thus the openness of a society is a means of change and renewal because open access allows innovative individuals to acquire both the resources and authority to implement their ideas for the satisfaction of changing needs.

Management of an Open System

A renewable society requires innovators and entrepreneurs; and unfortunately institutions produce guardians and conservators. The conservators guard their rights, prerogatives, resources, property, subsidies, charters, and laws. Conservators are interested in such things as getting reelected to perpetuate themselves, or in the cliche of "the bottom line," as a means of perpetuating their resources.

Entrepreneurs and innovators are interested in such things as creating a new idea and implementing it through a program of development. They are creation and program oriented rather than being institutional protectionists. They want to acquire new resources to build a new idea, rather than guard old subsidies by institutional acquisitiveness. They are doers rather than custodians.

A society of custodians is not only dull, but it is also growthless and unchanging. Institutions can exist as growthless and unchanging because they are mindless. Individuals cannot exist except by growth and change because new experiences are essential to learning and maturation of their minds. The conservator form of management represents all the skills commonly learned by elected officials, bureaucrats, and corporate executives—that is, to have and to hold what is.

Management of an open society requires a new set of managerial skills, in which all managers regard themselves as short-term program entrepreneurs, and none regard themselves as long-term institutional guardians. The innovator uses different and more difficult management skills that are inventive and program directed. These innovative program skills are those which have been covered in chapters 12, 13, and 14.

Note

1. Stahrl W. Edmunds, *Alternative U.S. Futures* (Santa Monica, Ca.: Goodyear Publishing Company, 1978).

15 The Meaning of Management Competence

The management of an open society is quite different and more complex in its requirements than the management of a predominantly institutional society. An open society requires change managers whose role is innovative renewal by means of new program implementation. An institutional society is most comfortable with guardians who extrapolate past practice and avoid change. Therefore the test of competency differs for each type of manager. Competent institutional management is defined as hanging or adding on to what the institution already has. Change management, on the other hand, demonstrates its competence by the extent to which it maintains an open system, capable of self-renewal; and it attends to the neglected consequences of decision making.

The Managed

We have seen, by way of summary of the book, that a management function is needed when individuals cannot perform desired services for themselves by reason of their own lack of time, knowledge, technology, or resources. Then individuals delegate a management function to an institution to perform the service for them. But we also saw (in chapters 1 through 3) that individuals consent to such delegations of authority only for the peripheral concerns of their lives, such as products, work or social order; but they jealously retain for themselves those emotional concerns that determine the deep meaning of their lives, such as love, marriage, family, friendships, learning, reading, art, and play. Hence there are large portions of individual living that are outside the sphere of management; and moreover, there are myriad ecological interactions between human activity and biological cycles that are beyond the knowledge of management.

The managed portions of a society or of institutions thus are composed of those needs, missions, and goals that are selected for accomplishment and toward which resources and tasks are directed by management authority; but these managed portions of society are only a small part of the total social and natural environment. Management's concentration focuses on a very narrow spectrum of the living ecosystem. This is necessary because (1) individuals constrain management delegations to the performance of their less important needs, (2) resources are limited and must be allocated carefully to accomplish the few selected goals that are possible, (3) management competence is limited

293

to understanding and directing a few parallel sets of activities at a time, and (4) understanding of the interworkings of the ecosystem has (so far at least) been beyond the comprehension of the human mind.

Thus given that management is selective, limited, narrow, focused and preoccupied with the housekeeping chores of the world, we should not be astonished to find that the environment is full of surprises for management. All the residual goings-on in the social ecology to which management pays little or no attention (and sometimes does not understand) provide feedback for and have unexpected effects on managment. For example, management made agricultural pesticides with mercury, and mercury in the environment came back to surprise management by lethally damaging nerve cells in man and animals. Or management suppresses competition and dissent as a means of maintaining order, and revolutionary violence comes back in the guise of alienated individuals to seize authority back from management. Clearly, the flux of mission selection, management direction, environmental reaction, and feedback surprises are a complex and continuous ongoing process.

The art of management is usually regarded, in learning and practice, as the direction of activity (these skills are covered in chapters 4 through 11 of this book). However, a competent manager knows that these skills, while essential, are simplistic. They allow an executive to manage a complex set of activities to achieve a goal, and this laudable achievement may be rewarded by bestowing wealth, authority, power, prestige, and position on him, which may indeed be satisfying to a recipient of such benefactions from society. However, the simplistic skills of management are also rewarded by environmental feedbacks, which may make the entire enterprise a monumental mistake from a social viewpoint in terms of meeting new human needs.

The meeting of new human needs, which are continually changing, requires a greater competence of management than sheer accomplishment skills; it also requires competence in change management and social renewal. The art of change management and social renewal has been considered in chapters 12 through 14, where it became clear that the perception of change through mission, competitive, and technological assessments are only part of the problem. The more subtle and difficult part of change management is to conceive of incentive and implementation scenarios that will enable new ideas to be carried out. Incentive scenarios represent alternative ways that resources and authority can be reallocated from old institutions to new entrepreneurs, so that innovation may unfold.

The failure of society to design incentive mechanisms for reallocating resources to meet new human needs brings the social process full circle to the point where unmet human needs bring about alienation, dissent, and violent change. In this dynamic cycle of change, orderly renewal occurs when change management has the competence to solve new problems and needs as they emerge out of the unmanaged.

The Unmanaged

Previous sections, particularly chapters 12-14, have dealt at some length with both the origin of surprise events in the form of feedback from the unmanaged environment, and the importance to social renewal of reallocatable resources to meet new human needs. The purpose of this section is to integrate the entire social process flow by showing that unmanaged environmental surprises and new human needs are, in fact, one and the same thing.

Environmental surprises and new human needs are one and the same thing because the surprise events present new problems that individuals want solved. Pollution emissions from automobiles were a surprise, which, when discovered, presented a new problem (representing a need for clean air) that individuals wanted solved. Mercury poisoning from pesticides was a new problem that people wanted solved. The increasing apathy of individuals and their alienation from the American society, leading to rising street crime and violence, presents a new problem that citizens want solved.

Unexpected environmental changes present new problems and new needs; and these environmental changes are the unmanaged portions of society. The unmanaged portions of the social process, which are by far the larger realm of activity, thus yield feedback surprises that are the stimulus for new needs that individuals want solved. Being unmanaged, these reactions are issues and events that management heretofore overlooked or neglected: the new needs of individuals come out of the prior neglect of management. If new needs of individuals originate in the negligence of management, then the demand for new ideas and change has a direct relation to management competence or incompetence. The more new demands for change, the greater the management incompetence of society.

The Accumulation of Unmanaged Neglected Issues

The accumulation of unmanaged neglected issues becomes the basis for counter-management strategies and successes. A revolutionary is a countermanager who wishes to offer a different mode of institutional (that is, constitutional) management to meet society's accumulated neglected issues. A revolutionary is, therefore, very sensitive to the state of accumulated grievances among a population. The state of accumulated grievances enables him to estimate the probable prospects for revolutionary change.

Revolutions are not made; they are the product of accumulated grievances. Revolutions are not fierce convolutions instigated by firebrands; they are the crumbling from within of a society caused by internal accumulated neglects. Revolutions are made not by the firebrands, but by the institutional conservators who attend to the wrong business too long. They attend to their internal maintenance, rather than to the accomulated neglected issues and problems from the unmanaged portion of their large environments.

If one prefers not to have revolutionary change, then competency in management requires the orderly renewal of society by tackling neglected environmental issues one by one as they occur, and not letting them accumulate into dissent and alienation. That orderly renewal process, as we have seen, implies the use of incentives for reallocating resources and authority continually so that institutions adapt to innovation and change.

The Neglected Issues as Sources of Change

The neglected present new needs for solution; and left unsolved, they are transformed into rising individual dissatisfactions. We saw earlier (in chapter 1) that individuals are loathe to resort to dissent, confrontation, and revolution because most of the matters with which institutional management deals are of secondary importance to their personal lives. Only when the accumulated grievances cross a critical threshold (at which individuals lose even the governance of their own private lives) do individuals resort to violent change. By then they have been deprived of so many choices over their private lives—such as no income, employment opportunity, entry, opportunity, or advancement—that they feel they have nothing to lose. Such is the threshold of revolt; and in fact, it is a high and reluctant threshold. Yet it is surprising how many times individuals have crossed that threshold, not only in the demise of the Greek, Roman, and Medieval societies, but also in the French Revolution, the American Revolution, the Russian Revolution, and even, on more limited scale, in contemporary U.S. society. That individuals come to the threshold of violence at all is an indication of monumental management incompetence historically, in letting the neglected issues pile up into grievances of such huge proportions that people will give up their current personal safety and private lives to change the social system.

Neglected Issues in Contemporary Society

Much can be said about the good things about the United States—its rising standards of living for the majority of the population, accessible education, open vocational choices, and private housing choices and life styles for those with means. Most important of all, perhaps, is that despite some shortcomings, the United States is perhaps the freest nation in the world in political activity and protection against false imprisonment.

Having recognized these and other satisfactions in and benefits of U.S. society, however, the competent change manager would be myopic not to see that U.S. society also has many neglected issues and a considerable history of violence. The violence has been kept below the threshold of broad revolt, but not to a great enough margin to allow us to become complacent about the change management problem. We define violent dissent as any event that involved armed forces, on either side, to forment or suppress conflict. We also include international violence (wars) as evidence of U.S. failures to adapt to orderly (peaceable) change, but exclude criminal activity defined as solely seeking property gains but not seeking reallocation of authority. While the following list does not pretend to be complete, it does give an indication of violence occurring in each decade:

1890-1900	Spanish American War Military used to suppress labor strikes
1901-1910	Assassination of President McKinley
1911-1920	World War I
1921-1930	None noted
1931-1940	National guard used to suppress strikes by farmers and labor Assassination attempt on President Roosevelt
1941-1950	World War II
1951-1960	Korean War Lebanese action
1961-1970	Cuban missile crisis and Cuban invasion attempt Assassination of President Kennedy Vietnam War Military used to suppress race riots in Watts and Detroit Assassination of presidential candidate Robert Kennedy
1971-1980	Vietnam War Military fire upon students at Kent State Symbionese Liberation Army Assassination attempt on President Ford

During the past nine decades, only one has been relatively free of violent conflict of one type or another. Eight decades have seen considerable numbers of wars, assassination attempts, and some military suppression of dissent. The use of troops against its own citizenry is a desperate act by government to suppress dissent, and it is a clear admission of the failure of society to meet the accumulated grievances of the dissidents—that is, the use of military force against citizens is an indication of incompetence in change management and social renewal.

Who have been the dissidents that the government has tried to suppress militarily? They have been, over the years, laborers, farmers, blacks, and students. This segment of the citizenry represents a large and diverse portion of the population. Moreover, the occasions for suppression have been more frequent in the last two decades than they were earlier. If military force has been needed to suppress dissent over a large segment of the population with increasing frequency, and if crime rates are rising as well, then we may conclude that the accumulated neglected issues and dissatisfactions of the society need attention. While neglected issues and dissent have been contained below the threshold of general revolt, military suppression bodes ill for orderly governance and renewal of society. The accumulated neglected issues are significant enough to cause us to question whether U.S. society has developed competence in change management.

What have dissident groups in the United States had in common? Farmers, laborers, minorities, and youth share low-skill levels, heavy dependence upon institutional management for continuous employment, or dependence on free market adjustment for their livelihoods. Youth and minorities have low-skill levels and have difficulty obtaining employment from existing institutions that are capital intensive, substituting capital for labor. Labor, youth, and minorities are highly dependent on large institutions for a livelihood through employment because they have little access to capital to go into business for themselves. Farmers and laborers are highly dependent on free-market price adjustments in demand or volume—that is, when farm prices or employment go down, farmers and laborers can only maintain themselves if all other prices go down in the market to balance supply and demand. But prices of industrial goods are not flexible, because large corporations keep their prices up. Hence, the burden of diminished employment or declining food prices falls heavily on laborers and farmers.

The issues of discontent, then, have been unemployment, unfair pricing, lack of opportunity, barrier to entry, inflation, and wars. These have been chronic problems of the U.S. society for a century; these are the accumulated neglected issues, which appear to become worse instead of better. Unemployment among youths and blacks is high and persistent. Inflation is high and persistent. Labor and farmers suffer the brunt of inflexible pricing in every recession. Recessions are more frequent. The economic growth rate is falling over time. Indeed, the bundle of accumulated neglected issues below the surface calm of society is formidable and chronic.

Not only are the accumulated neglected issues formidable and persistent, they are also systematically interrelated. We saw in chapter 14 that the pattern of authority in contemporary America on thirteen major policy issues was toward a closed, centralized institutional society, in which institutional barriers and maintenance tended to exclude individual freedom of choice on many of the thirteen issues. The exclusion of individual choice has been accomplished mainly by eliminating competition and closing the capital markets to individuals. The closing of access to capital by financial, competitive, and technical means has been a major factor underlying the accumulated neglected issues of American society, accounting directly or indirectly for a large portion of unemployment, inflexible prices, inflation, lack of opportunity, and ultimately wars to protect the economic interests of the large institutions.

The Social Overhead Costs of Neglected Issues

There are two major ways to deal with neglected social issues: to suppress them, or to abate them. We have seen in the previous section that the United States government has occasionally used military troops against its citizens to suppress dissent arising from accumulated grievances. These military suppressions have been the exception. To contain dissatisfactions among its citizens, the government usually has tried to abate the dissatisfactions by compensating citizens for their neglected or disadvantaged state. Crudely put, the government seeks to buy the allegiance of its citizens that it has been unable to earn by competent change management. These purchases of allegiance take the form of subsidies, welfare, or transfer payments, which become a form of social overhead cost—that is, to make the transfer payments to dissatisfied persons, the government has to add taxes (or inflation) on the productive population as a social overhead cost to be transferred to the neglected population.

The magnitude of social overhead costs may be measured by the amount of compensatory payments the government makes to ameliorate dissatisfactions and violence. Total government expenditures make up about one-fourth of the whole U.S. economy, and 80 percent of the expenditures are for welfare, transfer payments, the military, and regulation of the effects of oligopolistic competition on noncompetitive business. That is to say, the social overhead from the accumulated neglected issues in the United States is about one-fifth of the entire economy.

Social Feasibility Inversely Proportional to Social Overhead

An ideal social system would have no overhead costs, but rather, would achieve its allegiance and leadership by substantially satisfying the wants of the entire population. Accumulated neglected issues and social overhead would be kept to a minimum by adaptive change and renewal. Some societies have come close to achieving such an optimum, for example, Greece in the fifth century B.C., Rome in the fourth century B.C., and England and the United States in the nineteenth century. These were the golden ages of the societies, with much ideation, allegiance, idealization, and motivation.

As allegiance declines in a society, leaders find it necessary to placate the dissatisfied population suffering from unmanaged, neglected issues by trying to ameliorate their condition. The Roman society did this by distributing corn to the poor for food. U.S. society uses welfare and transfer payments. The purpose of the compensatory payment is to retain sufficient loyalty to make the society workable. The dissatisfied and neglected are given sufficient compensation or goods to make it just worth their while to refrain from confrontation and disorder. In this sense, their allegiance is being purchased.

The amount of compensatory payments or social overhead increases as neglects accumulated. The social overhead comes out of the economic surplus of the balance of productive society. The amount of economic surplus, or the resource margin of a society, is limited to the excess output after paying all production costs for labor, materials, management, and capital—that is, the economic surplus is a finite amount, and that finite amount limits and constrains the social overhead that is possible. As the social overhead goes beyond the limits of this resource margin, the productive system itself falters because there are insufficient remaining funds to pay all its costs, particularly the cost of new capital. Then economic growth begins to lag, recessions and unemployment become more frequent, and inflation becomes chronic. This pattern of lagging growth, rising unemployment, and chronic inflation has been characteristic of failing societies in the past. It happened to the Roman Empire, to Medieval society, to England, and to France. The symptoms are appearing in the United States.

The higher the social overhead grows to cover the costs of neglects and to maintain minimal allegiance of the neglected citizens, the less feasible the social process becomes, because society has absorbed its surplus in the neglected issues and has insufficient resources left for innovation, development, growth, and new capital facilities—that is, the feasibility of the social process is inversely proportionate to the amount of social overhead which the productive system must bear.

The Reduction of Social Overhead Costs

The reduction of social overhead costs is a principal requirement of competent change management. The purpose of change management is to renew the social process and develop its capacity to meet new human needs. This means that the change manager must have flexibility as well as leeway to use resources for new purposes. A principal way he can obtain such leeway is to cut the burden of social overhead costs, thus converting some of the economic surplus into new development capital instead of paying it out as transfer payments to compensate for accumulated neglected issues. The reduction of social overhead costs is an exercise in writing and realizing new incentive scenarios (discussed in the last chapter)—that is, the change manager must terminate old subsidies to create new incentives.

The common method of cutting social overhead cost is the crude approach of swinging a broad axe and chopping out anything vulnerable that those in authority do not like. This method is only moderately successful, because the meat axe method exacerbates old accumulated dissatisfactions without putting any positive new incentive in their place. A more subtle form of cutting social overhead is to trade off old subsidies for new incentives aimed at the disaffected population. We know from their past near revolts that laborers, farmers, students, and minorities have accumulated dissatisfactions and neglected issues related to unemployment, pricing practices, inflation, and wars. Many of the transfer and welfare payments go to families in their population groups. Moreover, many of the burdens and neglected issues from which they suffer are caused by a pattern of centralization of capital resources in large, noncompetitive institutions whose innovation and growth is lagging. Thus one form of incentive trade-off would be to diminish the welfare and transfer payments to the poorer population in exchange for freer access to capital markets as an incentive for them to become entrepreneurs. The obverse of the trade-off, of course, is that large institutions lose their old subsidies derived from monopolizing the markets, but in return they will benefit from greater sales and profits as the growth rate picks up with new increments of innovation and entrepreneurship entering the economy.

An objection to this revised incentive scheme might be that poor and unskilled managers are unlikely sources of innovation and entrepreneurship. Perhaps, but the poor and unskilled managers were the principal entrepreneurs of the nineteenth century who created the wealth the United States has. It is at least worth taking a risk on the common people of the United States, since present institutional management is unable to increase lagging growth rates.

In summary, the reduction of social overhead is a principal requirement of competent change management; and the most likely way to achieve such reductions is to trade off old subsidies for positive new incentives that will yield innovation and growth.

Points of No Return in Social Overhead Costs

Rich industrial nations have an economic surplus, beyond the costs of production and subsidence, that can be used in a variety of ways—for innovation, capital expansion, cultural development, or social overhead. But even for rich nations, this economic surplus, or resource margin, is limited. The limit begins to show as unemployment, inflation, lower growth rates, and a declining marginal productivity of capital. The marginal productivity of capital is the added increment of production obtainable from an added increment of capital facility investment. The marginal productivity of capital in the United States has been declining for the last decade or more. As a result, growth rates are lagging, and unemployment and inflation have been rising. These indicators suggests that the United States is moving toward the limit of its resource margin and overexpanding its economic surplus.

The amount of a nation's economic surplus, or resource margin, is probably not a fixed amount, nor the same for all nations. Still, the concept of a resource margin is useful because it tends to suggest limits beyond which the management of the society cannot go without debilitating the system. The point of no return for a society is reached when the sum of its social overhead costs and personal savings exceeds its economic surplus, and when the marginal productivity of capital beings to fall.

What is the resource margin or economic surplus of the United States? The composition of the U.S. resource margin, which is roughly 36 percent of the gross national product, is made up of a 16 percent savings rate and, as we saw earlier, a 20 percent social overhead rate—that is, the U.S. economy requires about 64 percent of its output to satisfy the costs of production and current living standards of the employed. The remaining 36 percent may be spent at the discretion of society. The United States has chosen to spend 20 percent on social overhead and 16 percent on savings. Savings are the principal source of funds for innovation, development, new capital investment, and economic growth. The 16 percent savings rate of the United States is among the lowest of any industrialized nation in the world, except Great Britain, which is in a state of serious economic stagnation. The Western European countries generally have savings rates around 20 percent, and Japan's savings rate is about 30 percent. Japan's growth rate has also been the highest in the world, over 9 percent annually. (The U.S. growth rate is about 3 percent annually, in real terms.)

The United States thus could improve its economic growth rate, well being, and living standards for everyone by increasing its rate of innovation and capital investment. Suppose the United States spent 20 percent on savings and 16 percent on social overhead. The savings rate and growth rate would increase to be comparable to other major industrial nations, and the likely economic growth rate would be around 4 percent annually instead of 3 percent. Perhaps this 1 percent differential does not seem like very much, but it makes the difference between a 71 percent increase in output over a decade, compared with a 48 percent gain. Or expressed as an increase in the gross national product of the nation, which is roughly $1.5 trillion, the gain in a decade from the extra 1 percent would be $340 billion, which is a very large resource margin to throw away; it would go a long way toward renewing society and relieving the accumulated neglected issues that have mounted over the years.

In summary, the United States is not yet at the point of no return on its social overhead costs, but it is close enough to resource margin for us to give serious thought to means for reducing the overhead rate and increasing the innovation rate.

Thin Margins of Survival and Turning Points in Evolutionary Change

The resources margins for survival are thinly divided between social overhead and innovation rates that, by slipping a few percentage points into overcommitment (either through catastrophe or insufficient management competence), can become the turning points to evolutionary or revolutionary change. The resource margins of a society are relatively thin compared to its commitments, particularly as the society ages. Social overhead costs tend to increase and accumulate gradually and become permanent rights from which there is no withdrawal. As the social overhead grows and becomes fixed, it gradually overcommits the resource margin in one of two ways. Either the resource margin shrinks suddenly through a catastrophic surprise from which the society has no reserves for recovery, or attrition on the savings rate from social overhead accretions causes growth and innovation rates to decline and languish until the society crumbles from within.

The collapse of Ankgor Vat and Chichen Itza are examples of the first case, where catastrophe overwhelmed what had appeared to be ample resource reserves. Both were rich and highly cultured societies. Both succumbed to climatic changes that catastrophically cut their resource margins and caused them to fail. The collapse of the Roman Empire illustrates the second case; and the crumbling of the Empire was very slow indeed. In the eight centuries of Rome's survival, the expansive phase covered about two and one half centuries, the period of stable prosperity and centralization lasted about one and one half centuries, and the demise occurred slowly over four centuries.[1] The demise was a long era of falling growth rates, declining morality and allegiance, waning innovation, rising inflation and dissent, and a crumbling of the Empire at its fringes from attacks by insurgent barbarian dissenters. The long decline of the Roman Empire suggests that its resource margins were originally wise, because its revenues came from military tribute and slave labor; its overhead accretions were slow (mainly the corn dole to dispossessed farmers, who became the urban unemployed as plebes); and its authoritarian repression of dissent were very powerful. Still, the society crumbled in time.

The patterns of social evolution and decline in the past indicate that the United States, or any society, has three major options as it matures and ages: (1) to move toward dictatorial, institutional authority over the society to control dissent or the social overhead rate; (2) to ride thinly along the resource margin until some catastrophe overtakes the society, for which it has no recovery reserves; or (3) to try to free up the commitments imposed on the resource margin by lowering social overhead, decentralizing social incentives and authority, and increasing the innovation rate.

The Meaning of Management Competence

The meaning of management competence is found in a simple test—that is, determining whether the society is capable of maintaining a steady growth rate without inflation while avoiding centralization of authority in its institutions. The main test of management competence is to determine whether it has the capacity for change management and social renewal. The capacity for change management and social renewal is measurable by the ratio of the savings rate to the social overhead rate within the resource margin. The higher the savings rate, compared with the overhead rate, the more flexibility the economy has to foster innovation or retain reserves against catastrophe. The simplest indicator of the maintenance of innovation and social renewal is a steady real-growth rate in the social economy.

The other test of management competence is to determine whether the steady growth rate is maintained without increasing the centralization of authority among its institutions. The centralization of authority is measurable by the relative size of government employment and expenditures, and the concentration ratios among industries. As government size increases relative to the economy, or as industrial concentration ratios increase, authority shifts from decentralized, individual decision makers to institutional authority. History and previous discussion show that institutions, under stress, become more authoritarian rather than less; that is, they tighten up on their authority and resources to deal with dissatisfactions and dissent. In time, this increasing centralization has (historically) become authoritarian and dictatorial, for the reason that the institutions cannot maintain themselves under narrowing resource margins without taking progressively more resources and authority from their citizenry in the form of taxes or inflation, or by repressing the dissatisfactions of the population. Therefore, the centralization of authority among institutions may be taken as an indication that social renewal is being sacrificed in favor of social control over dissent. Conversely, the decentralization of authority within a society is an indication that social renewal is succeeding as a trade-off against social control. Diminishing social control is possible when allegiances to the society are increasing in strength—that is, allegiance occurs when individual aspirations and motivations are increasing, which makes citizens loyal to a society that is providing them with the opportunity, resources, and authority to govern their own lives. The provision of opportunity, resources, and authority to individuals over their own lives is, in fact, the process of decentralization. The meaning of management competence thus is found in a management that provides a steady growth rate within a decentralizing decision process.

Note

1. Stahrl Edmunds, *Alternative U.S. Futures* (Santa Monica, Ca.: Goodyear Publishing Co., 1978).

Bibliography

Ansoff, H. Igor. *Business Strategy*. Baltimore, Penguin Books, 1969.

Argyris, Chris. *Organization and Innovation*. Homewood, Ill., Richard D. Irwin, 1965.

Baier, Kurt, and Nicholas Rescher. *Values and the Future*. New York, The Free Press, 1969.

Barnard, Chester. *The Functions of the Executive*. Cambridge, Mass., Harvard University Press, 1938.

_____. *Organization and Management*. Cambridge, Mass., Harvard University Press, 1948.

Basil, Douglas C. *Managerial Skills for Executive Action*. New York, American Management Association, 1970.

Bauer, Raymond, and Kenneth Gergen. *Policy Formation*. New York, The Free Press, 1968.

Bauer, R., I. Pool, and L. Dexter, *American Business and Public Policy*. New York, Atherton Press, 1963.

Bertanlanffy, L.V. *General Systems Theory*. New York, George Braziller, 1968.

Braybrooke, David, and Charles E. Lindbloom. *A Strategy for Decision*. New York, The Free Press, 1963.

Bruner, J.S., and J.J. Goodnow. *A Study in Thinking*. New York, John Wiley and Sons, 1956.

Buffa, Elwood. *Operations Management: the Management of Productive Systems*. New York, John Wiley and Sons, 1976.

Bureau of the Budget, U.S. *Measuring Productivity in the Federal Government*. Washington, D.C., Supt. of Documents, 1964.

Cartwright, D., and A. Zander. *Group Dynamics: Research and Theory*. Evanston, Ill., Row, Peterson, 1960.

Churchman, C. West. *The Design of Inuqiring Systems*. New York, Basic Books, 1971.

_____. *Challenge to Reason*. New York, McGraw-Hill, 1968.

_____. *The Systems Approach*. New York, Delacorte Press, 1968.

Dahl, Robert A. *Who Governs?* New Haven, Yale University Press, 1961.

Dale, Ernest, ed. *Readings in Management*. New York, McGraw-Hill, 1965.

Earley, James E. "Marginal Policies of Excellently Managed Companies." *American Economic Review*, March, 1956.

Easton, D., *Systems Analysis in Political Life*. New York, John Wiley and Sons, 1965.

Eckstein, Harry. *Pressure Group Politics*. London, G. Allen, 1960.

Editors of *Nation's Business*. "Lessons in Leadership." New York, Doubleday, 1965.

Edmunds, Stahrl. *Alternative Futures: A Policy Analysis of Social and Individual Choices for the U.S.*, Santa Monica, Ca., Goodyear Publishing Co., 1978.

_____. *Environmental Administration.* New York, McGraw-Hill, 1973.

_____. "Social Responsibility, Neglects, and Reticulation," *Business and Society*, Vol. 16, Spring, 1976.

Fayol, Henri. *General and Industrial Management.* London, Sir Isaac Pitman & Sons, 1949.

Federal Trade Commission, U.S. *Economic Papers.* Washington, D.C., Supt. of Documents, 1969.

Fiedler, Conrad. *On the Nature and History of Architecture.* Lexington, Ky., Victor Hammer (private printing), 1954.

Folsom, Marion B. *Executive Decision Making.* New York, McGraw-Hill 1962.

Galbraith, John D. *Economics of the Public Purpose.* New York, Signet, 1973.

Gordon, Paul J. "Heuristic Problem Solving," *Business Horizons* Spring, 1962, pp. 43-53.

Harrison, E. Frank. *The Managerial Decision Process.* Boston, Houghton Mifflin, 1975.

Haynes, W.W. *Pricing Decisions in Small Business.* Lexington, Ky., The University of Kentucky Press, 1962.

Haynes, W. Warren, and William R. Henry, *Managerial Economics.* Dallas, Texas, Business Publications, 1974.

Heidegger, Martin. *An Introduction to Metaphysics.* New Haven, Conn., Yale University Press, 1959.

Heller, Frank A. *Managerial Decision Making.* London, Van Gorcum/Tavistock, 1971.

Iannaccone, Laurence, and Frank W. Lutz. *Politics, Power, and Policy, The Governing of Local School Districts.* Columbus, Ohio, Charles E. Merrill Publishing Co., 1970.

Jung, Carl. *Man and His Symbols.* Garden City, N.Y., Doubleday, 1964.

Kaplan, A.D.H., Joel B. Dirlam, and Robert Lanzillotti. *Pricing in Big Business.* Washington, D.C., The Brookings Institution, 1958.

Kast, Freemont E., and James E. Rosenzweig. *Organizations and Management.* New York, McGraw-Hill, 1970.

Lasswell, Harold D. *A Preview of the Policy Sciences.* New York, American Elsevier, 1971.

Lazlo, Ervin. *The System View of the World.* New York, George Braziller, 1972.

Leavitt, Harold, ed. *Organizations of the Future: Interactions With the External Environment.* New York, Praeger, 1974.

McGuigan, James R., and R. Charles Moyer. *Managerial Economics.* Hinsdale, Ill., Dryden Press, 1975.

Nadler, G. *Work Design.* Homewood, Ill., Richard D. Irwin, 1970.

Nisbet, Robert. *Community and Power.* New York, Oxford University Press, 1967.

Porter, L., and J.R. Hackman. *Behavior in Organizations,* New York, McGraw-Hill, 1975.

Read, Herbert. *Icon and Idea, The Function of Art in the Development of Human Consciousness.* New York, Schocken Books, 1975.

_____ . *The Origins of Form in Art.* London, Thames and Hudson, 1965.

Reynolds, Lloyd G. *Principles of Economics: Micro.* Homewood, Ill., Richard D. Irwin, 1973.

Schumpter, Joseph. *Business Cycles.* New York, McGraw-Hill, 1939.

Shaner, E.L., *Environmental Theory of Management.* Austin, Texas, Saegert Publishing, 1961.

Simon, Herbert A. *The New Science of Decision Making.* New York, Harper & Row, 1960.

_____ . *Models of Man.* New York, John Wiley & Sons, 1957.

Simon, Julian L. *Applied Managerial Economics.* Englewood Cliffs, N.J., Prentice Hall, 1975.

van Gigch, John P. *Applied General Systems Theory.* New York, Harper & Row, 1975.

Vroom, Victor H., and Philip W. Yetton. *Leadership and Decision-Making.* Pittsburgh, University of Pittsburgh Press, 1973.

Webber, Ross A. *Management.* Homewood, Ill., Richard D. Irwin, 1975.

Wilson, T. and P.W.S. Andrews. *Oxford Studies on the Price Mechanism.* Oxford, Eng., Oxford Clarendon Press, 1951.

Index

accountability, 98, 133
adaptation, 108
   technical, 18
adaptive
   response, 107
   stages, 268
administrative regulations, 128
alienation, 10,42
allegiance, 41, 299
   business, 93
   decisions, 55
   government, 138
   voluntary organizations, 119
allocations, government, 134
alternatives, 12, 277
Ansoff, Igor, 210
antitrust laws, 181
Argyris, Chris, 201
art, of management, 205
Atahuallpa, 262
authoritarian, 97
authority, 41
   accession, 13
   assumption of, 287
   business, 84
   coercive, 55, 59
   consent to, 6
   decision, 60
   delegation, 85
   dispersal, 10
   nature of, 5
   persuasive, 57, 72
   protection against, 6
   realignment, 37
   reallocation, 123
   redistribution, 286
   reinforcement, 59
   succession, 14

balance sheet, 73
bargaining, 220
Barnard, Chester, 190, 198
barriers to entry, 34
Bauer, R., 221

behavioral
   decisions, 189
   models, 198
benefit-cost analysis, 132, 187
Braybrooke, David, 218
break-even analysis, 176
budget, 72
budgetary
   control, 144
   cycle, 136
   process, 133
business, 8, 63
   gaming, 97

capital
   equipment, 22
   flows, 25-6, 288
   intensification, 24
   investment, 173
   market, 286
Carnegie, Andrew, 74
case
   analysis, 194
   method, 192
caveat emptor, 64, 65, 77
change
   forces, 96, 121, 140
   management, 261
   mechanisms, 272
   open system, 291
checks and balances, 139
choices
   alternative, 282
   value and attitudinal, 44
closed system, business, 97
coalitions, 223
communications, 141
compensatory risk, 278
competence, management, 293
competition, 28, 180, 272, 285
competitive markets, 272
compromise, negotiated, 153
conflict, 37
   of interest, 16, 61, 92

models, 44
monetary policy, 25
morality, 139

Nader, Ralph, 213
need analysis, 107, 234
needs, 9, 12
    unmet, 152
networks, 83, 248
Nisbet, Robert, 11
Nixon, Richard, 205, 227
nonparticipation, 138
nonvoting, 139, 228

objective data, 156
objectives, business, 67
oligopoly, 18
open system, management of, 290-91
opportunity costs, 186
optimization, 18
order, 271
organization,
    business, 100
    government, 141
    voluntary institutions, 121
organizational capability, 17, 157
ownership, business, 98

participation, voluntary 108
partnership, 99
perceptual gaps, 201
performance, human, 21
    maximization, 61
    requirements, 154, 237
personnel function, 79
persuasion, 201
Piaget, Jean, 208
Pizarro, Francisco, 261
planning, 69
points of no return, 301
policies, U.S., 51
policy, 44, 69
    analysis, 282
    choices, 38
    evolutionary, 216
    resolution, 144
policymaker, self-interest, 220

policymaking, 45
political context, 216
politics, 221, 229
positional strength, 226
precedent, legal, 193
prescriptive, 104
present value, 183
pressure groups, 141
price elasticity, 178
pricing, 178
    public goods, 187
probabilities, 152, 197
problems, 43
process, 13, 42
    business, 83
    government, 137-38
    social agencies, 113
    society, 4
process of elimination, 147
procurement, 80
product concept, 67
production, 75
productivity, 133
    capital, 23
    human, 23
profit, 29, 91, 176
    maximization, 171
pro forma, 73
program management, 252
programming, 75, 85
progress, technological, 30
property rights, 27
proprietorship, 99
prospective management, 78
pyramidal values, 201

quantitative models, 256

Read, Herbert, 207
reciprocating balances, 73
referenda, 133, 287
regulated, the, 129
regulation, 92-3
reinforcement, innovation, 288
renewal, 272, 285
    management of, 273
research, 30, 69

About the Author

Stahrl W. Edmunds is professor and dean of the School of Administration, University of California at Riverside. He received the B.B.A. and M.A. degrees from the University of Minnesota and has twenty years' experience as a business executive for Hughes Aircraft Company, Ford Motor Company, Booz Allan Hamilton, National City Bank of New York, and Northwestern National Life Insurance Company. Dean Edmunds served in Ecuador as industrial development advisor to the U.S. Department of State in 1965-1967 and was vice chancellor of administration at the University of California at Riverside in 1967-1969. His current research and teaching interests are in environmental administration, business economics, systems management, and policy and planning.